CHILD CUSTODY, VISITATION, AND SUPPORT IN ILLINOIS

Second Edition

CHILD CUSTODY, VISITATION, AND SUPPORT IN ILLINOIS

Second Edition

Linda H. Connell
Attorney at Law

SPHINX® PUBLISHING
AN IMPRINT OF SOURCEBOOKS, INC.®
NAPERVILLE, ILLINOIS
www.SphinxLegal.com

Second Edition, 2008

Published by: **Sphinx® Publishing, An Imprint of Sourcebooks, Inc.®**

<u>Naperville Office</u>
P.O. Box 4410
Naperville, Illinois 60567-4410
630-961-3900
Fax: 630-961-2168
www.sourcebooks.com
www.SphinxLegal.com

This publication is designed to provide accurate and authoritative information in regard to the subject matter covered. It is sold with the understanding that the publisher is not engaged in rendering legal, accounting, or other professional service. If legal advice or other expert assistance is required, the services of a competent professional person should be sought.
From a Declaration of Principles Jointly Adopted by a Committee of the American Bar Association and a Committee of Publishers and Associations

This product is not a substitute for legal advice.

Disclaimer required by Texas statutes.

Library of Congress Cataloging-in-Publication Data
Connell, Linda H.
  Child custody, visitation and support in Illinois / by Linda H. Connell.
     p. cm.
  ISBN-13: 9781572486836 (alk. paper)
  ISBN-10: 157248683X
 1. Custody of children--Illinois--Popular works. 2. Child support--Law and legislation--Illinois--Popular works. 3. Visitation rights (Domestic relations)--Illinois--Popular works. I. Title.
KFI1304.6.Z9 C66 2002
346.77301'73--dc21

                                      2002152743

Printed and bound in the United States of America.
SB — 10 9 8 7 6 5 4 3 2 1

Contents

Citation to Discover Assets/Turnover of Personal Property
Wage Deduction and Non-Wage Garnishment
Incarceration
Creation of a Trust from Assets of Obligor Parent
Non-Support Punishment Act
Out-of-State Obligor Parent
Assistance of Illinois Department of Public Aid

Custody and Visitation
Removal of Child from State
Child Support Modification
Child Support Termination

Using Self-Help Law Books

Before using a self-help law book, you should realize the advantages and disadvantages of doing your own legal work and understand the challenges and diligence that this requires.

The Growing Trend
Rest assured that you will not be the first or only person handling your own legal matter. For example, in some states, more than 75% of divorces and other cases have at least one party representing him- or herself. Because of the high cost of legal services, this is a major trend and many courts are struggling to make it easier for people to represent themselves. However, some courts are not happy with people who do not use attorneys and refuse to help them in any way. For some, the attitude is, "Go to the law library and figure it out for yourself."

We at Sphinx write and publish self-help law books to give people an alternative to the often complicated and confusing legal books found in most law libraries. We have made the explanations of the law as simple and easy to understand as possible. Of course, unlike an attorney advising an individual client, we cannot cover every conceivable possibility.

Cost/Value Analysis
Whenever you shop for a product or service, you are faced with various levels of quality and price. In deciding what product or service to buy, you make a cost/value analysis on the basis of your willingness to pay and the quality you desire.

When buying a car, you decide whether you want transportation, comfort, status, or sex appeal. Accordingly, you decide among such choices as a Neon, a Lincoln, a Rolls Royce, or a Porsche. Before making a decision, you usually weigh the merits of each option against the cost.

When you get a headache, you can take a pain reliever (such as aspirin) or visit a medical specialist for a neurological examination. Given this choice, most people, of course, take a pain reliever, since it costs only pennies, whereas a medical examination costs hundreds of dollars and takes a lot of time. This is usually a logical choice because it is rare to need anything more than a pain reliever for a headache. But in some cases, a headache may indicate a brain tumor and failing to see a specialist right away can result in complications. Should everyone with a headache go to a specialist? Of course not, but people treating their own illnesses must realize that they are betting on the basis of their cost/value analysis of the situation. They are taking the most logical option.

The same cost/value analysis must be made when deciding to do one's own legal work. Many legal situations are very straightforward, requiring a simple form and no complicated analysis. Anyone with a little intelligence and a book of instructions can handle the matter without outside help.

But there is always the chance that complications are involved that only an attorney would notice. To simplify the law into a book like this, several legal cases often must be condensed into a single sentence or paragraph. Otherwise, the book would be several hundred pages long and too complicated for most people. However, this simplification necessarily leaves out many details and nuances that would apply to special or unusual situations. Also, there are many ways to interpret most legal questions. Your case may come before a judge who disagrees with the analysis of our authors.

Therefore, in deciding to use a self-help law book and to do your own legal work, you must realize that you are making a cost/value analysis. You have decided that the money you will save in doing it yourself outweighs the chance that your case will not turn out to your satisfaction. Most people handling their own simple legal matters never have a problem, but occasionally people find that it ended up costing them more to have an attorney straighten out the situation than it would have if they had hired an attorney in the beginning. Keep this in mind if you decide to handle your own case, and be sure to consult an attorney if you feel you might need further guidance.

Local Rules   The next thing to remember is that a book that covers the law for the entire nation, or even for an entire state, cannot possibly include every procedural difference of every county court. Whenever possible, we provide the exact form needed; however, in some areas, each county, or even each judge, may require unique forms and procedures. In our *state* books, our forms usually cover the majority of counties in the state, or provide examples of the type of form that will be required. In our *national* books, our forms are sometimes even more general in nature but are designed to give a good idea of the type of form that will be needed in most locations. Nonetheless, keep in mind that your *state*, county, or judge may have a requirement, or use a form, that is not included in this book.

You should not necessarily expect to be able to get all the information and resources you need solely from within the pages of this book. This book will serve as your guide, giving you specific information whenever possible and helping you to find out what else you will need to know. This is just like if you decided to build your own backyard deck. You might purchase a book on how to build decks. However, such a book would not include the building codes and permit requirements of every city, town, county, and township in the nation; nor would it include the lumber, nails, saws, hammers, and other materials and tools you would need to actually build the deck. You would use the book as your guide, and then do some work and research involving such matters as whether you need a permit of some kind, what type and grade of wood are available in your area, whether to use hand tools or power tools, and how to use those tools.

Before using the forms in a book like this, you should check with your court clerk to see if there are any local rules of which you should be aware, or local forms you will need to use. Often, such forms will require the same information as the forms in the book but are merely laid out differently, use slightly different language, or use different color paper so the clerks can easily find them. They will sometimes require additional information.

Changes in the Law   Besides being subject to state and local rules and practices, the law is subject to change at any time. The courts and the legislatures of all fifty states are constantly revising the laws. It is possible that while you are reading this book, some aspect of the law is being changed or a court is interpreting a law in a different way. You should always check the most recent statutes, rules, and regulations to see what, if any, changes have been made.

In most cases, the change will be of minimal significance. A form will be redesigned, additional information will be required, or a waiting period will be extended. As a result, you might need to revise a form, file an extra form, or wait out a longer time period; these types of changes will not usually affect the outcome of your case. On the other hand, sometimes a major part of the law is changed, the entire law in a particular area is rewritten, or a case that was the basis of a central legal point is overruled. In such instances, your entire ability to pursue your case may be impaired.

To help you with local requirements and changes in the law, be sure to read Chapter 2.

Again, you should weigh the value of your case against the cost of an attorney and make a decision as to what you believe is in your best interest.

Introduction

This book is meant to assist people who feel that they have a custody, visitation, or support issue occurring in their lives, by providing information about the laws themselves and the procedures used in implementing those laws. This book cannot, however, take the place of the competent advice of an attorney who is familiar with the individual set of facts at hand. No book on its own can provide a definitive answer to such a complex legal and factual situation.

Cases involving children can become contentious, and too often the parties focus on advancing a negative agenda against one another, rather than obtaining the best result for the children themselves. Child custody cases in particular are difficult to litigate because they may require expert testimony from physicians or child psychologists, for example. In addition, the law in Illinois relating to child custody, visitation, and support may change at any time. A change in the law may alter the rights and responsibilities of the parties. These cases are fraught with difficulties for the parties, even for those with legal experience, and are best handled by an attorney who has a background in the practice of family law.

It is our hope at Sphinx that we can help you, the non-lawyer, with a potential custody, visitation, or support issue, by providing you with insight into what is involved in litigating such cases. This, in turn, will give you more power over your own situation, and will enable you to make informed decisions as that situation progresses.

The purpose of custody, visitation, and support laws in Illinois is to determine the rights and responsibilities of relevant parties as to children in whom the parties have an interest. In general, custody and visitation cases involve the questions of who has access to, contact with, and the power to make decisions regarding a child. Generally, support cases deal with issues of who is responsible for the financial support of a child.

Most often, custody, visitation, and support laws are applied to situations involving the children's parents, but sometimes others, such as grandparents, stepparents, or even non-relatives, may be considered parties in such a case. While custody, visitation, or support issues often arise in the context of a divorce proceeding, they often come up in situations in which the parties were never married. In the latter case, sometimes there is a question of paternity that must be answered before a custody, visitation, or support issue can be decided.

The key element in custody, support, and visitation cases in Illinois is the best interest of the child. This means that the judge in the case will base his or her decision upon what is the best result for the child, rather than upon what either of the parties may desire. Regardless of what standard a judge applies in reaching a legal decision, this element is going to be the one that usually carries the most weight, and you will see this phrase repeatedly during the course of this book.

Chapters 1 and 2 of this book will discuss some preliminary matters for you to consider: whether and how to find a lawyer and how to find the laws used in Illinois to decide questions of custody, visitation, and support. Chapters 3 through 7 will take you through custody and visitation cases in Illinois. Custody and visitation will be examined together, because they both pertain to issues of the parties' access to the child. Chapters

8 through 10 will discuss the child support case in Illinois, including the enforcement of support orders previously handed down by a judge. Chapter 11 will explain the procedures for changing or terminating prior court orders pertaining to custody, visitation, or support. Finally, appendices found at the end of the book will provide you with Illinois statutes governing custody, visitation, and support issues, forms similar to those that you may need to fill out and file in your particular case, a sample visitation schedule, and a list of resources in Illinois for those seeking legal assistance.

Hiring an Attorney

Once you have decided that you have a custody, visitation, or support issue, the next question is whether you will go it alone, which is known as proceeding *pro se*, or will hire someone to represent you. Some of the factors to think about in making this decision have already been discussed. Again, it is important to emphasize that people with custody, visitation, and support issues are advised in most cases to go forward with counsel rather than pro se.

There are other considerations as well. You should weigh the advantages and disadvantages of retaining an attorney.

Advantages   On the plus side, an attorney is probably your best source for advice concerning your particular situation because of his or her experience in the legal arena. He or she can also serve as a neutral sounding board with whom you can share confidential information and from whom you can receive an objective opinion about your chances for success in your case.

An attorney should know the procedural rules in your jurisdiction, such as filing deadlines and technical requirements for documents that must be prepared in your case. These rules sometimes can prove to be a minefield to the nonlawyer.

Finally, if you have an attorney, the other parent, his or her attorney, and even the judge in the case are more likely to take you seriously. Although pro se litigants should be given the same consideration in court as people who have representation, in reality, those who have legal counsel are more likely to achieve satisfactory results in the event of a lawsuit than are those who represent themselves.

Disadvantages The main disadvantages of hiring a lawyer are twofold. First, if your attorney does a poor job in representing you, you still will be bound by the outcome of the case. If your attorney's performance is so inadequate that it rises to the level of malpractice, you may have a cause of action against him or her, but that will be of small comfort if you have lost your child custody case. That is why it is so very important to research prospective attorneys by asking for references and reviewing the attorney's credentials.

The other negative to retaining a lawyer is the expense involved. Attorneys in family law cases generally charge for their services on an hourly basis. Fees may reach several hundred dollars an hour and up. Under certain circumstances in Illinois, an attorney may take a case on a *contingent basis*, which means the attorney takes a percentage of what-ever amount of money he or she wins for you. In divorce and other sup-port cases in Illinois, however, this is not allowed. Many attorneys will meet with a potential client for an initial consultation at no charge, at which time you can discuss your legal options as well as any fee arrange-ments for continued representation.

Legal Clinics Even if you do not believe you can afford an attorney, you still may be able to obtain legal representation. There are legal clinics in Illinois that provide assistance to people in financial need. Private attorneys operate some of these clinics. Others may be run by law schools, using student interns who practice law in a limited manner under a special rule of the Illinois Supreme Court. Typically, in order to utilize the services of these clinics, you will have to show that your income level is inadequate to allow you to retain and pay for an attorney on your own. Included in Appendix C at the end of this book is a list of some of the organizations in Illinois that may provide legal services to qualified individuals at a reduced charge or no charge.

Locating An Attorney

Once you have decided to retain an attorney to represent you, the next question is how to find one. If you do not have an attorney, there are a number of resources for finding lawyers familiar with handling family law issues.

Advertisements Many attorneys advertise in publications, on television or radio, or in the Yellow Pages.

Lawyer Referral Services Most counties in Illinois have professional organizations for lawyers called *bar associations*, in which many of the attorneys practicing in the county belong. Many bar associations offer lawyer referral services that provide the names of local attorneys practicing family law. You then are responsible for contacting the attorney of your choice to set up an initial consultation.

Legal Directories Your local library may have one of the state or national legal directories that list almost all of the attorneys practicing in the geographical area covered by the directory. Examples of directories commonly found in Illinois libraries are Martindale-Hubbell and Sullivan's.

Internet Websites If you have Internet access, there are a number of websites that you can use to search for attorneys practicing in family law. A few of them available are:

www.Findlaw.com
www.AllLaw.com
www.IllinoisLawyerFinder.com
www.chicagobar.org

Scheduling a Consultation

After locating an attorney who practices family law, you should contact his or her office to schedule an appointment, called an *initial consultation.* As noted previously, some lawyers will meet with you for a reduced fee or no fee at all. When you contact the attorney to set up a meeting, you probably will be asked for some preliminary information, such as the number and ages of the children involved, how long you have been with your spouse or significant other, and whether you are living together or separately. You also should be prepared to bring copies of any other judicial orders or other court documents that may exist concerning the particular children who are involved in your current case.

Finally, you should be asked for the name of the other party. This is because lawyers are required to avoid conflicts of interest. In other words, if an attorney has represented the other parent in a substantially related matter, that attorney may not represent you, unless the other parent consents after the conflict has been disclosed to him or her. Even if the other parent has merely consulted with the attorney, he or she may have divulged confidential information to the attorney, which would trigger the conflict of interest rules.

Attorney-Client Confidentiality

If you do retain an attorney, it is imperative that you provide him or her with all the information asked for, even if you think the information will hurt your case. Attorneys in Illinois are governed by a code of professional responsibility, which is a set of legal ethics rules. One of the most important of these rules is that of confidentiality. Anything you discuss with your attorney relating to the custody, visitation, or support case will remain between you and your attorney. This is the case even if you only consult with the attorney one time and do not end up retaining him or her.

The attorney's staff must maintain the confidentiality of your information as well. Therefore, it is in your interest to be completely straightforward and honest with your attorney. Otherwise, some information that is negative to your case could come to light during the actual proceedings, and your attorney could be unprepared. This would be a much worse position for you than if your attorney were aware of the information well in advance and had time to counteract any negative effect.

Initial Consultation with the Attorney

Once you have found an attorney, the next step is to contact his or her office to schedule an initial consultation. At this meeting, you will have a short period of time, perhaps a half hour or an hour, to speak with the prospective attorney to determine if he or she is the right person to represent you. This is time to discuss the attorney's qualifications, experience in family law, and style of representation.

Attorney Demeanor

This last item refers to the attorney's demeanor and manner of presenting your case. Is the attorney laid-back or aggressive? Does the attorney seem to promote settlement of a case or a fight to the bitter end? How do you yourself feel about the attorney? It is important for you to feel comfortable with the attorney's professional style. If you do not agree with the stance he or she takes while representing you, you should keep looking for another lawyer.

Fees

The initial consultation is also the time when you should discuss fees with your attorney. As has been discussed previously, custody, visitation, and support cases are often contentious and usually quite expensive. Remember that attorneys in these cases will usually charge a set per-hour fee for all services rendered. Some attorneys charge one rate for office work and a higher rate for time spent in court.

NOTE: *Be wary of any attorney who tells you that you have an open-and-shut case that will not require a substantial expenditure of fees.*

Attorneys routinely require a *retainer*, or a lump-sum advance payment to cover a certain amount of attorney's fees and costs to be charged. The attorney will take his or her fees out of the retainer first, and then will bill you, often on a monthly or other periodic basis, for whatever fees are incurred above and beyond the retainer.

Attorneys also routinely advance court costs to their clients and then include those charges on their bill. For example, if the clerk of the court charges a filing fee for a particular document, the attorney generally will pay that fee out of an account held by the law office when the document is filed. The filing fee will then be added to your bill, along with the charges for any work performed by your attorney on the case.

The fee arrangement on which you and the attorney agree should be in writing, signed by both you and the lawyer. In fact, a law called the *Illinois Marriage and Dissolution of Marriage Act* requires certain written language to be included in fee agreements in order for an attorney to pursue a case for unpaid fees against his or her client. (750 ILCS 5/508(f).)

NOTE: *If you do retain an attorney, be sure that you will receive itemized bills, specifically stating what activities the attorney spent time on, and how much time was spent on each item.*

Although it is possible to ask the court to order the other parent to pay your attorney's fees, the burden of proof will be on you to show that you are financially unable to pay your attorney and that the other parent has the financial means to do so. In addition, you will have to show that the fees charged are reasonable. Sometimes, one party will run up a large amount in fees under the mistaken belief that the other party will eventually be stuck paying them. Unless the court orders otherwise, you will be responsible for paying for whatever services your attorney renders, and the attorney may take legal steps to collect payment as would any other creditor. It is wise not to assume that your obligation to pay your attorney will be placed on the other party.

Attorney-Client Relationship

If you find you are not in tune with the first attorney that you speak with, do not worry. There are a large number of qualified attorneys who practice in the area of family law. Even if you feel comfortable with the first attorney you contact, it would not hurt to speak with more than one, if time and your financial situation allow. Consulting with a second, or even third attorney, may give you a clearer picture of your chances of succeeding with your case, and will also give you the opportunity to locate the lawyer that will best represent your interests.

The relationship between you and your attorney may have a great impact on the outcome of your case. A successful attorney-client relationship is one in which the client feels free to discuss concerns about the case and to ask questions about all aspects of the representation. The attorney should be open to constructive criticism and should be willing to explain the relevant law and all procedural and strategic steps the attorney plans. Likewise, the attorney should be satisfied that the client is providing him or her with complete and truthful information regarding the facts of the case so that the attorney is fully prepared to present the client's case.

If you do not feel that you and your attorney have this type of relationship, or if you are intimidated by him or her, are afraid to ask questions, or do not receive satisfactory answers, then you may want to consider looking for a new attorney.

Finding the Relevant Law

Hopefully, by now you can appreciate the importance of having an attorney in a custody, visitation, or support case. If you should decide to attempt it alone, or if you have an attorney and simply wish to understand what is happening with your case, then you need to know how to perform legal research. This is the science of finding the law that applies to your particular case.

You should know the law, not only in order to support the arguments you are making, but also to know what position is best for you to take.

Example: Let us say that you are in the midst of a custody matter and want sole custody of the children involved. Under the circumstances of your case, if the law indicates you probably would not be entitled to sole custody, then you can save a great deal of time, effort, and expense by adopting a position that is more in line with what the law provides.

The best places to seek out the relevant law are law libraries and the Internet. In Illinois, fairly comprehensive law libraries can be found in the courthouses of most counties and on the campuses of law schools throughout the state. These libraries are generally open to the public, although those who are not lawyers or law students may not be able to check the materials out. For that reason, the Internet can be a good alternative.

When using the Internet, materials often can be downloaded in the privacy of your own home. Moreover, there is a wealth of secondary materials that interpret the many cases and statutes that may apply to your case. The downside to the Internet is that there are no guarantees that the materials are accurate, and there are very few controls on the information that is posted.

Sources of Law

Legal researchers often describe the various sources of law that attorneys use to support their clients' cases as either primary or secondary.

Primary Source

Primary sources of law are comprised of the actual statutes, ordinances, and regulations that have been enacted by federal, state, and local legislative bodies. Primary sources of law also include the judicial opinions, also known as a *case law*, that have been handed down by judges who interpret the legislation. Primary sources are the best places to find the law that supports your particular position because statutes and case law are the most definitive statements of what the law actually is.

Secondary Source

Secondary sources of law, on the other hand, are those that have been formulated to explain statutory and case law, or to categorize the law by topic. Some examples of these sources are digests and legal encyclopedias. Judges and lawyers may look to these sources for assistance in understanding the law, but they are not as strongly supportive of a particular legal argument as a primary source would be.

Statutory Codes

The entire statutory code of the State of Illinois, as enacted by the state legislature, is called the *Illinois Compiled Statutes* (ILCS). Statutes referred to in this book are often abbreviated according to a standard reference form, called a *citation*.

Example: The *Illinois Marriage and Dissolution of Marriage Act* is Chapter 750, act 5 of the Illinois Compiled Statutes, which is abbreviated as 750 ILCS 5. The section of the

Illinois Marriage and Dissolution of Marriage Act that deals with marital settlement agreements is in Section 502 of the act. This section would be cited as: 750 ILCS 5/502. To find this provision in the statute, which is voluminous, you would first look for the chapter (Chapter 750). Once you locate the chapter, find Act 5, then Section 502. These provisions should be cited in the standard form throughout the research materials you are using.

Illinois Compiled Statutes also come in an annotated form, which means that each statutory provision includes citations to Illinois case decisions that relied on that particular provision.

Federal laws are published in a similar manner, in, for example, the United States Code (U.S.C. or U.S.C.A.) and the Code of Federal Regulations (C.F.R.).

Case Reporters   Judges rely on statutory law, as well as established case law from earlier judicial opinions. The judge in a particular case will then apply this law to the sets of facts before the court. Your attorney may refer to some of these decisions in earlier cases that have facts similar to your own case, as support for your position in a custody, visitation, or support dispute. Previous case law is called *precedent*. Judicial opinions can be found in published volumes called *case reporters*.

Several different case reporters provide access to Illinois judicial opinions. The official reporters of Illinois cases are *Illinois Reports* (abbreviated as Ill. or Ill.2d, depending on the series) and *Illinois Appellate Court Reports* (Ill. App., Ill. App. 2d, or Ill. App. 3d). West's *Illinois Decisions* (Ill.Dec.) and the *North Eastern Reporter* (N.E. or N.E.2d) are unofficial sources for judicial opinions. The *North Eastern Reporter* is a regional reporter, which means it also contains opinions from certain other states besides Illinois.

As in the *Illinois Compiled Statutes*, citations to cases found in these reporters have a standard form: the case name (which is made up of the names of the litigants), the volume number of the reporter, the standard abbreviation used for the particular reporter, the relevant page number, and the year of the decision. An example of this standard form of citation is *Marriage of Eckert*, 518 N.E.2d 1041 (1988). This 1988 opinion appears in Volume 518 of the *North Eastern Reporter*, Second Series, and begins at page 1,041.

It is important to note that only Illinois Supreme Court and Appellate Court opinions are published. Trial court opinions are not published in Illinois and do not make good precedent.

Federal court cases are published in the *Federal Reporter* (F., F.2d, F.3d) and the *Federal Supplement* (F.Supp.). Decisions of the United States Supreme Court are reported in the *United States Reports* (U.S.), the *United States Supreme Court Reports Lawyers' Edition* (L.Ed. or L.Ed.2d), and the *Supreme Court Reporter* (S.Ct.).

Digests *Digests* take the legally relevant points from a judicial opinion and organize those points according to topic. When the researcher looks up a particular legal topic, he or she will find citations for a number of cases pertaining to that topic. West's *Illinois Digest* and West's *General Digest* are examples of digests that contain citations of Illinois cases.

Legal Encyclopedias *Legal encyclopedias* are valuable tools for the legal researcher because they provide a summary of a number of legal topics. The most commonly found encyclopedias are *American Jurisprudence* (Am. Jur.) and *Corpus Juris Secundum* (C.J.S.).

Internet There are many websites devoted to legal research that are geared toward attorneys and nonattorneys alike. Examples of sites providing access to Illinois law are: **www.Findlaw.com** and **www.law.siu.edu/ lawlib**. Various Illinois governmental websites also may offer assistance, such as **www.illinois.gov**. If you have Internet access, a good search engine will assist you in locating other online resources.

Changes in the Law

Keep in mind that the law can change at any time. Even though research materials in law libraries generally are kept up-to-date, there is a lag time between the passage of an amendment to a law and its publication and distribution to the libraries. Moreover, information obtained from the Internet may not be accurate or current. If the Illinois Supreme Court reverses an appellate court case that you were planning to use in support of your own case, the appellate court opinion no longer will be a good precedent. For these reasons, you must be diligent in checking any supplementary materials to the statutes and cases you cite to ensure that they remain good law.

Custody and Visitation—General Considerations

The terms *custody* and *visitation* refer to a collection of rights and responsibilities held by a person with regard to certain children. Usually, the person is one of the parents of the children, but under certain circumstances, other parties may receive custodial or visitation rights. Most often, the non-parent seeking custody or visitation is a grandparent or stepparent. A non-parent seeking custody of or visitation with a child must establish that he or she has *standing* to file a custody or visitation petition. *Standing* is a legal term that refers to whether a person has a right to be involved as a party to a lawsuit.

In order for a non-parent to even have the right to seek custody of a child, the parent must not have physical possession of the child. This does not mean that leaving a child for a brief visit with the non-parent confers standing on the non-parent. The biological parent has to leave the child in the care and control of the non-parent with the intent that the child remain with the non-parent indefinitely. (*In re Marriage of Feig*, 694 N.E.2d 654 (3rd Dist. 1998).)

The right of grandparents, great-grandparents, and siblings to visitation has been a contentious topic in Illinois and many other states in recent years. In the past, an Illinois statute allowed these third parties to seek visitation with a child, even though the child was in the physical possession of one of the parents. The Illinois Supreme Court has now held this statute unconstitutional. (*Schweigert v. Schweigert*, 772 N.E.2d 229 (Ill., 2002).) Third-party custody and visitation is discussed more fully in Chapter 7.

Types of Custody

Physical vs. Legal Custody

Physical custody refers to both the actual possession and the physical control of the child. *Legal custody*, on the other hand, is the power to make decisions on behalf of the child, such as his or her education, activities, and religious upbringing. Both types of custody may be vested in a single person, or the rights and responsibilities may be divided between the parents as the court sees fit. Custody determinations are made according to the *best interest of the child* standard, which is discussed later in this section.

Joint Custody

Section 602.1 of the *Illinois Marriage and Dissolution of Marriage Act* (750 ILCS 5/602.1) provides that a court may make an award of *joint custody*. Generally, this means that both physical and legal custody is divided between both parents. Again, joint custody must be in the best interest of the child. The court will take into account, among other factors, whether the parents are able to cooperate in matters covered by the court's *joint custody order*.

Note: *Joint custody does not necessarily mean each parent will have equal time with the child. One parent may be given primary residential custody of the child in a joint parenting situation with the other parent receiving a lesser amount of contact.*

Temporary Custody

If you become a party to a custody proceeding, whether as the person who files the petition for custody or the person who must respond to a petition, there usually will be a court order fixing *temporary custody* during the pendency of the case. Just as it sounds, temporary custody is not the final determination of the rights and responsibilities at issue. Keep in mind, however, that courts very often will continue the provisions of a temporary custody order when the final custody determination is made.

Example: If the child's mother receives the lion's share of the physical custody of the child during the time a divorce case is being litigated, and the case goes on for a year before a final divorce decree is entered, the court is more likely to allow the mother to have greater access to the child at the time of the final award of custody.

Because the child has now spent many months in this living situation, the court will be hesitant to disturb the child's routine after the passage of so much time unless there is a very good reason for doing so. Therefore, it is important to obtain a favorable temporary custody award as early as possible, as the provisions of the temporary order may end up carrying over to the final custody award.

Best Interest of the Child

In making a determination of custody, the court will look to the *best interest of the child.* The court will evaluate all relevant factors in applying this standard. Some of the most important factors are included in 750 ILCS 5/602 and are discussed here.

NOTE: Even though this section is part of the *Illinois Marriage and Dissolution of Marriage Act,* the provisions of Section 602 apply to children of unmarried parents as well.

Wishes of the Parents
Although important, the parents' wishes as to who receives custody will not be the lone factor of the actual award. Too often parents seek custody for reasons other than what is best for the child. Some parents may be motivated by a desire for revenge against the other parent. Others may petition for custody in the hope that they can bargain for a lesser spousal or child support obligation. Courts, therefore, will consider the parents' wishes, but generally will not base an award of custody on those wishes without other evidence of the child's best interest.

Wishes of the Child
A court will sometimes ask the child with which parent he or she prefers to live. Whether the court does inquire, however, and the amount of weight the court will give to the child's preference, will

depend on the age and level of maturity of the child. Children under the age of eight usually will not be consulted about their choice of custodial parent. Courts, on the other hand, often give considerable weight to the wishes of children aged fourteen and above. Remember, though, that the child's preference should be based on his or her relationship with the preferred parent and not on some other factor.

📖 In one case, the court declined to honor the child's stated desire to live with his mother, because the mother had been physically and verbally abusive to the child. The child's preference was based only on his wish to remain near his friends. (*In re Marriage of Apperson*, 574 N.E.2d 1257(4th Dist. 1991).)

Interaction and Interrelationship

These factors refer to the relationships between the child and those people who have important interactions with the child. Most often, that means members of the child's family, but it can include anyone who "may significantly affect the child's best interest." The court will examine both the manner in which the present relationships affect the child, and the way in which a particular custody award might affect their relationships.

Child's Adjustment

Under this subsection, the court will look at how the child is faring in the three most important parts of his or her environment—home, school, and community. Over the years, Illinois court opinions have enumerated a variety of situations that could impact the child's adjustment in these areas. One example is where one parent has a job that requires long hours or extensive travel and is apart from the child for substantial amounts of time, leaving the child with a sitter. Another such situation would be when one parent moves several times in the course of a few months.

📖 In a case in which both the mother and father were deemed to be good parents, but the mother had been the primary caregiver for the child's life and the father spent long hours at work and much of his time working while at home, custody was given to the mother. (*Cooper v. Cooper*, 497 N.E.2d 805 (5th Dist. 1986).)

📖 The instability of the child's home life was considered in a situation in which the mother took the children and left the marital home without informing the father. Furthermore, the mother moved three different times in the course of one year. Custody was awarded to the father. (*In re Marriage of Stone*, 518 N.E.2d 402 (1st Dist. 1987).)

Mental and Physical Health of all Individuals Involved

This refers to the condition of not only the child, but also those others who live in the house or who have similarly close and substantial contact with the child, such as extended family members. This consideration includes both the medical and the emotional state of each of these people.

Physical Violence

Physical violence or the threat of physical violence by the person seeking custody, no matter if it is directed toward the child or toward someone else, is of course going to have great impact on the court's determination of what is in the best interest of the child.

Abuse

This subsection is similar to the previous provision regarding violence. However, *abuse* encompasses harassment and intimidation by the potential custodian. This abuse may be directed at *any* person for the court to consider the effect of the petitioning parent's conduct on the best interest of the child.

Relationship with Other Parent

A large number of Illinois cases address the importance of the parent's facilitation of the relationship between the child and the other parent. Attempts by one parent to turn the child against the other parent, or to interfere with the other parent's contact with the child, are against the best interest of the child.

Other Factors

Beyond those listed in the statute, Illinois cases have provided a number of other circumstances to examine in determining the best interest of the child. Among these are:

- ✪ false allegations by one parent of abuse by the other parent;

- ✪ substance abuse by a parent;

- ✪ failure of a parent to pay child support; or,

- ✪ attempts by one parent to change the last name of the child from that of the other parent.

The remarriage of one parent is not enough on its own to count against the best interest of the child. The wealth of one parent is also not a lone determinative. All of these factors must be considered together in the context of how they impact the child's interests.

Paternity

In custody, visitation, or support cases, it is necessary to establish who the child's father is because paternity is required to be shown in order to enforce a right to custody or visitation or a duty to pay support.

Presumption of Father

Often, questions arise when the parents are not married. The chapter of the *Illinois Compiled Statutes* that addresses paternity is the *Illinois Parentage Act of 1984*, 750 ILCS 45. If a child is born to a married woman, there is a presumption that the woman's husband is the child's father. This presumption may be rebutted by clear and convincing evidence to the contrary.

Paternity may be established if the parents are not married at the time the child is born, but marry later on, and the father is named, with his written consent, as the child's father on the child's birth certificate. A conclusive presumption of paternity arises if both parents sign an acknowledgment of paternity in accordance with Section 6 of the statute.

Paternity Suit

When paternity is disputed by either of the alleged parents, it may become necessary to establish custody by means of a paternity suit. The suit may be brought by either the child, the child's mother, a pregnant woman, a person or public agency who has provided financial support to the child, or a man who alleges that he is the father of the child. Once the paternity action is filed, the court will set a trial schedule, which should include a conference before trial, called the *pretrial*.

The pretrial is extremely important. In general, the pretrial is when the court will order a DNA test to provide evidence of paternity—with a DNA test, the genetic makeup of the alleged father and the child are compared to determine the likelihood that the man in question is in fact the child's father. In many Illinois courts, the pretrial order for DNA testing is required before the case will be set for a trial. In the case in which a party is receiving public assistance, paternity also may be determined by an administrative hearing conducted by the Illinois Department of Public Aid (IDPA).

DNA tests sometimes are utilized in cases in which the parents are married, but most often they are used when the parents have never married. A test is sought when the mother is seeking support from the alleged father. However, the alleged father also may use DNA testing, either to establish a right to custody or visitation or to avoid an obligation to pay support. The cost of the testing is charged to the person requesting the test; if the court has determined the person to be indigent, the cost will be borne by the county in which the case was brought, unless the indigent person is represented by a public agency such as the IDPA. In that case, the agency will bear the expense.

An action to determine paternity, whether by the child, either parent, or the Illinois Department of Public Aid, must be brought no later than two years after the child reaches the age of eighteen. However, if a public agency other than the Department of Public Aid has provided financial support for the child and wishes to bring a paternity action, it must do so no later than two years after the agency has stopped providing aid.

In the case where a man has been adjudicated the father based on presumptions in the statute (for example, if he was married to the child's mother at the time of the birth and believed he was the father), and later learns that he is not the father, he may bring an action denying paternity no later than two years after obtaining knowledge that he is not the father. During that two-year period, if either the mother or the child refuse to submit to DNA testing, the two-year period ceases to run until the DNA testing is completed. If a party continues to refuse to submit to DNA testing, the court may rule against that party in the proceeding without the testing.

Father's Rights

During the pendency of a paternity case, the court may order the alleged father, called the *putative father*, to pay temporary child support. In that case, the support order is established and treated just as an order for support in a case where paternity has already been established.

A final note concerns men who wish to establish paternity for the purpose of preventing the mother of their out-of-wedlock child from placing the child for adoption. In Illinois, the state's Department of Children and Family Services (DCFS) has established a Putative Father Registry to maintain information about men who believe they have fathered children in Illinois and wish to protect their rights as fathers to those children. The father must register by submitting information about himself, the mother, and the child to the registry on the necessary DCFS form, and must commence proceedings to establish paternity. This must be done within thirty days after the birth of the child in order to have rights with regard to the child. Registration also may be accomplished online at **www.putativefather.org**.

Registration alone does not set paternity; that is why the putative father must begin a paternity action as well. Once registered, the putative father has the right to be notified if the mother attempts to place the child for adoption.

Parentage in Assisted Reproduction Cases

Illinois is one of the few states with a statute that specifically allows gestational surrogacy contracts. The *Illinois Gestational Surrogacy Act*, enacted in 2004, is found at 750 ILCS 47, and it outlines the requirements for an enforceable surrogacy agreement. In general, the statute mandates that both the biological parents and the surrogate meet certain conditions, and that the agreement be in writing.

For the parent or parents, the act requires the following:

- that he, she, or they contribute the sperm and/or the egg that will be used in the fertilization procedure resulting in the embryo to be used in the surrogacy;
- that a qualified physician provide an affidavit, to be attached to the written contract, showing that the parents have a medical need for such a surrogacy arrangement;

- that they complete a mental health evaluation; and,

- that they consult with an attorney regarding the terms and consequences of the surrogacy arrangement.

As for the surrogate, the act provides:

- that she must be twenty-one years old or more;

- that she has already given birth to at least one child;

- that she must complete both a medical and a mental health evaluation;

- that she must consult with an attorney regarding the terms and consequences of the surrogacy arrangement; and,

- that she must obtain health insurance to cover the duration of the pregnancy, up until eight weeks after the birth.

The contract itself must meet the following conditions:

- it must be in writing;

- it must have been entered into before any actual medical procedures in furtherance of the surrogacy are commenced;

- it must be executed by the biological parents, the surrogate, and the surrogates's husband if she is married;

- the parent or parents must be represented by a different attorney than the one representing the surrogate;

- both the surrogate and the parent or parents must execute a written acknowledgment that they have received information regarding the "legal, financial, and contractual rights, expectations, penalties, and obligations of the surrogacy agreement";

- any compensation provided for in the agreement must be placed in escrow before any medical procedures are commenced;

- it must be witnessed by two competent adults;

- it must provide for the express written consent of the surrogate to undergo embryo transfer procedures, to carry and give birth to the child, and to surrender custody of the child to the biological parents immediately upon the birth of the child (the surrogate's husband must also agree in writing to the surrender); and,

✪ it must provide for the express written consent of the intended parents to accept custody of the child immediately upon the birth and to accept sole responsibility for the support of the child.

An enforceable surrogacy contract gives rise to a number of legal consequences. The intended parents are the legal parents of the child immediately upon the child's birth, and sole custody vests in the intended parents. The child is the legitimate child of the intended parents immediately upon the child's birth. Neither the surrogate nor her husband have any parental rights over the child. If the medical clinic performing the medical procedures involved in the surrogacy makes a mistake and the resulting child is not genetically related to the intended parents, they remain the legal parents of the child.

A controversial provision of the act is that it allows for the payment of compensation to the surrogate, above and beyond reimbursement for medical expenses, for the service she is providing. Popular opinion tends to run counter to allowing payment, because some see this as baby selling.

Illinois may prove to be a popular state for couples looking to contract with a surrogate. One thing that statute does not require is residency of any of the parties to the agreement. This raises the possibility that residents of other states will come to Illinois in order to enter into surrogacy contracts. Another feature of the act that will appeal to parties seeking a surrogacy arrangement is the ease with which the parents can obtain a birth certificate—that is, without having to go to court. Because the Gestational Surrogacy Act is fairly recent, time will need to pass before the full effect of the statute on custodial issues can be evaluated.

Visitation

The Illinois legislature, as well as the courts of this state, have taken the view that, whenever possible, it is desirable for a child to have a relationship with both parents. The statute on visitation, 750 ILCS 5/607, clearly states that a parent who has not been awarded physical custody of a child is entitled to reasonable visitation with the child unless visitation would seriously endanger the child. Thus, to deny or limit visitation requires a more stringent showing than the best interest standard.

Courts often order what is known as *standard visitation*: the non-custodial parent has the child on alternate weekends (Friday evening to Sunday evening) and alternating holidays (for example, the mother has the child on Christmas in even-numbered years, and the father has the child on Christmas in odd-numbered years, and so on), the father has the child every year on Father's Day and the father's birthday, the mother has the child every year on Mother's Day and the mother's birthday, and the non-custodial parent has the child for approximately one-half of the child's summer vacation (four or five weeks).

The non-custodial parent may be able to convince the court that standard visitation is not in the best interest of the child, if he or she can show why the child needs to spend more time with him or her. The most effective way to accomplish this is to show that some or all of the best interest factors previously listed would not be served by limiting visitation to the standard order.

Example: The non-custodial parent can make a case for expanded visitation by providing evidence that the custodial parent is unwilling to facilitate the other parent's relationship with the child. That the custodial parent has a history of attempting to turn the child against the other parent or has unreasonably refused to allow the other parent to have contact with the child can be viewed as a case for expanded visitation.

Settlement Prior to Trial—Custody or Visitation Agreements

Many parents are able to work out a custody or visitation agreement with each other without having to go to trial. You need to decide whether this is the best option for you and, if so, how you will draft your agreement and what to include. This chapter tells you what you should consider when making these important decisions.

Whether to Settle

Once you realize that you are part of a custody dispute, you should evaluate your possible courses of action. Think about what outcome you hope to achieve, and more importantly, try to look honestly at your reasons for wanting that outcome. Also, take into account the standing of the other parent. Has he or she commenced or threatened to commence a proceeding for custody? If not, do you believe he or she would be willing to negotiate a custody arrangement that is satisfactory to you both, or is it more likely that he or she will not budge on what he or she demands?

Please also take into account the costs of a custody dispute; not just the financial expenses, which may be considerable, but also the emotional toll, upon both you and your child. Before deciding to embark upon a full-fledged course of litigation, you should consider whether a custody battle may be avoided.

Whether or not the parents are married to each other, it is preferable in most cases for the parties to come to an agreement on custody and visitation issues before a judicial determination becomes necessary. The parents are more likely to know what is best for the child than the judge. If both parents are motivated by the child's well-being, the resulting custody agreement will most likely be beneficial to the child. In addition, if the parents come to agreement on their own, they will be more likely to want to see the custody arrangement succeed, again with a resulting benefit to the child.

Win-Win Situation   Finally, parents who have fashioned their own agreement regarding custody will see themselves as part of a win-win situation. Once a custody determination is left to a judge, it becomes a win-lose proposition, with one party, or sometimes even both, feeling as though they have been defeated in the proceedings. Although it is the judge's decision as to whether he or she will approve a custody agreement reached by the parents outside of court, a judge is likely to give great deference to an arrangement that appears to have been formed on the basis of the child's best interest.

Out-of-Court Agreement   Although it is usually best to avoid an approach that strives to intimidate the other parent, it most certainly is advisable to consult with an attorney if you are considering an out-of-court agreement. In fact, you probably should advise the other parent to get an attorney as well, if he or she has not already done so. Although it might seem as though you would have an advantage if you are represented and the other parent is not, an attorney often serves the purpose of giving the other parent an objective opinion about the position he or she has adopted. Therefore, if the other parent truly has been taking an unreasonable position about one of the issues at stake, an attorney may be able to convince that parent that he or she should abandon the position because he or she will not succeed.

Example: Ford and Maria are separated and are considering divorce. Ford has asked for shared custody of their children, but Maria will not agree. Maria is angry with Ford for leaving her, and she wrongly believes that Ford is entitled only to supervised visitation every other week. Perhaps if Maria retained an attorney, the attorney would be able to explain the legal principle to Maria. The legal principle states that the supervised visitation is proper only if Ford posed a danger to the children, and this position is not appropriate just because she feels she has been wronged by Ford.

Also, the court will have more confidence in custody agreements reached in situations where both parties are represented, because their consent is more likely to be informed and voluntary.

Sometimes a parent might be hesitant to try to work out a settlement in a custody dispute because the parent believes that he or she will have to give up too much, whereas if a judge were to hear the evidence, the judge would see how obvious it is that the parent is the natural choice to be custodian. However, even if the case were to proceed to trial, a court-ordered arrangement rarely is a slam dunk one way or the other.

If you decide that you and the other parent may be able to negotiate a custody agreement, the next thing you need to do is to take an honest look at both your and the other parent's positions. This means, as discussed earlier, evaluating both your weaknesses as well as the other parent's strengths as potential custodial parents. Some of the factors you should consider are as follows.

- ✪ Whether you have drug or alcohol problems, domestic abuse tendencies, or mental or emotional disabilities. If so, are you willing to seek out help in overcoming these obstacles?

- ✪ Whether you honestly wish to spend as much time as possible with your kids, or want to have the responsibility for making lifestyle decisions for them, or just want to make sure the other parent has less time with them or less control over their upbringing.

- ✪ Who has been the primary caregiver? This does not necessarily mean the person who has spent the most time with the children, but rather the one who has met their basic needs. That is, who is responsible for seeing that the children are fed, dressed, changed, bathed, and cared for when ill? Who plays with the children and takes them to their activities, the doctor, school, religious education classes, and friends' houses?

Mediation

Sometimes parents want very much to reach an out-of-court agreement regarding custody, but are unable to do so on their own. In these cases, *mediation* may be helpful. In fact, there is statutory authority allowing the court to order mediation if necessary to resolve visitation issues or to help determine if an award of joint custody is appropriate.

Finding a Mediator

Mediation is a way to resolve disputes as an alternative to litigating in court. It is a process where the parties meet with a neutral third party who has been trained specifically in the methods of alternative dispute resolution. Often in family law matters the mediator is also an attorney. Sometimes the mediator will meet with both parties at the same time. Other times, the mediator will shuttle back and forth between the parties, trying to get them to reach an agreement. Sometimes the parties' attorneys are present, sometimes they are not. A resolution reached through mediation is not legally binding on the parties. The success of mediation therefore depends on the willingness of the parties to find a middle ground. As a result, there is no way to determine which method of mediation is most effective.

There are a number of ways to locate and evaluate a potential mediator. Your attorney will most likely know one or more professionals in that area that he or she can recommend. If you do not have an attorney, your local bar association may have a list of attorneys or others who specialize in dispute resolution. The Yellow Pages also has listings under "Mediation Services." If your potential mediator was not recommended to you by someone trustworthy, you should interview the mediator to determine whether he or she is someone you would be comfortable working with.

Ask the mediator about his or her qualifications and education, how many years he or she has worked in this field, whether he or she belongs to any professional associations, how he or she approaches the mediation process, and what his or her fees are. Your comfort level with the mediator should be one of your paramount concerns. If you do not believe this is the right person to assist you in reaching a resolution, you should continue your search. The other party to the mediation also must be satisfied with the choice of mediator, or the likelihood of reaching a settlement both parties can live with may be lessened.

Facilitating Negotiation

The goal of the mediator is not to convince one side that the other side is correct. The mediator's purpose is to facilitate negotiation between the parties so they can reach their own agreement on the issues at stake. A resolution that is mutually agreed-upon is more likely to be accepted by the court in a litigation scenario. It also is more likely that the parties will abide by the agreement. A good mediator should be able to identify the issues of contention between the parties and distinguish those issues that are being used by one party merely as points upon which to bargain for other concessions. Moreover, an effective mediator should make the parties feel they are not disadvantaged or powerless in the negotiation process.

If you are in a situation where you are unable to agree on a custody or visitation arrangement with your child's other parent and are contemplating either filing a custody petition or challenging a petition that has been filed against you, it would be beneficial for you and your child for you to honestly examine your motivation. A great deal of expense and anguish may be avoided if parents keep their child's well-being as their top priority.

Mediation Alternative

Unfortunately, parents often are driven by improper motivation, such as a desire for revenge. In cases like these, agreement may not be possible and it will be necessary to submit the matter to the court, which will issue a custody award. If you do reach agreement, it should be presented to the court as a judicial order so the court has the authority to enforce the agreement if it becomes necessary.

Drafting the Agreement

In the event that you and the other party find common ground, the next step will be to put the agreement in writing. Before drafting a custody agreement, you must decide what you want to get out of it. In particular, you should determine how much flexibility you need to write into the agreement. In some cases, a party will want a great deal of flexibility; for example, a father who has a fluctuating work schedule and different days off every week. In other cases, it will be necessary to spell out every detail with very little room for interpretation. An example of this case is where one of the parties uses loopholes in the agreement terms to harass the other parent. In such a case, every issue covered by the agreement will have to be set out with all foreseeable contingencies explained in writing. Unfortunately, situations like this are often not good candidates for mediation in the first place.

The following are issues that usually should be addressed in a custody agreement. Your particular circumstances may require that fewer or more items be included. Consider the following:

- which days of the year the child resides with each parent;

- how school vacations and holidays are to be divided between the parents;

- where and at what time the child is to be dropped off and picked up;

- who makes major decisions about the child, such as major medical issues, dental or orthodontic work, body piercing, dating, schooling, and religious education;

- whether the custodial parent must provide notice of forthcoming or recent doctor visits by the child;

- who has access to school and medical records;

- ✪ who can give consents, for example, to go on class trips, etc., and who is allowed to sign important documents, for example, a passport application for the child;

- ✪ how often, when, and for how long must the custodial parent allow telephone contact between the child and the other parent;

- ✪ that the custodial parent will provide the child with any mail sent to the child by the other parent;

- ✪ whether physical punishment (spanking) is to be allowed;

- ✪ how much input into the child's upbringing will be allowed by either parent's new spouse or significant other;

- ✪ which parent is allowed to take a dependent deduction for income tax purposes;

- ✪ that each parent will provide the other with any change in address or telephone number;

- ✪ that visitation may not be denied to the other parent due to illness of the child or unwillingness of the child to visit the other parent;

- ✪ that neither parent may move with the child out-of-state (or out of the county of residence) without permission from the court;

- ✪ that neither parent will take the child out of the country without the other parent's written consent;

- ✪ that neither parent will intimidate, threaten, harass, stalk, or assault the other;

- ✪ whether the child's grandparents will be allowed visitation with the child in the event of the death of the grandparents' child (for example, paternal grandparents if the father dies);

- ✪ whether the parents agree that one parent will receive custody if the other parent dies; and,

✪ how to handle later disputes; for example, whether additional mediation will be required and who will pay for it.

It also is routine to include a provision saying that, if one of the parties does not follow the agreement and enforcement proceedings become necessary, the person whose actions are the reason for the proceedings will pay the other party's attorney's fees.

Preparing and Litigating a Custody or Visitation Case

An action for custody is commenced in Illinois by filing a petition for either dissolution of marriage, legal separation, or declaration of invalidity of marriage (*annulment*). If the parents are not married to each other, an action is commenced by filing a petition for custody in the county of the child's residence.

Gathering Information and Preserving Evidence

Whether you are attempting to negotiate a custody agreement or have decided to pursue litigation, it is absolutely crucial for you to have as much relevant factual data as possible, as quickly as possible. This will enable you and your attorney to evaluate your position and adopt the best stance possible for your case. In order to prepare your case, you must do two things: gather information and preserve evidence.

The information you need to collect is anything that will show that you are a parent who deserves to have the custody or visitation award that you are seeking. You also need to be prepared, if necessary, to show that the other parent should not have the award he or she seeks. While it is true that in a negotiation situation you usually are better off avoiding a combative or accusatory position, you have to be prepared for the possibility that negotiation may not succeed. In this case, you will have to leave it to the court to make the custody or visitation determination. For this reason, information favorable to you is important, as is information that may be unfavorable to the other parent.

It is equally important for the preparation of your case that you provide your attorney with information that is *unfavorable* to your position. The reason for this is that your attorney may be able to neutralize the negative effect of such information. If your attorney is not aware of the unfavorable information in advance and hears it for the first time when it is presented to the judge in your case, he or she will not be in a position to soften its impact.

Evaluating Witnesses

In assessing the weaknesses in your own position, it will be necessary to consider what others may say about you, should the time come when witnesses are called in to court to give testimony. You should evaluate your relationships with those around you, from your own family members to the other parent's relatives and friends, to others with whom you have had regular contact. In particular, beware of the neighbor or other non-relative with whom you have had an ongoing spat. A person with an agenda against you and no familial ties with the other parent may, perhaps wrongly, give the appearance of being a neutral, objective witness should he or she be called to testify.

The testimony of such witnesses may be very damaging to your case because the judge may give the testimony more weight than he or she would to the testimony of the other parent's relatives. The judge would expect those relatives to automatically give evidence that reflects negatively upon you, but would not have the same expectation of non-relatives. Unfortunately, a neighbor or other outsider with a grudge against you may not necessarily be motivated to be fair or even honest in giving testimony. In such a situation, you should be prepared to explain to your attorney why the seemingly neutral witness is not credible and should not be believed.

Preserving Evidence

Preserving evidence is something you should think about as soon as you have determined that you have a custody or visitation issue. Especially if you are considering leaving a home that you share with the other parent, having in your possession copies of important documents, photographs, and other items that may be needed to present your case is strongly advised. It is best to start a file of these items, and to keep it in a safe place. If it is not possible or practical to have original documents in this file, be sure to make photocopies. Some of this information also may be useful when determining what child support should be paid and by whom.

If you have access to them, the information in your file should contain the following:

- federal and state income tax returns, from at least the last two years, for both you and the other parent;

- bank statements for any separate or joint accounts, held either by you or the other parent, for at least the last six months;

- Social Security numbers for you, the other parent, and the child;

- any health insurance or prescription records pertaining to the other parent, particularly if the physical condition of or prescription drug abuse by the other parent is an issue;

- any documentation regarding the other parent's employment history, including any disciplinary warnings or termination notices;

- any credit card account numbers, loan account information, such as mortgage, car loans, or student loans, whether in your name alone, in the name of the other parent alone, or held jointly;

- any documentation showing other property, whether real estate, personal property, or intangible property, such as a patent or copyright belonging to the other parent;

- any correspondence in your possession written by the other parent, particularly if it is complimentary to you as a parent, or on the other hand if it is threatening to you or another person, or otherwise shows that the other parent may not act in the best interest of the child;

❂ any public records indicating violations of the law or unlawful harmful conduct on the part of the other parent, including court records of criminal violations, previous court orders prohibiting domestic violence, or lawsuits filed against the other parent by third parties; and,

❂ any previous court orders that have been entered concerning the custody of any of the children involved in the current case.

In addition, you should know and be able to provide as much information as possible about your child's life, including personal preferences and interests. This is especially important if you are trying to show that you are the child's primary caregiver and you should be the custodial parent.

The following are some of the things you should know about your child:

❂ birth date;

❂ favorite color, foods, toys, songs, etc.;

❂ clothes and shoe sizes;

❂ names and phone numbers of doctor and dentist;

❂ names of day care providers and/or teachers;

❂ names of friends; and,

❂ extracurricular activities, sports, and hobbies.

Of course, every custody or visitation situation is different. Some of the documents and information listed here may not apply to your particular case, and others not listed may be very useful. This list is meant to give you an idea about where to start in your search for evidence and information. If you are unable to obtain information or documents you believe are important to your case, there are court procedures that may help you gain access to them, but this usually requires that a custody case actually has been filed.

Commencing a Court Case

Jurisdiction and Venue

An attorney seeking to file a petition for custody on behalf of a parent first must determine which court has the power to hear the case, termed *jurisdiction*. There are set rules by which this determination is made; otherwise, there could be no final settlement of the issues because competing custody orders from different courts would have no authoritative value. Simply put, jurisdiction refers to which court has the authority to rule on the issues in a particular case. *Venue* refers to the location of the proper court with which to file a custody action. Illinois has joined a number of other states in adopting a version of the *Uniform Child Custody Jurisdiction and Enforcement Act* (UCCJEA) to answer the question of which courts have jurisdiction over custody matters. The Illinois UCCJEA can be found at 750 ILCS 36/1.

According to the UCCJEA, jurisdiction is proper in the Illinois circuit courts if:

✪   Illinois is the home state of the child at the time the proceeding is commenced (the home state is the state where the child has continually lived with the parent for six months);

✪   Illinois has been the home state of the child but the child is now absent from the state due to his or her removal or retention by one claiming custody, and a parent or other person acting as a parent still resides in Illinois;

✪   the child and his parent or parents have a significant connection with Illinois, and there is substantial evidence available in the state regarding the child's present care, future care, protection, training, and personal relationships; or,

✪   any other state that could properly hear and decide the case (or *exercise jurisdiction*) has specifically refused to exercise jurisdiction because Illinois courts are better suited to decide the case.

Once the attorney determines that Illinois is the proper jurisdiction in which to commence a custody case, he or she next must decide *which* Illinois court is the appropriate venue. Generally, the proper court will be in the county where the child resides.

Preparing Court Documents

If you decide it is necessary to litigate your custody or visitation case, whether you are the one initiating the case or are responding to a petition filed by the other parent, there are a number of documents you will need to prepare and file with the court. If you are the person who commences litigation, you are called the *petitioner*. If the custody petition has been filed against you, you are the *respondent*.

Petition

As previously mentioned, the court case begins when the petitioner files the petition. In the case of parents who are married to each other, this will be either a *petition for dissolution of marriage*, a *petition for legal separation*, or a *petition for declaration of invalidity of marriage* (annulment). If the parents are not married to each other, the petitioner will file a *petition for custody of the child*.

If you are the petitioner, your petition should be in paragraph form. Each fact you are relying on to support your petition should be a separate paragraph. Likewise, as the respondent, you should reply to each of the allegations of the petition against you with a separate paragraph that either admits, denies, or claims insufficient knowledge for each specific allegation. (Blank petitions for custody and support, and for visitation, are found in Appendix E. (see form 1, p.237 and form 8, p.255.))

UCCJEA Affidavit

For the petitioner, it also is very important to prepare and file, along with the petition, a document commonly known as a **UCCJEA AFFIDAVIT**, which is required by Section 209 of the *Uniform Child Custody Jurisdiction and Enforcement Act*. Through the affidavit, the petitioner states under oath that Illinois is the proper jurisdiction for the matter at hand. An example of the **UCCJEA Affidavit** can be found in Appendix E. (see form 5, p.247.)

When one parent files an action in court for custody, the United States Constitution requires that the other parent receive notice of the proceeding and an opportunity to be heard in the matter. Therefore, in addition to the petition, it is necessary to prepare a document called a *summons*, which is a notice of the pending action. A sample petition for custody and summons are included in Appendix D of this book. Often in Illinois, however, a particular county will have its own summons form that must be used.

If a parent is pursuing a custody or visitation case and the other parent lives out-of-state, the petitioner's attorney will have to follow the rules of procedure in that state to provide adequate notice. The petitioner's attorney will have to use that state's forms as well.

Filing the Documents

Once the documents have been prepared, they must be filed in the appropriate court. The attorney will bring an original and at least one copy of the summons and the petition to the office of the clerk of the court. The attorney will file the originals with the court and should request the clerk to stamp the copies with the date and time filed. The attorney should also request the extra copies for the attorney's file. The case begins at the time the summons and petition are filed.

Filing Fees

It is standard for the clerk to require the petitioner to pay a filing fee for the documents. The fee will vary from county to county. Often the fee will include a charge for having the county sheriff *serve* copies of the summons and petition to the other parent. In some cases, an indigent petitioner can ask the clerk to waive the fees. Usually the petitioner will be required to first submit an *affidavit*, a written statement made under oath, showing why he or she cannot afford to pay the fees.

Service of the Summons

Service of the summons and petition, called *service of process*, must be made either by the sheriff of the county where the respondent resides or by a special process server who is registered with the county sheriff. The summons must be given to the respondent directly or must be given to a resident of the respondent's household who is older than thirteen years of age, and a copy of the summons should be mailed to the respondent.

Illinois also provides for notice by publication in a newspaper. This happens only in cases where the petitioner files an affidavit stating that he or she made a good faith effort to locate the other parent, has been unable to do so, and does not know where the other parent is.

Once the sheriff or process server serves the respondent, he or she will fill out an affidavit of service, stating under oath that the respondent was served with the summons. This affidavit is proof that the respondent has notice of the pending custody proceeding. Anyone who has received such notice and fails to respond to the petition does so at his or her peril, as you will see in the following section.

Responding to a Petition

Upon receiving service of a summons and petition in a custody matter, a respondent generally has thirty days to file a response, called a *responsive pleading*. Absent some sort of technical problem with the petition or summons themselves, the respondent should file a document answering each specific allegation of the petition, either with an admission, a denial, or a statement that the respondent has insufficient knowledge of the facts of the allegation to admit or deny.

Agree or Disagree   If you are a respondent, you will have to decide whether you agree or disagree with the allegations of the petition and the request for relief. If you wish to contest the custody arrangement being asked for by the petitioner, you should set out in your response your reasons for disagreement. If the other parent is requesting sole or primary custody, as opposed to joint custody, you may wish to make your own request for custody in your response. (An example of a RESPONSE TO A PETITION FOR CHILD CUSTODY AND SUPPORT is included in Appendix E; see form 2, p.239.)

Thirty-Day Time Period   If the respondent is unable to file a response within the thirty-day period, the respondent's attorney must file a request to extend the time allowed before the end of the thirty days. If a person who is served with a summons and petition for custody fails to file any responsive pleading or request for more time in which to answer, he or she may be found in default by the court. This means that he or she may be barred from filing documents in the case at all and may be denied an opportunity to present his or her case. The petitioner may therefore be automatically awarded whatever he or she asked for in the petition. For that reason, it is imperative that if you are served with a petition for custody, you seek legal counsel as soon as possible so your attorney may meet the filing deadline and avoid default. There usually is no filing fee for a response to a petition for custody.

Litigation

Litigation begins upon the filing of the documents previously discussed. If no responsive pleadings have been filed within the deadline, the respondent can be held in default and the petitioner may be granted whatever he or she requested without further action. If an answer is filed, however, the next steps are geared toward preparing for trial and *temporarily* resolving certain issues until final judgment is entered.

The next stages are *discovery*, *pretrial*, *trial*, and *judgment*. During discovery, information and evidence are collected under the supervision of the court. During the pretrial hearing, which is often informal, the issues to be ruled upon by the court at trial are fixed. If the case does not settle, it proceeds to trial, where physical and testimonial evidence is heard by the judge in a formal setting. After considering the evidence, the court will enter a final judgment that will include a custody award and any visitation provisions that the court deems proper. A party who believes the court made an error in the final judgment has a right to appeal the decision to the Illinois appellate court.

Temporary Motions

Either party to a custody proceeding may ask the court for a *temporary custody* order. In such a case, the court may award temporary custody based on what is in the best interest of the child. Temporary custody orders are addressed in the Illinois statutes at 750 ILCS 5/603.

When filing a petition for custody, the petitioner's attorney usually will simultaneously file a motion asking the court to grant temporary custody of the child to the petitioner. If this motion is granted, it usually will allow the petitioner to retain custody of the child throughout the pendency of the custody case. Other temporary motions that may be made at this time are for the payment of temporary child support and for possession of the home where the child lives, where applicable. The need for financial support and a home for the child depends on whether the petitioner receives temporary custody of the child. Therefore, the outcomes of these motions are interconnected.

Representation for the Child

The court may appoint an attorney to represent a child who is the subject of a custody proceeding. There are several different forms that such a representation may take:

- ✪ an attorney to represent the child's wishes;

- ✪ a *guardian ad litem*, who argues for whatever he or she deems is in the child's best interests; or,

- ✪ a child's representative (discussed as follows).

The provisions related to representation for a child are found at 750 ILCS 5/506. There are several differences between the three types of representatives.

The attorney appointed to represent the child's wishes does just that— he or she strives to achieve the child's desires in the custody dispute, even when the child's wishes do not appear to follow his or her own best interest. Both the guardian ad litem and the child's representative, on the other hand, investigate and make a determination regarding the child's best interest, and then advocate that position before the court. For this reason, the court is more likely to appoint an attorney to serve as a guardian ad litem or a child's representative in the case of a younger child, and will appoint an attorney to represent the child's wishes only in the case where the court believes the child is competent to make decisions that conform to his or her best interest.

Whether the appointment is of a guardian ad litem or a child's representative, the main purpose of the appointment is to review the facts of a case and make a recommendation to the court as to custody. The attorney will investigate all relevant aspects of the case, including:

- the preference of the child as to custody;

- the positions of each of the parents as to custody;

- drug or alcohol abuse by either parent;

- abuse of the child by either parent;

- the relationship between the child and others in his or her household;

- the ability of each parent to provide for the child's physical needs, such as food and clothing;

- the method each parent uses to discipline the child;

- the living environment each parent provides for the child, such as the quality of the neighborhood and schools;

- the amount of time each parent spends with the child, and conversely, the amount of time each parent is unavailable due to job requirements; and,

- any other factor that impacts the best interest of the child.

When the court appoints one of these representatives, it usually will include an order directing how payment to the representative is to be made. The court may require one or both parents to pay, or may order payment to come from the marital estate or even the child's assets. Such payments are considered to be similar to child support, and as a result are not able to be avoided by filing bankruptcy.

Discovery   The process of discovery is the means by which a party to a custody action can gather information when the other party will not provide it voluntarily. The rules of the Illinois Supreme Court allow certain methods that each side can use to demand information and evidence from the other. The rules also provide penalties for refusal to comply with discovery requests. Various types of discovery are discussed as follows.

Interrogatories

Interrogatories are a series of written questions that are submitted to the other party to be answered under oath. In Illinois, the maximum number of interrogatories that may be propounded without further permission of the court is thirty, including subparts of questions. Under Supreme Court Rule 213, the Illinois Supreme Court has approved standard interrogatories that will serve to maximize information gathering in most cases. These INTERROGATORIES are included in Appendix E. (see form 14, p.267.)

If there are circumstances in your own case that render the standard interrogatories insufficient, it is important that your attorney phrase the questions in such a way that requests as much information as possible within the thirty-question limit. Otherwise, it will be necessary to move the court for permission to propound additional interrogatories. Such a request will be granted only in limited circumstances where good cause is shown.

Request to Admit Facts

If you believe there are facts that are not being disputed by the other party, you can submit a request to admit facts to the other party. This is a series of written assertions of fact to which the other party must respond under oath. The response will be in the form of an admission, a denial, or a statement that the other party is unable to admit or deny and the reason why. Having admissions of the other party to a set of facts will save time and effort at trial by narrowing the scope of issues that are in dispute.

Subpoenas/ Requests to Produce

If you find from the other party's responses to your interrogatories and request to admit facts that there are documents in existence that would be helpful to your case, the next step is to compel production of those documents. If the documents are in the hands of the other party, you should serve him or her with a *request to produce*. If the documents are in the possession of a third party, such as a bank or the other party's employer, you will need to serve the third party with a subpoena for documents.

You must be particular about the documents you are seeking and they must be relevant to the issues at stake in your case. Otherwise, the other party may object to the subpoena or request to produce as being over-broad. While the court will not allow a fishing expedition for documents, discovery is meant to help ascertain the truth, and so subpoenas usually will be liberally interpreted to allow the documents to be discovered.

Depositions   In a *deposition*, a witness (called the *deponent*) is placed under oath and asked a series of questions by the attorney for one of the parties. The testimony is recorded by a court reporter and can be used as evidence at trial. The deponent can be one of the litigants or may be a third party. Parties themselves are called to a deposition by means of a *notice to appear*, delivered to the party's attorney. Third-party deponents must be summoned by a *subpoena*, which can be served by certified or registered mail and must include a witness fee and mileage costs.

If the person you seek to depose is expected to give testimony favorable to your case, consult with him or her to schedule the deposition, at his or her convenience if possible. You do not want to alienate the deponent by having a subpoena show up unexpectedly, ordering the person to appear and submit to a deposition. Even though a deposition is a routine procedure, it may be intimidating to one who is unfamiliar with the course of a legal proceeding.

As with a request to produce, the questions asked of the deponent must be relevant to the proceeding giving rise to the deposition, or the attorney for the other party is likely to object. If that happens, the objectionable question will have to be presented to the court for a determination as to whether it is proper.

When preparing interrogatories, your attorney should include a request that the other party list all witnesses the other party intends to call at trial and the subject of the testimony of each witness. You can then determine which of the potential witnesses should be deposed. Although the cost of taking depositions, including court reporters and transcripts, can be prohibitive, you probably should err on the side of caution and depose as many of the listed witnesses as possible to avoid unpleasant surprises at trial. In addition, deposing witnesses will get their testimony on the record so that if a witness attempts to change his or her story at trial, your attorney will be able to use the prior deposition testimony to *impeach*, or discredit, the witness.

Of course, in a typical case, you also will be called to give a deposition by the other side. Your attorney should be present during the deposition, should prepare you for giving testimony beforehand by foreseeing and going over questions with you that are likely to be asked, and should object at the time of the deposition to any question that is improper.

Remember that even if you do not feel you make a particularly good witness, depositions are different than live testimony. Whatever you say will be transcribed by a court reporter, and if your testimony comes up again at a later time during the litigation, it will only be read out loud. In other words, if you stammer or your hands shake because you are nervous, or if you take a long time to answer questions, it will not show up in the written transcript. Giving testimony before the judge, however, is another matter, which is discussed as follows.

Request for Mental or Physical Examination

If you believe that the mental or physical condition of either the other parent or the child is at issue, you can ask the court to order a mental or physical evaluation of that person. In addition, the court may require such an examination on its own or may order an approved social service agency to conduct an investigation in the child's custodial arrangement, under 750 ILCS 5/605. In that case, the investigator may send the child to a professional for a mental or physical exam.

A psychiatric evaluation of the child may be useful if you believe the other parent is doing psychological harm to the child, or if you wish to show that the other parent has psychiatric or psychological issues affecting his or her ability to adequately care for the child. In a psychiatric evaluation for custody purposes, the subject is likely to be given several tests to assess his or her personality traits and responses to various real-life situations. The tests are designed to correct for the possibility that some subjects may give answers they consider to be the "right" answer, even if the answer given is not honest. Some of these tests are also used to uncover indicators of the potential for mental illness.

The evaluator will also interview the subject and may interview others who the evaluator believes can provide relevant information. Sometimes the evaluator will ask the subject to provide the names of people who know the subject and are willing to answer questions about him or her. The evaluator might then speak to these people or might provide them with a written questionnaire to complete and return.

The evaluator will take the information provided by all concerned, along with the test results and his or her own opinions and make a report of his or her findings, which may include a recommendation as to custody. The determination of the custody evaluator is a crucial piece of evidence, one to which a court may give a great deal of weight.

Evaluation of the Child's Best Interest

Upon motion by a party, parent, custodian, guardian ad litem, or other representative of the child, an evaluation of the best interest of the child may be ordered by the court. The court itself may consult with an expert, in which case the parties' attorneys may examine the expert in the same manner as any other witness.

Interview with the Child

The judge in a custody case has the authority to interview the child in the judge's chambers in order to ascertain the child's preference for custody arrangements. Generally, parents are not present at the interview, although the parents' attorneys are allowed to attend unless the parties agree otherwise.

Pretrial

The purpose of a pretrial hearing or conference is to focus the issues that the judge will be asked to rule upon at trial and to clear up any lingering matters that need to be settled prior to trial, such as any outstanding discovery requests or objections to evidence or witnesses that the other party will seek to produce at trial. The judge will ask the attorneys to state their clients' positions, in the hope that the judge can recommend a resolution the parties can agree on and avoid going to trial. If there is no settlement at the pretrial hearing, the judge will set a trial date.

Trial

The trial is the formal presentation of evidence and legal arguments in support of each party's case. The admissibility of evidence presented in court is subject to formal requirements found in the Illinois Supreme Court Rules. An in-depth discussion of the rules of evidence is beyond the scope of this book. In general, however, any physical evidence, photographs, documents, or witness testimony that you want the court to consider must be credible and must be relevant to the issues at stake in your case. In addition, documents must be shown to be authentic.

The procedure at trial generally follows a certain pattern. First, the petitioner's attorney presents an opening statement, in which he or she provides an overview of the petitioner's position and the evidence that will be presented at trial. Next, the respondent's attorney makes his or her own opening statement. After this, evidence is presented in the form of both physical evidence and witness testimony. Witness testimony is discussed in more detail as follows.

If one side does not believe that the court should consider a certain piece of evidence or a witness statement, that attorney should object to the admission of the evidence. The court will rule on each objection as it is made, either by *sustaining the objection* (agreeing with the objection and refusing to allow the evidence) or *overruling the objection* (disagreeing with the objection and allowing the evidence). It is necessary to object to any problematic evidence in order to be able to raise the issue on appeal if objectionable evidence is admitted.

After all the evidence has been submitted, each party may make a closing argument. This is a summary of what has been presented to the court, along with citations to the applicable law, and argument as to why the court should rule in favor of that particular party. The petitioner's side goes first. This is your last chance to impress the merits of your case upon the judge, so it is best to be sure the argument is well-organized, to the point, and supported by the evidence that has been presented.

Witness Testimony

At trial, both parents will have the opportunity to present evidence in support of their respective positions. Much of the evidence will be oral testimony given by various witnesses, including the parents themselves. Other potential witnesses are grandparents and other family members, friends, neighbors, the child's doctor, teacher or sports coach, and others who have a relationship with either parent or the child who can provide relevant testimony as to the factors affecting the best interest of the child. Prior to trial, the witnesses who will be called by each side usually have been disclosed, either in response to interrogatories or at the time of the pretrial conference.

As discussed previously, it is advisable to take depositions of all the other party's witnesses before trial to minimize the likelihood that there will be testimony during the trial for which your attorney is unprepared. Depositions serve the additional purpose of allowing you to see how a potential witness conducts himself or herself under examination by attorneys. This will help you evaluate which of the other party's witnesses will be most credible.

By the same measure, your attorney should interview the witnesses that you intend to call to testify. Your attorney can then prepare your witnesses for giving testimony and can ascertain what they will say when on the stand. It is possible that the other side will take depositions of your witnesses, for which your attorney should be present.

Each of your witnesses will be *examined* by your attorney at trial. After one witness is examined directly, the other party will have the opportunity to *cross-examine* the witness regarding the answers the witness gave on direct examination. Prior to deposition or trial, your attorney should go over the questions he or she plans on asking the witness and also should discuss the questions that may be asked of the witness on cross-examination.

Your attorney can evaluate the witness's demeanor, and can prepare to soften the impact of any negative testimony that may be given. Keep in mind that the attorney cannot put words in the witness's mouth. The witness will be under oath when testifying at trial and will be subject to prosecution for perjury if he or she lies on the stand.

You, as a witness in the case, also need to be prepared by your attorney to testify. For many people, a case such as this will be the first time they have ever found themselves on a witness stand. It can be an intimidating experience. The most important thing to remember is to tell the truth. If you have been honest with your attorney so far, hopefully he or she can mitigate the effect of negative testimony. At the same time, you should take care not to volunteer more information than that for which you are asked, whether it is your attorney or the other party's attorney who is asking.

Some people, because they are nervous on the witness stand, keep talking even after they have responded to the examining attorney's most recent question. Give your answer, make it short and sweet, and then sit silently until the next question is asked. If you do not know the answer to a question, simply state that you do not know.

If the other party's attorney asks you an inappropriate question on cross-examination, it is your attorney's job to object to the question. If the other attorney asks you a question that is confusing to you, or that assumes an answer, state that you do not understand or are not able to answer the question as it has been posed. If the other attorney asks you a question requiring you to give an answer that has a negative effect on your case or that impeaches your credibility, your attorney will have a chance to rehabilitate your testimony on redirect examination.

Above all, try not to let your nerves get to you. Take a calming breath, if necessary, before answering. Try to remain fairly still on the stand, because leg-bouncing, finger-tapping, and other nervous behaviors can be distracting to the judge as he or she tries to listen to your testimony.

Expert Testimony

The testimony of experts is often of key importance in a custody case. Health care professionals and physicians, in particular, may be invaluable in shedding light on many of the factors that the court considers in determining the best interest of the child. Experts may be appointed by the court or may be called by the parties to testify in support of a party's particular position. In the latter case, the expert witness, along with the subject of his or her expected testimony, must be disclosed to the other party prior to trial.

Courtroom Demeanor

It is important to understand the behavior that is expected of those appearing in a courtroom. Even if you have an attorney representing you, your own appearance and manners may have an impact on the judge's decision in your case.

First of all, you should appear in court well-groomed. It is not necessary for you to have an expensive suit or designer clothes, but you should be clean and your outfit should be in good repair. Men with long hair, beards, and so on, should not be unkempt. If you show that you care how you look, it sends a message to the judge that you also will take care of your child.

Second, you should not be late to court. If your case is called and you are not present, your attorney will have to ask that the case be held until the judge has finished the rest of his or her business. This will inconvenience the court, and also may tell the judge that this proceeding is not of the utmost importance to you, as it should be.

Finally, you should use proper manners before the judge, even if you are in the spectator area waiting for your case to be called. Do not speak loudly or rudely, do not use bad language, and do not make any threatening remarks or gestures. There are bailiffs present who will remove you from the courtroom. Beyond that, use common manners. Do not chew gum or bring food or drinks to court. Do not bring a newspaper; turn off your pager and cell phone. Many judges instruct their bailiffs to forbid parties from bringing these items into the courtroom at all.

When speaking to the judge, address him or her as "Your Honor," "Sir," or "Ma'am." Regardless of the outcome of your court date, tell the judge "Thank you" when the proceedings are finished and save any outbursts for your attorney once you have left the courtroom. Particularly in contentious cases where you may find yourself before this judge on a number of occasions, it is important to give the impression that you are serious about your case and also that you respect the court's authority in the matter.

Judgment   After hearing all the evidence and arguments by the parties' or child's attorneys, reviewing pleadings and document evidence, and considering any independent or court-ordered reports, evaluations, or recommendations, as necessary, the court will enter a final judgment. In the case of a dissolution of marriage action, there will be a judgment of dissolution, which may well include a number of other provisions related to issues such as child support and property division.

If the parties have agreed to a custody arrangement outside of court, whether before or after the court has heard evidence, the agreement must be submitted to the judge for his or her approval. If the judge accepts the agreement, it will be encompassed in the final judgment order. Custody and visitation agreements are discussed more fully in Chapter 4.

Appeal
If each party decides that it can live with the custody award given by the court, the litigation ends.

NOTE: *There may be issues of enforcement or modification of the award at some point down the road. Those issues are discussed later in this book.*

If, on the other hand, the award is unacceptable to one or both of the parties, the next step is to take the matter to a higher court, through a process called an *appeal*.

In Illinois, there are three levels of courts: the circuit, or trial, court; the appellate court, and the Illinois Supreme Court. The trial court is the court where evidence is considered, and the order fixing custodial rights is entered. The kind of litigation discussed up to this point takes place in the trial court. Taking a case to the appellate court is, in effect, "going over the head" of the trial court judge. Illinois is divided into five appellate districts, each one made up of a number of judicial circuits. The City of Chicago, for example, is part of the Circuit Court of Cook County (trial level) and is within the First Appellate District (appellate level).

The party wishing to file an appeal is called the *appellant*, and the one responding to the appeal is the *appellee*. Sometimes, both sides file appeals; in that case, the parties are *cross-appellants*. No new evidence is heard by the appellate court; only the transcribed record of the trial court proceedings, pleadings filed by the parties, and in some cases, additional oral arguments presented by the attorneys are considered on appeal.

As in making a decision to proceed to trial with a custody issue, you should carefully examine your motives if you are considering filing an appeal of a final custody determination. Appellate work is quite involved and may be expensive. The standard for reversal of a trial court decision is fairly high, and it is more likely than not that the appellate court will refuse to overrule the trial court. Emotions run high in custody matters and sometimes the desire to achieve total victory over the other party can cloud an honest assessment of the merits of your position. Consider whether you want to take the chance of losing whatever you were granted by the trial court, because there is no guarantee that the end result will be different, even if you manage to have the trial court overruled. The case could be returned to the trial court for a new hearing, and the results of that hearing conceivably could be less favorable than what you received the first time around.

Unless otherwise provided by the Supreme Court Rules, appeals can be taken only from a *final* judgment by the trial court. By and large, an order that leaves many issues unsettled usually will not be considered final by Illinois courts. On the other hand, a judgment that resolves all the main issues of the case, such as custody, property division, and maintenance (which used to be called *alimony*) in an order for dissolution of marriage, usually will be considered final.

The appellant must have grounds for challenging a final order by the trial court. The most common grounds for appeal are that the trial court made a mistake in applying the law or that the trial court judge could not have reasonably come to his or her decision. This is very difficult to show since the trial court judge is the one who heard the testimony and reviewed the other evidence firsthand. Appellate courts are very hesitant to reverse a case solely on the basis that the trial judge incorrectly evaluated the facts.

Filing an Appeal   The procedural rules for appeals are found in Article III of the Illinois Supreme Court Rules. In order to initiate an appeal, you must file a document called a *notice of appeal* and serve a copy of the notice to the other parent. The notice of appeal is filed with the clerk of the circuit court that heard your case at the trial court level. The notice of appeal must be filed within thirty days of the judgment, or, if there has been a post-trial motion, within thirty days of the ruling on that motion. If the thirtieth day falls on a Saturday, Sunday, or court holiday, the deadline for filing will be the next business day after that. If, on the other hand, you are the appellee—that is, you are the one who is served with a notice of appeal filed by the other parent—you have ten days after being served to file a cross-appeal if you wish to do so.

NOTE: *The Illinois Supreme Court Rules are very specific regarding filing deadlines. While trial courts sometimes are lenient with litigants, often giving parties a second or third chance to correct pleadings and file documents late, the appellate courts are not so forgiving, even in the case of an appellant who is representing himself or herself.*

Docketing Statement

Within fourteen days after the notice of appeal is filed, the appellant must file a *docketing statement*. This document provides the appellate court with background information about the case, for example, by identifying the parties, their attorneys, and the statute that gives the court jurisdiction to hear the appeal, among other information.

Record on Appeal

The appellant also is responsible for seeing that the record of proceedings in the trial court is given to the appellate court. The record consists of all pleadings, transcripts of court hearings, and any exhibits that have been submitted into evidence at the trial court level. First, within the fourteen days allowed for filing the docketing statement, the appellant must make a written request to the court reporter who transcribed the trial court proceedings to provide a certified copy of the transcript, which the appellant then must file with the circuit court clerk. Once the clerk's office receives the transcript, the clerk prepares, binds, and certifies the record. The clerk may then transport the record directly to the appellate court or, in many cases, will turn the record over to the parties to use in preparing their briefs. As an appellant, you must take care to ensure that nothing is left out of the record, because it will be the only factual material that the appellate court will consider.

Appellate Briefs

Aside from the record of the trial court proceedings itself, the most important part of a party's case on appeal is the brief. The appellate brief summarizes the case and provides a roadmap of the party's position for the appellate justices. Illinois Supreme Court Rule 341 gives specific guidance for the layout of the parties' appellate briefs, from the number of pages allowed to the requirements of the brief's cover to the required order of the parts of the brief. Again, the rules here are quite strict. Failure to produce a brief that is in compliance with Rule 341 may cause the appellate court to strike the brief, which may seriously impede your ability to present your case. Following is a sample cover of an appellate brief.

No. 3-02-2976
IN THE
APPELLATE COURT OF ILLINOIS
THIRD JUDICIAL DISTRICT

| IN RE THE MARRIAGE OF:
JANE X. SMITH,

Petitioner-Appellant,

and

JOHN Z. SMITH,

Respondent-Appellee. |)
)
)
)
)
)
)
)
)
)
)
) | Appeal from the Circuit Court
of Will County, 12th Judicial
Circuit

Case No. 02 D 14587

The Honorable
JOAN Q. DOE
Judge Presiding |

BRIEF OF JANE X. SMITH,
PETITIONER-APPELLANT

JEAN Y. ROE
Attorney at Law
164 W. Jefferson Street
Joliet, Illinois 60431
(815) 555-0000
Attorney for Petitioner-Appellant

ORAL ARGUMENT REQUESTED

Oral Argument

Oral argument is the opportunity to present your case to a panel made up of appellate justices. It must be specifically requested at the bottom of the cover of your brief. The court is authorized to deny oral argument when no substantial question is presented, although this power is used sparingly. Despite that admonition, one appellate court staff member has said that in his district, only about 10% of the cases on appeal are allowed oral argument. If neither side requests oral argument, the case may be decided on the briefs and the trial court record; however, the appellate court may order the attorneys to appear and argue if it deems oral argument necessary.

Arguments usually are made before a panel of three justices. There are strict time limits for oral argument. Each side gets twenty minutes to present its case, and the appellant also receives ten minutes to give a rebuttal argument. During argument, it is possible that the justices will interrupt the attorneys to ask questions. For this reason, it is crucial that the attorneys not only be prepared to present the strengths of their client's case, but that they also be ready to discuss the weaknesses in their arguments.

Appellate Court and Further Appeals

Eventually, the appellate court will hand down its ruling in the appeal. The court might affirm the trial court, in which case the trial court's final order will be enforceable once the time for filing a further appeal has passed. However, the appellate court might reverse the trial court, in which case the trial court's judgment will be void and unenforceable. This will usually leave the parties' rights and responsibilities unsettled, so the case must be sent back to the trial court with instructions that the trial court must follow.

If either party is dissatisfied with the appellate court decision, it is possible to try a further appeal to the Illinois Supreme Court. In custody and support cases, however, it is up to the Supreme Court to decide if it will hear the appeal. In order to commence a Supreme Court appeal, a party must file a petition asking the Court to hear the case. Realistically, the chances of having the Court review a custody case are extremely slim, unless there is a truly unique legal issue involved.

Visitation Difficulties and Other Abuse

No matter how a custody issue is resolved, whether by the court's order or an agreement between the parties, there is no guarantee that the parties will abide by the terms of the resolution. The emergency situations discussed in this chapter often occur before and during, as well as after, a custody matter is litigated or negotiated. Nowadays, state and federal statutes that prohibit the particular conduct discussed cover all the circumstances listed as follows. Sanctions can range from criminal penalties to changes in a custody award from one parent to the other.

Domestic Abuse

The *Illinois Domestic Violence Act of 1986* is found at 750 ILCS 60. It serves to protect:

- ✪ any person abused by a family or household member;

- ✪ any high-risk adult with disabilities who is abused, neglected, or exploited by a family or household member;

- ✪ any minor child or dependent adult in the care of such person; and,

- ✪ any person residing or employed at a private home or public shelter that is housing an abused family or a household member.

The Domestic Violence Act allows courts to issue orders meant to prevent domestic abuse, called *orders of protection*. Actions for orders of protection can be commenced either by filing a petition for an order of protection by itself or by petitioning for an order of protection as part of a dissolution of marriage or other proceeding. An action also can be commenced by filing a petition for an order of protection as part of a criminal prosecution. To obtain an order of protection, the petitioner must show that it is more likely than not that the abuse occurred.

Orders of protection under the Domestic Violence Act may:

- ✪ prohibit conduct by the respondent that amounts to harassment, interference with personal liberty, intimidation of a dependent, physical abuse, or willful deprivation, neglect, or exploitation;

- ✪ prohibit the respondent from entering or remaining in the residence of the petitioner;

- ✪ order the respondent to stay away from the petitioner or any other person protected by the order of protection, or prohibit the respondent from entering or remaining at the petitioner's school, place of employment, or other specified places at times when the petitioner is present;

- ✪ require or recommend that the respondent undergo counseling;

- ✪ award temporary legal custody to the petitioner. If a court finds after a hearing that the respondent has committed abuse of a child, there is a presumption that awarding temporary legal custody to the respondent would not be in the child's best interest;

- ✪ restrict or deny the respondent's visitation with a child if the court finds that the respondent has done or is likely to do any of the following:

  - ✪ abuse or endanger the child during visitation;

  - ✪ use the visitation as an opportunity to abuse or harass the petitioner or petitioner's family or household members;

- ✪ improperly conceal or detain the child; or,

- ✪ otherwise act in a manner that is not in the best interests of the child;

✪ prohibit the respondent from removing the child from Illinois or concealing the child within the state;

✪ order the respondent to appear in court, alone or with the child, to prevent abuse, neglect, removal, or concealment of the child, to return the child to the custody or care of the petitioner, or to permit any court-ordered interview or examination of the child or the respondent;

✪ grant the petitioner exclusive possession of personal property (such as a car), and if the respondent has possession or control, direct the respondent to promptly make it available to the petitioner; however, title to the property is not affected by an order;

✪ forbid the respondent from taking, transferring, concealing, damaging or otherwise disposing of any real or personal property;

✪ order the respondent to pay temporary support for the petitioner or any child in the petitioner's care or custody when the respondent has a legal obligation to support that person;

✪ order the respondent to pay the petitioner for losses suffered as a direct result of the abuse, including medical expenses, lost earnings or other support, repair, or replacement of property damaged or taken, attorney's fees and court costs, and moving or other travel expenses, including additional reasonable expenses for temporary shelter and restaurant meals;

✪ prohibit the respondent from entering or remaining in the residence or household while under the influence of alcohol or drugs that constitute a threat to the safety and well-being of the petitioner or the petitioner's children; and,

✪   order the respondent to reimburse a shelter providing temporary housing and counseling services to the petitioner for the cost of the services.

In addition:

✪   if the court believes there is any danger of the illegal use of firearms by the respondent, it must require that any firearms in the possession of the respondent be turned over to the local law enforcement agency for safekeeping; and,

✪   if an order of protection prohibits the respondent from having contact with the child, or if it is necessary to prevent abuse or wrongful removal or concealment of a child, the court must deny the respondent access to school records or any other records of a child who is in the care of the petitioner.

Kinds of Protective Orders   There are several kinds of protective orders with varying standards and requirements. *Emergency orders* are effective between fourteen and twenty-one days and may be granted *ex parte*, or without giving the respondent prior notice of an opportunity for a hearing. However, a court may not order any of the aforementioned remedies related to counseling, legal custody, support, or monetary compensation. *Interim orders* are effective for up to thirty days and may include all statutory remedies if the respondent has entered an appearance in the case or has been served personally. *Plenary orders* of protection are valid for up to two years. The respondent must be served with notice in order for either an interim or plenary order to be issued.

Harmful Exercise of Visitation

Visitation abuse is the failure to abide by the terms of visitation set in a court order regarding custody. Sometimes, it is the parent with visitation rights who exercises visitation abuse. For example, the failure of one parent to return the child to the custodial parent at the time or place specified in a custody order is a direct abuse of a visitation order.

In some cases, the parent may actually pose a danger to the physical, mental, emotional, or moral health of the child. One example is where the parent has a history of mental illness and may do harm to himself or herself or the child. In response to such a possibility, courts have the authority to restrict visitation or to require that visitation by that parent be supervised, under 750 ILCS 5/608. Supervision is conducted through the Illinois Department of Children and Family Services (DCFS), a state social service agency.

Interference with Contact

Family Law Remedies

In some cases, it is the custodial parent who engages in visitation abuse. A common tactic of a parent seeking to get even with the other parent is to interfere with the other parent's access to and relationship with the child. Sometimes the interference is blatant; that is, the offending parent simply refuses to turn the child over to the other parent for that parent's court-ordered visitation.

Other times, the interference is more subtle. When it is time for the offending parent to drop off the child with the other parent, there will be some excuse for why the offending parent cannot or will not turn the child over.

Example: Mary and Frank's judgment for dissolution provides that Mary is the custodial parent of Mary and Frank's child, Charlie. Frank is entitled to four one-week vacations per year with Charlie, upon thirty days' notice prior to each vacation. Frank's attorney, knowing that interference by Mary with Frank's contact has been a problem in the past, sends Mary a letter two months early, notifying Mary that Frank intends to take a Caribbean vacation with Charlie starting on May 1.

On April 30, Frank receives a telephone call from Mary stating that Charlie has an ear infection. Mary has a note from a physician, who is not Charlie's regular doctor, stating that Charlie should not fly. Therefore, Mary says, she will not be dropping Charlie off with Frank for the vacation. It is possible that Mary has shopped for a doctor who would provide the recommendation that Charlie not fly. In addition, Mary could have given Frank the option of spending the week with Charlie, but not traveling to the Caribbean. Her outright refusal to drop Charlie off indicates that her motive is to interfere with Frank's contact with Charlie.

In such a case the wronged parent can petition the court for an order holding the offending parent in contempt of court for refusing to follow the court's final order. Penalties for being found in contempt include ordering the parent to pay both a fine and the petitioner's attorney's fees incurred in pursuing the contempt charge and ordering the parent to provide make-up time with the child. Unfortunately, judges may be reluctant to hold a parent in contempt unless the conduct is blatant or frequent; this may mean returning to court repeatedly as each incident of interference occurs.

While interference with contact alone is not a sufficient reason to change custody from one parent to another, if the interference is part of a pattern of alienation on the part of the offending parent, the court may find that a change of custody in favor of the wronged parent is necessary.

Criminal Law Remedies

The Illinois Criminal Code provides for the criminal offense of unlawful visitation interference, at 720 ILCS 5/10-5.5.

> *Every person who, in violation of the visitation provisions of a court order relating to child custody, detains or conceals a child with the intent to deprive another person of his or her rights to visitation shall be guilty of unlawful visitation interference. . . . A person committing unlawful visitation interference is guilty of a petty offense. However, any person violating this section after two prior convictions of unlawful visitation interference is guilty of a Class A misdemeanor.*

The statute lists several defenses to the offense:

- ✪ a person or lawful custodian committed the act to protect the child from imminent physical harm, provided that the defendant's belief that there was physical harm imminent was reasonable and that the defendant's conduct in withholding visitation rights was a reasonable response to the harm believed imminent;

- ✪ the act was committed with the mutual consent of all parties having a right to custody and visitation of the child; or,

- ✪ the act was otherwise authorized by law.

If you are a parent who is the victim of unlawful visitation interference, you should contact the proper local law enforcement agency and file a complaint. The Criminal Code provides that the agency must issue a notice to appear in court to a person who has committed a crime under this statute. If the police are uncooperative, take your complaint to the State's Attorney of the Illinois county where the other parent resides.

Parental Kidnapping

Whether a parent can remove a child from Illinois should be addressed in a final custody order, whether the order was formulated solely by the court or was entered by an agreement between the parties. The standards for allowing removal of a child are discussed more fully in Chapter 11. If a parent removes a child from Illinois in violation of a custody order, there are several state and federal statutes that apply to the parent's conduct.

The *Parental Kidnapping Prevention Act* (PKPA) (28 U.S.C.A. Sec. 1738A) is a federal statute saying that if a custody determination was properly entered in one state, all other states must enforce that order. Once a state has exercised jurisdiction over the custody matter, no other state may exercise jurisdiction at the same time. The purpose of the PKPA is to prevent one parent from removing a child from one state where a custody order is already in place and attempting to obtain a more favorable custody determination in another state.

Under 750 ILCS 5/611, a court may specifically prohibit a parent from removing a child from the court's jurisdiction, and may enter a judgment directing law enforcement authorities to assist the petitioning parent in recovering the child.

Harassment

The Illinois Domestic Violence Act includes *harassment* in its definition of abuse. Harassment is defined as "knowing conduct [that] would cause a reasonable person emotional distress, and does cause emotional distress to the petitioner." According to 750 ILCS 60/103, the following types of conduct are presumed to cause emotional distress:

- ✪ appearing at the petitioner's workplace or school and creating a disturbance;

- ✪ repeatedly telephoning the petitioner's workplace or home;

- ✪ repeatedly following the petitioner around in public places;

- ✪ repeatedly showing up and loitering at the petitioner's workplace, etc.;

- ✪ hiding the child from the petitioner, repeatedly threatening to improperly remove the petitioner's child from the state, repeatedly threatening to hide the child from the petitioner, etc.; or,

- ✪ threatening physical force or restraint.

The parent who engages in harassment is subject to the remedies under the abuse provisions of the Illinois Domestic Violence Act, as discussed previously under "Domestic Abuse."

False Claims of Abuse

Just as there are many legitimate claims of domestic abuse made to authorities, many times people lie in order to get revenge against a custody opponent or gain an advantage in the dispute. False domestic abuse claims made under the Illinois Domestic Violence Act are addressed at 750 ILCS 60/226:

> If a parent alleges abuse without justification and the claim is later found to be untrue, he or she might have to pay the expenses and attorney's fees the other parent paid, provided it is reasonable. The same may happen if a parent falsely denies an abuse claim. Also the parent risks being prosecuted for perjury.

> If a parent makes repeated false claims and acts as if he or she is trying to destroy the relationship between the child and the other parent, the custody order might be modified in favor of the other parent.

False claims can take a number of forms. A malicious parent may make claims to the State's Attorney, local law enforcement officers, DCFS, or all three. Sometimes a person who is unrepresented and who does not have the means or desire to pay an attorney will resort to "working the system" to achieve a goal of revenge against the other parent. This person will go from one agency to the next with a series of untrue allegations meant to subject the other parent to a risk of conviction. If you find yourself a victim of this tactic, the best way to protect yourself is to document, document, document.

Example: Melinda filed a claim with DCFS stating that her child, Dana, returned from the home of Dana's father, Fred, with a cut and bruises around her right eye. Fred knew that Dana had no such injuries when he dropped her off after their weekly visit. Now Fred takes two photographs of Dana every week—one right after he picks her up from Melinda and another right before he drops her off with Melinda. He also has invested in a camera that prints the date the photograph was taken right on the photograph.

Example: Melinda sought a protective order through the Doe County State's Attorney stating that Fred had attempted to force his way into her home by breaking a door frame on her house on October 1 at 7:00 p.m. At that date and time, Fred was at his work, an hour away from Melinda's home. Because Fred punches a clock at his workplace, he was able to provide proof that he was not at Melinda's at the time in question. Now when he is home alone and unable to rely on another person or a work log to account for his whereabouts, he has made it a habit to make periodic telephone calls to family members from his home phone so that some evidence might exist to show where he was at a particular time.

Another way of providing evidence to refute a false claim is to keep a journal of your daily activities so that if the other parent accuses you of some kind of illegal conduct that allegedly took place in the past, you can reconstruct the events of that day even though you may not independently recall the date in question. An easy way to keep track is through the use of a calendar desk pad or an appointment book. Simply make a quick note, such as "Dana and I baked cookies, then watched a video before bedtime." Anything that can jog your memory will be helpful if you find you have to defend yourself from a false claim.

On the other hand, if something does occur, for example, if Dana trips and skins her knee, take care how you would note that. It may be helpful to have in writing that a minor injury happened on a particular day and how the injury occurred. Take care, however, in the event that you are ordered by the court to produce your notes. If you are the victim of a pattern of false reports, it probably is best to keep your own notes as brief as possible and try to limit them strictly to facts. This will avoid providing ammunition to the other parent who is trying to use social service and law enforcement agencies to railroad you into the position of a criminal defendant.

Emergency Custody Situations

Sometimes a parent will be in a situation where a custody determination on an emergency basis is necessary. The most likely situation is where circumstances make it imperative that custody be changed to the non-custodial parent because the custodial parent is either physically or mentally incapable of caring for the child, or because the parent has placed the child in harm's way. Examples would be where the custodial parent has been involved in some sort of accident, has become seriously ill, or has physically abused the child.

If you believe your custody issue needs to be determined on an emergency basis, the most common way to proceed is to file an emergency motion asking for immediate temporary custody. An emergency motion may be heard on a fast-track basis without setting the motion for hearing or serving notice on the other party. It is necessary, though, to consult the civil practice rules of your particular Illinois judicial district for any other procedural requirements that may exist with regard to emergency motions.

Rights of Non-Parents to Custody or Visitation

In some situations, a person other than the child's parent may believe he or she should have custody or visitation rights. A common example is where one of the parents has died and the other parent refuses to allow the parents of the deceased person to have contact with their grandchild. Another situation is one of abandonment, where the parents leave the child in the care of a third party with no intention of seeing the child again.

Custody

The first question to ask when a non-parent wishes to seek custody of a child is whether the non-parent has standing to file a petition for custody. *Standing* refers to the right of a person to be involved as a party to a lawsuit. It has nothing to do with whether the person would be successful if he or she were a party.

For a non-parent to have standing to seek custody of a child, the non-parent must have physical possession of the child. Case law has stated that the biological parent must have left the child in the care and control of the non-parent with the intent that the child remain with the non-parent indefinitely. (*In re Marriage of Feig*, 694 N.E.2d 654 (3rd Dist. 1998).)

Once the non-parent is able to establish standing to petition for custody, he or she may file the petition in the county where the child resides. Notice must be given to the child's parents, guardian, and custodian, if applicable, in the same manner as in any custody proceeding. The court then will consider all the factors discussed in Chapter 3 to determine the best interest of the child.

Visitation

The issue of non-parents' visitation rights has been a hot topic in the state courts as well as in the United States Supreme Court. The case of *Troxel v. Granville*, 147 L.Ed. 2d 49 (2000), is a United States Supreme Court decision where the Court refused to uphold a trial court order granting visitation to the paternal grandparents of two children. The grandparents petitioned for visitation after the children's father died. The Court held that the trial court's order violated the mother's right to make decisions about the care and control of her own children.

In *Wickham v. Byrne*, 769 N.E.2d 1(Ill. 2002), the Illinois Supreme Court held that the Illinois grandparent visitation statute was unconstitutional, using similar reasoning as that in *Troxel v. Granville*. In response to Troxel and Wickham, that state legislature revised the original visitation statute, 750 ILCS 5/607, in 2004. It remains to be seen, however, whether this new version will ultimately prevail in a constitutional challenge.

The problem, from the point of view of a grandparent being denied visitation, is that parents generally are presumed to be fit and proper decision-makers regarding those who will be allowed to associate with their child. The new statute provides specific situations for giving a grandparent (or great-grandparent or sibling) the right to seek visitation. If the parents have lost or given up their parental rights, as in the case of adoption, the biological grandparents have no legal standing to ask a court for visitation.

In general, the denial of visitation must be found to be unreasonable, and certain other conditions must exist as well:

- ✪ the other parent must be deceased or missing for at least three months;

- ✪ one of the parents must be legally incompetent;

- ✪ one of the parents must be incarcerated;

- ✪ the parents are divorced or separated, or there is a pending custody proceeding, and at least one of the parents does not object to the grandparents' visitation; or,

- ✪ the child is born out of wedlock and the parents are not living together.

The statute mainly applies to situations in which one parent is in control of the child and the other parent is not in a position to allow visitation to the grandparents. In other words, if both parents are in agreement that the grandparents should be denied access to the grandchild, it will be very difficult to successfully petition a court for visitation. If you are a grandparent being denied contact with your grandchild by both parents, your only option from a legal standpoint may be to show that the child's parents are not fit to make decisions about whom the child may see, and that the decisions the parents are making are actually harmful to the child.

Prior case law in Illinois indicates that even when non-parent visitation is granted, it usually does not include overnight visits and amounts to only a handful of days allowed per year. (*McVey v. Fredrickson*, 590 N.E.2d 996 (3rd Dist. 1992)—grandparents were allowed visitation with grandchild on one Saturday per month.)

Other Third Parties

The *Illinois Marriage and Dissolution of Marriage Act* also provides that a stepparent may request visitation.

The court may grant reasonable visitation privileges to a stepparent if he or she petitions to the court, but only if the court determines that it is in the child's best interests. A stepparent's petition for visitation privileges may be filed if the following circumstances are met:

- the child is at least twelve years old;

- the child resided continuously with the parent and stepparent for at least five years;

- the parent is deceased or is disabled and is unable to care for the child;

- the child wishes to have reasonable visitation with the stepparent; and,

- the stepparent was providing for the care, control, and welfare of the child prior to the initiation of the petition for visitation.

The Illinois Compiled Statutes do not specifically give any other person, besides those discussed in this chapter, the right to petition for visitation privileges with a child.

Child Support

Child support refers to expenditures on behalf of a minor in order to meet the child's physical, mental, and emotional needs. This means, among other things, food, clothing, shelter, health care, recreation, and education. The duty to support a child belongs to his or her parents or to those acting as parents and this duty does not depend on whether the parents are married or not. Several chapters of the Illinois Compiled Statutes, including the *Illinois Marriage and Dissolution of Marriage Act*, deal specifically with child support and are reproduced in relevant parts in Appendix A.

Child support may be ordered as part of a dissolution of marriage, a declaration of invalidity of marriage, a legal separation, or in response to a petition for child support. Most commonly, a court will order payment of support money to be made on a regular basis. Courts also are authorized to set aside property of the parents to be used for child support, rather than requiring periodic payments from income. For example, the court may award possession of the parents' home to the custodial parent as a form of child support.

Entitlement to Support

The child has a legal right to be supported. As a result, the parents are not allowed to agree that one will be relieved of the duty to pay child support in return for signing away rights to custody or visitation. If one parent is allowed to negotiate away the duty to support, and the other parent then becomes disabled and cannot meet the child's needs, the child may end up in the welfare system. In this case, the government, using funds collected from Illinois taxpayers, becomes responsible for supporting the child. By prohibiting agreements to relieve one parent of his or her legal obligation, the government hopes to avoid unnecessary placement of children on the welfare rolls. For the same reason, parties may not agree to make child support non-modifiable.

By the same measure, a parent's right to visitation is separate from the duty to support. If one parent is not contributing to the child's support, the custodial parent may not refuse to allow visitation. However, the failure to pay support may be one factor that impacts the best interest of the child and may be considered by a court in determining parties' respective custody or visitation rights.

Both parents have a duty to financially support their child. If one parent is providing more than his or her fair share of the money to pay for the child's necessities, that parent can petition the court to order the other parent to contribute. The right to receive child support payments belongs to the recipient parent, even though the support is ordered for the benefit of the child.

Determining Amount and Duration

In Illinois, as in most states, the legislature has provided statutory guidelines for determining the proper amount of support for which each parent is responsible. This is the starting point for any discussion of child support. Support often is ordered to be paid out of the income of the paying parent, although, as will be discussed as follows, support may come from the assets of his or her estate.

The minimum amount required is set forth in 750 ILCS 5/505:

Number of Children	Percent of Supporting Party's Net Income
1	20%
2	28%
3	32%
4	40%
5	45%
6 or more	50%

Net income is defined in section 505 as "the total of all income from all sources, minus the following deductions":

- federal income tax;

- state income tax;

- FICA (Social Security) payments;

- mandatory retirement contributions (required by law or by the employer);

- union dues;

- medical insurance premiums, for oneself or dependents;

- prior court-ordered support or maintenance obligations that were actually paid; and,

- various other expenditures, such as reasonable and necessary business expenses, medical expenditures necessary to preserve life or health, and reasonable expenditures for the benefit of the other parent or the child (but not including gifts).

When one parent's income differs greatly from one year to the next, the court may average the parent's income over several prior years to determine his or her income level.

If the court is not able to determine a parent's net income, for example, because the parent has failed to respond to the petition for support and is in default, then the court is authorized to order an amount of support "considered reasonable in the particular case."

Courts are required to follow these minimum guidelines unless the court finds that doing so would not be in the best interest of the child. In making such a finding, the court should consider all relevant factors, such as:

- the child's financial needs and resources;

- the custodial parent's needs and resources;

- the non-custodial parent's needs and resources;

- in the case of a dissolution of marriage, the child's standard of living had the marriage remained intact;

- the child's physical and emotional condition; and,

- the child's educational needs.

If the court disregards these statutory guidelines, it must explain why in its findings. The burden of proof is on the parent seeking the deviation to prove to the court that it should ignore the minimum guidelines. Keep in mind that the statutory guidelines are minimum requirements only; just as the court may order less support in a proper case, it also may order support in excess of the guidelines, so long as it makes express finding as to why it is doing so.

The following is an example of a situation where the court might deviate from the guidelines:

Example: Fred Father and Maria Mother are granted a divorce. They have one child, Charles, custody of whom is awarded to Maria. The court rules that Fred is responsible for child support. He also is responsible for paying all of the parties' marital debt, which includes substantial bills incurred by the couple for remodeling their home during the marriage. Fred then declares bankruptcy and receives a discharge of liability for the bills. The creditors have no choice but to pursue Maria for payment of the debts. This causes a substantial change in circumstances for Maria, who now has less money with which to contribute to the support of Charles. As a result, the court orders an upward deviation from the support guidelines, requiring Fred to pay a greater amount in child support.

What if the non-custodial parent has a very high or very low income? These situations are factors to be considered by the court in deciding whether to deviate from the guidelines, but there is no hard and fast rule. As noted in the list on the previous page, the court may consider the standard of living the child would have had if the parents remained together. If the previous standard of living was superior to that allowed by the application of the guidelines, it is necessary for the party seeking increased support to show what that standard of living was.

Sometimes an obligor parent will leave a job or take a lower-paying job in order to avoid the responsibility for support. Or, because the court may consider all of a parent's assets, not just income, in determining his or her ability to pay, the parent might attempt to transfer his or her property to a third person in order to appear to have fewer resources with which to pay child support. If the recipient parent can show that either of these is the case, the court can impute resources to the obligor. In other words, the court can set the obligor's income at a higher dollar amount, even if the obligor's paycheck is less, *if* the court decides that the lowered income is an intentional attempt to avoid paying child support. Then the court will make the parent pay what he or she would have to pay if employed according to his or her actual earning capability.

The court may order either parent or both to pay support, but in a typical case the non-custodial parent will be ordered to pay support to the custodial parent, according to the guidelines. This is because the custodial parent is more likely to incur greater expenses on behalf of the child than is the noncustodial parent. But what if the parents have joint custody? In such cases, the court may deviate from the guidelines and instead base a support award on the factors previously listed. Courts in a number of states now reduce the amount the obligor parent must pay when that parent spends close to half of his or her time as the physical custodian of the child. In Illinois such a result is not as common, although the Illinois Compiled Statutes allow it.

Another wrinkle is the case where a non-custodial parent is already paying support for the benefit of children from an earlier relationship. Prior court-ordered child support that is actually paid is deductible from gross income. Therefore, the resulting net income is less, and it follows that the applicable guideline percentage will yield a lesser amount of support for the second family.

Finally, the marital misconduct of either parent does not impact whether or how much support is ordered. Abuse or infidelity, for example, by or against the paying parent, generally has no bearing on the application of the minimum statutory child support guidelines.

Support Agreements

As in the case of child custody and visitation, it is desirable for the parties to formulate a child support agreement on their own rather than fighting it out in court. Of course, the agreement has to be acceptable to the court, in light of all relevant circumstances. If the amount to be paid is less than that set forth in the minimum guidelines, the parties will have to justify the deviation to the judge. An out-of-court agreement is not binding on the court, and the court will not enter a support order based on such an agreement unless it is in the best interest of the child.

If you are considering negotiating a child support agreement, you should ask yourself some of the same questions that were discussed regarding custody and visitation agreements. In particular, what is your motivation? Is it to ensure that your child is well cared for? Is there any agenda at work that is not focused on your child's best interest? This goes both ways. Those who may be support recipients sometimes believe they should receive more than they are entitled to because of what they had to put up with during the course of the relationship between the parents. By the same measure, the obligor parent may believe he or she should have the obligation reduced because of all the suffering he or she endured while with the other parent. Remember, marital misconduct is not a factor in determining child support, so you should not view the other parent's wrongful acts in that manner if you wish to negotiate a support agreement successfully.

On the other hand, those who are responsible for child support may feel that the money they end up paying will be spent on luxuries for the other parent rather than being used for the benefit of the child. For that reason, it is necessary to carefully consider the amount of money that will accomplish the quality-of-life goals you have for your child. You should take into account the child's needs and also the resources of each parent. *Resources* include not only current income, but also assets and future income potential. For example, the other parent may not be currently employed because he or she is a stay-at-home parent, but may have a college degree or a marketable skill. In that case, you would not want to settle on an amount that is based upon the other parent's unemployed status.

Other factors you should consider in writing a support agreement are:

- tax considerations;

- health insurance for the child;

- life or long-term disability insurance for the obligor parent, with the child as the beneficiary;

✪   duration of the agreement;

✪   educational expenses of the child, in particular, expenses incurred for higher education or for schooling after the child reaches the age of eighteen;

✪   special needs of the child, whether currently existing or arising in the future; and,

✪   other expenses either directly or indirectly affecting the amount of support needed or available for the child.

Most of these factors are discussed later in this chapter.

It is important to note that if the parties reach an agreement regarding child support, the terms of the agreement should be written so they are as specific as possible. In one Illinois case, the parents drafted an agreement that made each parent equally responsible for paying for the child's "special activities." The father refused to contribute to the cost of the child's music lessons and bat mitzvah, and the mother attempted to have him held in contempt. The court refused, saying that the wording of the settlement agreement was too vague to make the father liable for such costs. (*In re Marriage of Steinberg*, 706 N.E.2d 895 (1st Dist. 1998).) The moral of the story is that any agreement must be drafted so that every foreseeable circumstance is addressed right on the face of the agreement, in the hope that future differences in interpretation may be avoided.

Collecting Support Payments

Illinois law requires child support payments to be made to the State Disbursement Unit, which is the Illinois agency set up to collect and pay out child support. The State Disbursement Unit is currently located in Wheaton, Illinois. The court may direct that payment be made in another manner, if necessary. (750 ILCS 5/507.1)

Under the *Illinois Income Withholding for Support Act*, found at 750 ILCS 28, all child support orders are required to be accompanied by an income withholding notice, which is kept by the court. In the event the obligor stops making support payments, the notice is served on the obligor's employer. The employer then must deduct the amount set forth in the order, starting with the next paycheck due fourteen days after the time the withholding notice was served. The employer may not deduct less than what is ordered, even if the employer already is withholding money because of previous wage garnishments or other required deductions.

However, the federal *Consumer Credit Protection Act* places a limit on the total amount that may be withheld. An employer or prospective employer may not discipline, fire, or refuse to hire someone simply because the person is subject to income withholding. The income withholding notice directs the employer to pay the required amount directly to the State Disbursement Unit.

Child Support Enforcement Agencies

The governmental agency charged with assisting in the collection of child support in this state is the Child Support Enforcement Department of the Illinois Department of Healthcare and Family Services (HFS). The HFS's Customer Service Center may be reached at 800-447-4278. However, a number of other agencies, both state and federal, play a role in recovering delinquent child support from parents who fail to pay, including the following.

- *Illinois Office of the Comptroller*, which has the power to intercept tax refunds of deadbeat parents and apply them to the payment of delinquent child support.

- *Illinois Department of Employment Security*, which tracks new hires in the state and provides employment information on deadbeat parents to the HFS.

✪   *Illinois Secretary of State*, which can help the HFS to locate dead-beat parents and can suspend the driver's licenses of those who fail to pay child support.

✪   *Federal Office of Child Support Enforcement*, which oversees enforcement of federal laws regarding child support.

✪   *United States Department of Revenue*, which may intercept federal income tax refunds against child support delinquencies.

A good source for more information is the Illinois Department of Healthcare and Familiy Services website, **www.hfs.illinois.gov.**

Tax Considerations

No one who is considering pursuing an action related to child support can ignore the effects of federal income tax law on child support payments. The main points to remember regarding taxes in a custody or support situation are: (1) that the amounts paid by one parent to the other parent for child support are not deductible by the payor parent, nor are they included in the recipient parent's gross income; and, (2) absent an agreement or court order to the contrary, the custodial parent takes the dependent exemption on his or her tax return. The right to the exemption may be divided between the parties in a joint custody situation; for example, by allowing one parent to take the exemption during even-numbered years, with the other parent taking it during odd-numbered years.

A good attorney will be able to explain the tax consequences of the child support order in your case or a support agreement that you are contemplating. However, an in-depth discussion of income tax and child support is beyond the scope of this book.

Other Considerations

Whether you are negotiating a settlement concerning child support or litigating a child support case in court, you should take care that all necessary expenses related to the child are taken into account. Food, shelter, and clothing are obvious costs to consider. However, a number of other child-related expenses should be addressed in any support order.

Day Care Expenses

A court may order the obligor parent to cover the day care expenses incurred by the custodial parent. Generally, this means expenses the recipient parent pays for childcare while he or she works. This does not include babysitting charges for times when the recipient parent is engaging in social activities.

Life Insurance

As will be discussed in Chapter 11, the obligation to support a child does not end with the death of the obligor parent. Often in support cases, the court will require the obligor parent to keep life insurance, with either the child or the other parent listed as primary beneficiary, in order to secure the payment of support in the event of the obligor's death. If you are seeking child support, either by agreement or in a contested court case, it is advisable to require the other parent to maintain life insurance in an amount sufficient to provide financial support for your children until they have reached at least the age of majority. You also should include a provision requiring the other parent to provide periodic proof that the insurance premium has been paid on time.

Health Insurance

Parents also must address health care expenses in their child support agreement or court case. Under 750 ILCS 5/505.2, courts are required to include a health care provision covering the child. If the obligor parent has health insurance available through his or her employment, the court can require that the child be named as a beneficiary of that policy. If there is no job-related insurance, the support order that eventually is entered should contain a provision directing one or both parents to obtain medical insurance for the child, and to provide proof of coverage for the child on a periodic basis. It also should set out how non-covered expenses, such as a deductible, will be allocated between the parents.

Insurance premiums paid for court-ordered health care insurance are considered additional child support. These premiums are deductible from the obligor's gross income for purposes of determining net income. Although the statutory and case laws are not specific, it seems that a court would be giving an obligor a double dip if it allowed the obligor to lower his or her income with the premium deduction, and then consider the premium as satisfying part of a support obligation. If the obligor parent fails to pay the insurance premium, he or she will be liable to the other parent, not only for the amount that has not been paid, but also for any health care expenses the child has that would have been covered by the insurance if the premium had been paid.

Education and Extracurricular Expenses

Illinois law says that parents in a child support case may be ordered to pay for a child's educational expenses, even if the child is a college student or is still in high school and has reached the age of majority. Whether and how much a parent is ordered to pay will depend on the child's needs and the parent's ability to pay. This is decided on a case-by-case basis according to the court's discretion.

Special Needs

Be sure to include any expenses for activities beyond those that are school-related. Summer camps, music lessons, sports, and hobbies all should be accounted for in trying to determine an equitable amount of child support.

Aside from medical expenses, a support agreement or order also should address any other special needs of the child. These needs could result from the parents' breakup, such as the need for psychological counseling, or could be special educational requirements stemming from a child's disability. If you are negotiating a support agreement or seeking a support order in court, be sure the support amount covers any such needs.

Preparing and Litigating a Child Support Case

This chapter discusses the process of litigating a child support case. Whether you have an attorney or are representing yourself, you need to know what happens before, during, and after your child support trial. This information is essential if you are representing yourself. If you are represented by an attorney, you still should be familiar with what a trial involves. It will help your lawyer prepare a better case, and will give you more confidence and comfort during this difficult time.

Gathering Financial Information

The basic information needed to prepare a child support case is: (1) the dollar amount representing the needs of the child; and, (2) the assets and income of each parent. Whether you are the petitioner or the respondent, you must compile as much information as you can so that your attorney may prepare your case. One resource for the necessary information is the other parent; information can be obtained through the use of discovery requests, as in custody cases.

Non-Custodial Parent Income

The most important determination for the petitioner is the income of the other parent. This means, as stated in 750 ILCS 5/505, "all income from all sources." Be sure to obtain, through the use of discovery if necessary, copies of the other parent's tax returns for the past several years because these documents can be greatly informative. If you have any reason to believe the other parent has earned income that has not been reported to the Internal Revenue Service (IRS), you should inform your attorney so he or she may pursue discovery of that information as well.

Keep in mind that income is not necessarily limited to a base salary. Commissions, stock options, and other bonuses should be taken into account. Income can take other forms as well, such as interest or other investment returns. Lastly, be sure to provide your attorney with any information you may have regarding assets belonging to the other parent, as they may produce income. An example of this is a rental property owned by the other parent.

Calculating Support

In calculating the amount of support you will be asking for, start with the minimum guidelines provided for in the Illinois Compiled Statutes. Then, in deciding whether it is necessary for you to ask the court to deviate from the guidelines, you should take into account the following factors as they relate to your child:

- housing costs, including utilities;
- food costs;
- clothing costs;
- educational and extracurricular activity costs;
- health care costs, including dental costs;
- recreation costs, including sports and hobby equipment;
- child care costs; and,
- other necessary expenses, such as utilities and transportation costs.

Petition and Affidavit

If you are petitioning for child support, you will need to file a petition for support, along with a financial affidavit. If you are seeking either a dissolution of marriage, a declaration of invalidity of marriage, a legal separation, or custody, you will make the request for support part of whichever action you are filing. The financial affidavit provides a summary of information for the court. A standard form affidavit is found in Appendix D. While the final child support determination is pending, it is likely that your attorney will request the court to order the payment of temporary support.

The petition must be served upon the respondent, just as with a petition for dissolution or other similar legal proceeding. Service is discussed earlier in Chapter 5.

The Illinois Department of Public Aid maintains a Delinquent Parent Information web page, to disclose information about parents who are more than $5,000 in arrears with their support obligations. The page can be found at **www.ilchildsupport.com/deadbeats**. Also, the United States Department of Health and Human Services operates the Federal *Parent Locator Service* (FPLS), a computer network that you can utilize if you are unable to locate the other parent. The FPLS assists state agencies in locating parents who owe child support by providing employment, home address, and other information that may be found in the computer databases of various federal agencies.

Responding to a Petition for Child Support

If you are served with a petition requesting child support, the first question is whether the petition is timely. In Illinois, a petition may request child support at any time until two years after the child reaches the age of eighteen. This time limit to bring a legal action is called a *statute of limitations*. If the petition has been filed too late, the respondent should respond with a motion to dismiss the petition based on the running of the statute of limitations.

The next issue to address is whether you are the child's parent. Obviously, this is an issue only when the respondent is male. If you believe you are not the child's father, your attorney may advise you to file a response that denies paternity. Paternity is discussed more fully in Chapter 3.

If you do not raise parentage as a defense, your next best bet is to respond by attacking the allegations of the petition as to the child's needs and your income, through the use of your own financial affidavit. You may also make the argument that the statutory guidelines themselves should not apply in your case for one or some of the reasons for deviation that were previously listed.

Of course, if you believe that you should be the custodial parent, you should consider filing a counterpetition asking that you be awarded custody and support. As discussed earlier, however, you should evaluate your motives honestly before taking this step; decide if you desire custody because you truly wish to have the lion's share of the responsibility for your child, or if you are trying to gain a financial advantage or seeking revenge for a bad relationship.

Motion for Temporary Support

When a petitioner prepares the petition for support, it is routine and advisable to ask for temporary support directly in the main petition. If you have reason to believe that the other parent will try to hide money or property, or will try to remove the child from the state, the court might even grant temporary relief without giving the other parent a hearing before entering the order. A motion that is made without notice to the other party is called an *ex parte motion*. If you make such a motion, 750 ILCS 5/501 requires you to include an affidavit stating the factual basis that makes an ex parte proceeding necessary.

Request for Attorney's Fees

The Illinois Marriage and Dissolution of Marriage Act provides that courts may order one of the parties to a custody, visitation, or support proceeding to pay all or part of the attorney's fees incurred by the other party, after considering each party's ability to pay. The statute also allows a party to request payment by the other party for interim attorney's fees and attorney's fees incurred by the requesting party during the time that the case is pending. It is the sole discretion of the court as to whether a party will be charged with the other party's attorney's fees.

Child Support Order

Any child support order entered by the court, whether made by agreement between the parties or not, should at the very least include provisions setting out how much the payments will be, how the payments will be made, under what circumstances the order will be modified, and when the order will terminate.

The obligor parent probably will seek to have the support amount reduced as each child reaches the age of majority, which is eighteen years of age in Illinois. An order may be *self-adjusting*, which means the reduction and its effective date are written into the order and are automatic without further court action. If the support order is not self-adjusting, the obligor parent will have to go back to court to seek a modification.

Sometimes in a dissolution of marriage proceeding, the final dissolution decree provides for *spousal support* (formerly known as *alimony*) in addition to child support. Spousal support, unlike child support, is deductible by the obligor and is included in the income of the recipient. In some dissolution cases, support is awarded in a single payment and does not specify which amount is child support and which is spousal support. This is called *unallocated support*.

If support is unallocated, and the support order provides that the amount is to be reduced within six months before or after a child reaches eighteen years of age, the Internal Revenue Service will consider the payment to be child support—not spousal support, and, therefore, the obligor will not be allowed to take a tax deduction for the payment.

Enforcing a Child Support Order

Once a child support order is in place, it often becomes necessary to enforce it. Sometimes the obligor parent simply refuses to pay. Even if there is a withholding order in place, a payor may attempt to avoid his or her support obligation by terminating or changing his or her employment. When enforcement becomes necessary, the recipient parent has a number of options for assistance. Both civil and criminal remedies are available. In Illinois, interest accrues at a rate of 9% on child support that is more than thirty days late.

It is advisable to return to court to reduce any arrearages to a money judgment. In other words, the party who is entitled to the unpaid child support should ask the judge to enter a court order awarding the party the past-due amount. That way, the recipient parent will have all the civil enforcement options of any other person who has been awarded money damages in a lawsuit. Keep in mind, however, that a statute of limitations applies to the enforcement of past-due child support. As with any other money judgment, enforcement must be undertaken within twenty years, or the right to enforcement will be lost.

Contempt

As with the enforcement of a custody order, a support recipient can ask the court to hold the delinquent obligor parent in contempt. If the court finds that the obligor parent's failure to pay is unjustified, the court is required to order the obligor to pay the attorney's fees incurred by the recipient parent.

To request a contempt finding, the recipient parent must file a petition, called a *petition for rule to show cause*. The petition must be verified; that is, the petitioner must sign the petition and swear out an affidavit stating that the statements contained in the petition are true. The petition must specify the amount owed and should request that the court enter a judgment for the amount past due. Once the arrearage is reduced to a judgment, the petitioner may pursue collection of the amount due in the same manner as for any other debt. Finally, the petitioner should include an affidavit setting out any attorney's fees incurred in pursuing the petition. If the obligor parent is unemployed, the court can order him or her to seek employment and to keep records of his or her job search efforts.

A petition for rule to show cause must be served on the obligor parent. Unlike the petition for support, service may be either personal by process server or by regular mail to the obligor's last known address.

Suspension or Revocation of Licenses

The State of Illinois, particularly in recent years, has begun to crack down on deadbeat parents. One way the legislature has done this is by enacting statutes allowing the revocation of an obligor's driver's or other license, including a professional license. The driver's license may be suspended where the obligor parent is ninety or more days delinquent in support payments and may remain suspended until the parent is in full compliance with the support order. The Department of Professional Regulation and the Secretary of State's office have the authority to suspend or revoke the appropriate licenses.

Interception of Tax Refund

Another statutory weapon that can be used against deadbeat parents is the interception of the obligor's tax refunds. A recent report by the United States Department of Health and Human Services estimated that the federal government has collected over $1.4 billion in delinquent child support by this method.

It is the Illinois Department of Healthcare and Family Services that has the authority to seize refund money in the state of Illinois. A recipient seeking assistance in collection should contact the department for more information.

Lien on Real Property

As each support payment becomes due and is not paid, the delinquent amount automatically becomes a lien on the obligor's real property. (735 ILCS 5/12-101) The recipient parent does not need to go to court to ask that a lien be placed on the obligor's property. The recipient can simply prepare a *memorandum of lien* form and file it with the office of the recorder in the county where the property is located. Liens can be quite effective when they are recorded against real estate because most real estate transactions are highly regulated and usually will not be completed if there are any outstanding liens on the property.

Unlike the statute of limitations for the enforcement of money judgments, a lien on real estate for delinquent child support does not run out and can remain fixed to the property indefinitely.

Citation to Discover Assets/Turnover of Personal Property

Section 12-111 of 735 ILCS 5 allows enforcement of a judgment against the obligor's personal property through what is called *levy and sale*. The recipient must obtain a judgment order against specific personal property belonging to the obligor and must serve a certified copy of the judgment on the sheriff. The sheriff then will confiscate and sell the obligor's property to satisfy the judgment amount.

In order to determine what non-exempt personal property the obligor has that is available for the satisfaction of the judgment amount, the recipient should request the court to issue a citation to discover assets. This document is served on the obligor parent, who must appear in court and answer questions under oath about the assets he or she owns.

Wage Deduction and Non-Wage Garnishment

Once a child support arrearage has been reduced to a judgment, it may be enforced by all methods available to petitioners for collection of a judgment. Among the methods that may be used are wage deduction and non-wage garnishment.

Wage deduction is a court-ordered withholding of a certain amount of money from each of the obligor's paychecks until the arrearage is satisfied. The respondent in such a case is the obligor's employer. A *non-wage garnishment* is the taking and turning over of the obliger's property that is being held by a third-party respondent, for example, a savings account held by a bank. In a non-wage garnishment, the respondent is called the *garnishee*.

In both cases the necessary pleadings are filed and served upon the respondent, with delivery of a copy to the debtor. The respondent, whether garnishee or employer, must respond to the pleadings, and unless there is some objection to the propriety of the garnishment or deduction, the respondent must turn the money over to the petitioner. The rules covering wage deductions and non-wage garnishments are found in 735 ILCS 5/2–1402.

Incarceration

In addition to other penalties for contempt, 750 ILCS 5/505(b) provides that the court may sentence the delinquent obligor parent to imprisonment for up to six months. The court may allow the delinquent parent to be released for a period during the day or night to work or conduct business, with part or all of the earnings during the sentence being paid to the recipient parent for child support.

Creation of a Trust from Assets of Obligor Parent

Under certain circumstances the court may find it necessary to place some of the assets of the obligor parent into a trust for the benefit of the child. Usually, this is done when there is some misconduct by the obligor, for example, if the obligor hides property or works for under the table cash that he or she then conceals. These may be difficult factual situations to prove in court.

Non-Support Punishment Act

Illinois law provides a criminal provision to address obligor parents who willfully fail to pay support for their children without a lawful excuse. The statute is found at 750 ILCS 16. The penalties provided by the statute become more severe depending upon the violation.

NOTE: *Willful failure to pay a child support arrearage in the amount of $5,000 to $10,000 is a misdemeanor, while willful failure to satisfy an arrearage of over $10,000 is a felony. In addition to restitution of the amounts due and assessment of a fine, a court may order the debtor to be incarcerated according to the statutes covering imprisonment.*

Out-of-State Obligor Parent

One problem that frequently arises is how to enforce a child support order when the obligor parent lives in another state. All states now have enacted the *Uniform Interstate Family Support Act* (UIFSA) to deal with this situation. Prior to UIFSA, it usually was necessary to follow the other various procedures in order to make an Illinois support order enforceable in that state. Under UIFSA, however, Illinois has the authority to enforce child support orders directly against out-of-state residents in child support matters.

The recipient parent who lives in Illinois may enforce a wage deduction against the out-of-state obligor parent simply by serving the wage deduction order directly upon the out-of-state employer. A recipient parent also may seek enforcement through the appropriate government agency of the obligor parent's state without having to register the order. Registration in the other state is required in order for the recipient to utilize other enforcement methods. Conversely, a recipient parent who resides in another state may enforce an order from that state against an Illinois obligor parent, through the obligor's employer, in the same manner.

Illinois has continuing authority over child support orders issued in Illinois, so long as one of the parents or the child resides in Illinois. This means that a parent living out-of-state who wishes to modify a support order must do so in the courts of Illinois. Modification is discussed in greater detail in Chapter 11.

Registration in the other state is required for the recipient to utilize other enforcement methods, and is accomplished by submitting a copy of the order (which usually must be certified) to the proper court in the other state, according to that state's procedures.

Assistance of Illinois Department of Public Aid

The State of Illinois provides assistance for child support enforcement to recipients of support payments from Illinois residents who fail to pay. The *Illinois Department of Healthcare and Family Services* (HFS) offers a number of services on behalf of recipients' children, even if the children do not reside in Illinois. The HFS will help locate the obligor parent, take steps to establish paternity, and assist in obtaining a child support order if one is not already in place. The HFS also will undertake some of the collection actions against the obligor parent that are previously listed, including the interception of tax refunds, the withholding of money due from the state, such as unemployment benefits, and the placing of liens on property within the state. To apply for HFS assistance, contact the Department's Child Support Customer Service Center at 800-447-4278, or contact your Child Support Enforcement Regional Office. You may find the appropriate regional office online at **www.ilchildsupport.com.**

Modification and Termination of Custody, Visitation, and Support Orders

Custody and visitation orders are modifiable, as are orders for child support. The statutory provision covering modification of a custody or visitation order is found at 750 ILCS 5/610, and modifications of support orders are addressed at 750 ILCS 5/510.

Custody and Visitation

Modification Unless the parents agree there is an issue of endangerment to the child's well-being under the present circumstances, neither parent may petition to modify a custody order until two years have passed from the date the original order was entered. Unless there is endangerment to a child, the court will allow a modification only if:

> 1. either there has been a change in circumstances that occurred since the current custody order was entered, or facts affecting the custody award were unknown to the court at the time of the original order; and,
>
> 2. it is in the best interest of the child that custody be modified.

Simply meeting the best interest of the child standard alone is not enough to warrant a modification. To modify the order, the court must find by clear and convincing evidence that the basis for modification exists. This means that the court must have a "high level of certainty" that there is a change in circumstances and that modification is in the best interest of the child. This is a very difficult burden for a parent seeking a change in custody. Some situations in which Illinois courts have found a change in circumstances include:

❂ frequent moves by the custodial parent;

❂ psychological problems in the custodial parent;

❂ psychological problems in the child;

❂ physical or sexual abuse by the custodial parent;

❂ substance abuse by the custodial parent;

❂ failure to obtain health care for the child; and,

❂ difficulties in the relationship between the child and the new spouse of the custodial parent.

Other circumstances have been found insufficient to justify a change in custody. Cohabitation by the custodial parent is not enough to warrant a change in custody, nor is remarriage. However, if the cohabitation or remarriage negatively impacts the child's environment and well-being, then a change of custody may be ordered. Also, the court will not consider a petition to modify that is based upon allegations made during the original custody proceeding. There must be new evidence to show that the child's best interest would be served by a modification.

One common situation is where a parent seeks a change in custody because the other parent has interfered with the contact between the child and the petitioning parent. In general, visitation abuse by itself is not enough for modification of custody. However, if the abuse is part of a pattern showing that the interfering parent is attempting to sabotage the relationship between the petitioning parent and the child—a situation called *parental alienation syndrome*—a custody change may be warranted.

However, in a case under the Domestic Violence Act, the parent seeking a change in custody must prove the grounds for modification only to a preponderance of the evidence. This means that it must be more likely than not that the basis for modification exists and is a much easier burden to meet than the clear and convincing evidence standard. Cases under the Domestic Violence Act are discussed earlier, in Chapter 6.

Keep in mind that a petition for modification may be an expensive proposition. If the moving parent is alleging that the current arrangement is causing harm to the child, physical and/or psychological examinations of some or all of the parties may be ordered. Testimony by experts may also be advisable. In some ways, the process may be similar to the original custody hearing, with depositions and subpoenas. Also, remember that the statute provides that the respondent's attorney's fees may be charged to the petitioner if the court finds that the petition was filed in order to harass the respondent. For that reason, it is a good idea to assess your motivation for seeking a custody modification if you are considering requesting one; be sure you are primarily seeking to protect your child's best interest.

Filing and Petition Modification

To commence an action to modify a prior custody order, you must file two documents:

1. a **PETITION TO MODIFY CUSTODY** (form 10, p.259), and

2. a **UCCJEA AFFIDAVIT** (form 5, p.247), which has been discussed previously in Chapter 5.

The petition itself must be verified, which means the petitioner states under oath that the contents of the petition are true. The petitioner's signature on the document is notarized. A sample of a verified **PETITION TO MODIFY CUSTODY** and a **UCCJEA AFFIDAVIT** can be found in Appendix D. Just as in an original proceeding to determine custody, notice of the petition must be served upon the respondent according to Illinois civil practice rules.

In a case in which both parents seek a modification of a prior order of joint custody, the parties do not have to prove a change in circumstances, even if each parent seeks sole custody. If the parties themselves agree to a change in custody, the agreement probably will be given great weight by the court. Court approval still is necessary before the original custody order will be modified; however, it is unlikely that the court will require the parties to present much in the way of proof of the two requirements for modification. In other cases, in which proof is necessary, the party seeking modification must produce evidence both of the change in circumstances and of the best interest of the child. This may require a full-blown proceeding, including discovery, an evidentiary hearing, and the calling of expert witnesses. Professional custody evaluations, often done when custody originally is determined, may be advisable for a parent seeking a modification as well.

In many cases, the party seeking the modification must start from scratch. This is because courts are hesitant to change current custody arrangements for fear of bringing instability to the child's life. In a contested modification case, the parties may have to send out new interrogatories, conduct new depositions, and retain psychiatrists as experts for the hearing. A guardian ad litem may be appointed where there had not been one before. Remember that the change in circumstances that has been alleged must be subsequent to the original custody order. Therefore, most of the evidence to be presented will not have existed at the time custody was previously awarded, and now will be considered by the court for the first time. It is almost an entirely new proceeding, except there is the added obstacle of the court not wishing to disturb a custody situation that is already in place. Remember, too, that the standard of proof is by clear and convincing evidence. As a result, it is difficult to effect a change in custody without the court having a very clear-cut reason for doing so.

Termination of Custody Orders

Prior custody orders are no longer effective and the court loses authority to make custody decisions regarding the child once the child is emancipated or no longer under the control of his or her parents.

Emancipation occurs upon the happening of one of the following events:

- ✪ the child reaches the age of eighteen;

- ✪ the child marries;

- ✪ the child joins the military; or,

- ✪ the child is self-supporting and living on his or her own.

NOTE: *The death of the custodial parent does not automatically vest custody in the other parent. The surviving parent still must petition for a change in custody in such a case. However, courts generally find it appropriate to award custody to the non-custodial parent, so long as he or she is found to be fit.*

Removal of Child from State

Under the Illinois Marriage and Dissolution of Marriage Act, a parent seeking to permanently remove a child from Illinois must petition the court for permission to do so. Under 750 ILCS 5/609, the court may grant leave to remove the child if doing so would serve the best interest of the child. Note that this section does not apply when the parents have never been married; in such a case, no petition for removal is required.

The court opinion in the case of *In re Marriage of Eckert*, 518 N.E.2d 1041 (1988), discusses several factors courts should consider in ruling on a petition to allow removal:

- ✪ whether the removal is likely to improve the quality of both the child's and the custodial parent's lives;

- ✪ whether the motive of the parent seeking removal is to interfere with visitation by the non-custodial parent;

✪   whether the motive of the non-custodial parent in opposing removal is to use the issue as a bargaining chip, for example, to negotiate for a lesser child support obligation; and,

✪   whether an adequate visitation schedule can be formulated to replace the current arrangement, which will allow for the continued relationship between the child and the non-custodial parent.

The Illinois judicial districts have held differing views on the first factor, improvement in the quality of life. Some districts have held that the parent seeking removal need prove only that the parent will benefit from the move, and that this is enough to show that the child's life will improve as well. Other districts have ruled that the positive effect of removal on the *child's* life must be shown specifically. The burden of proof of the child's best interest with regard to these factors is on the person seeking removal.

Section 609 also provides for temporary removal of a child from Illinois, such as for an out-of-state vacation. The removing parent must supply the other parent, either directly or through the other parent's attorney, with the address and telephone number where the child may be reached, and the date when the child is returning to Illinois.

Child Support Modification

Section 510 allows for modification of a child support order if there is a substantial change in circumstances, or, if this cannot be shown, if there is a 20% or greater inconsistency between the amount of support actually ordered and that required under the minimum statutory guidelines (unless the court intentionally deviated from the guideline amount). Support payments that are already past due may not be modified. Only payments becoming due after the petitioner has given notice of the petition for modification may be changed.

Change of Income of Parent/ Change in Needs of Child

Both parents have a duty to support their child. A change in the income of either parent may be considered in ruling on a petition to modify support. The court also will look for a change in the child's needs in deciding whether to grant the order for modification. Therefore, if the parent seeking modification wants an increase in support, he or she will have to show both an increase in the obligor parent's ability to pay, and a corresponding increase in the child's need for support. In Illinois, one can presume that need has increased simply because the cost of living has gone up and the child has become older. (*In re Marriage of Sweet*, 735 N.E.2d 1037 (2d Dist. 2000).)

It is required that a decrease in the income of either parent not be the result of bad faith. In other words, the parent claiming a decreased ability to pay must not have voluntarily changed or terminated employment in order to avoid his or her support obligation.

Remarriage of Custodial Parent

In the case of remarriage, the financial resources of the parent's new spouse generally are not to be considered in determining whether to modify a support obligation.

Subsequent Family Obligations of Obligor Parent

If the obligor parent remarries and has children as a result of the later marriage, the obligor's expenses related to his or her second family are one factor to be considered by the court in deciding whether to reduce the support obligation. This is a change from the previous rule that the children of the first marriage were to receive support according to the statutory guidelines before the later-born children were to be taken into account. However, the income of the obligor parent's new spouse may be considered in determining what resources are available to the obligor for the support of his or her new family.

Filing and Litigating a Petition to Modify Child Support

As in the case of a petition to change a prior custody order, actions to modify child support awards begin with the filing of a verified *Petition to Modify Judgment for Child Support*. The petition must be accompanied by an updated financial affidavit. Notice must be served upon the payor parent. The court then will hold a hearing on the petition where evidence of the alleged substantial change in circumstances is presented and ruled upon. Remember that if a modification is granted, it applies only from the date the order is entered. Support that is due prior to the modification accrues at the rate previously ordered by the court and may not be changed.

Child Support Termination

Section 510 specifically states that, unless the parents have agreed or the court has ordered otherwise, a child support obligation is terminated upon the emancipation of the child. Emancipation is discussed in the previous section regarding termination of custody orders. Moreover, the adoption of a child of the obligor with a concurrent termination of the obligor's parental rights terminates the obligor's duty to provide child support.

If the parties have agreed or the court has ordered that the obligor parent will be responsible to pay the child's educational expenses beyond high school, then the duty will continue even after the child has reached the age of 18. Moreover, 750 ILCS 5/513 provides that the court may continue a support obligation on behalf of a mentally or physically disabled child, even though the child has reached the age of eighteen, if the child has not been emancipated by some other means. A petition for such post-majority support must be made prior to the disabled child's eighteenth birthday.

NOTE: *The support obligation does not end with the death of the obligor parent. The recipient parent may file a claim against the deceased obligor's estate for the amount the court finds equitable to cover the support or educational expenses.*

Finally, if the obligor parent owes past-due child support, and enforcement proceedings against the obligor are on the horizon, a petition by the obligor to modify or terminate child support will not delay the enforcement action. In other words, a parent who is delinquent in his or her support payments will not be able to avoid a wage deduction, non-wage garnishment, or other collection activities simply by filing a petition to revisit the child support obligation.

Afterword

Family law issues are among the most contentious legal matters a person may encounter in his or her lifetime. Custody and support cases are often extremely stressful, not only due to the emotional toll taken on the parties, but also because of the added upheaval that may result from the expense involved. Of course, these cases may have the greatest effect on the children at the center of the conflict. Following are some suggestions to lessen the negative impact of the legal processes, both upon yourself and your children.

First, find emotional support. For you, this may mean close friends in whom you are comfortable confiding, or perhaps a trusted member of the clergy. Many towns have support groups for single parents or for those who are going through a divorce. Having others to talk with who are going through the same things you are can be of great value to your emotional well-being. There also are support groups for children of divorce; check with local churches or even the local courthouse. Professional counseling also can be very useful for both parents and children, although some may find therapy to be an expensive alternative.

Second, make sure you are taking care of yourself physically. Some people have trouble eating during times of great stress; others may binge on unhealthy food. Some will find it difficult to keep a normal routine or may be unable to sleep. Unfortunately, some people will commence a destructive pattern, such as drinking or drug use; some who already have a substance abuse problem will sink more deeply into their addiction. Have your physician evaluate your physical condition periodically and attempt to keep a routine in which you allow yourself plenty of time to sleep. Watch your diet and take special care to avoid overindulging in alcohol. If you do not have a history of drug abuse, do not start. If drug use is a part of your life, continuing that pattern will only harm your case. If you are not able to abstain on your own, seek professional help.

Third, keep your motives in the front of your mind as you proceed through your case. Be honest with yourself and remember that your children's well-being is the most important factor in the case. Avoid taking actions in the proceedings that are meant solely to harm the other parent, and do not place your children in the middle of the conflict by asking them to choose between you and the other parent. Do not make gratuitously insulting comments about the other parent. In most cases, your children love both you and the other parent and hearing hurtful things about the other parent only makes your children feel bad. Moreover, in time, they probably will figure out which parent, if any, has taken the high road and nurtured their relationship with the other parent. They may come to resent one parent when they realize he or she tried to turn them against the other parent. At the very least, they will grow up to be very confused adults, and may end up without the ability to work out their own interpersonal conflicts in a reasonable manner.

Remember, as a parent, you are the primary role model for your children. You have a responsibility to act in their best interest, even if your own personal preference is to act otherwise. You will have the satisfaction of knowing that you are doing the best job you can as a parent. More importantly, your children will appreciate you for it and will have a much better chance of growing up to be well-adjusted adults.

Finally, regardless of the status of your custody, visitation, or support situation, keep in mind that the issue always can be revisited at a later date. The current arrangement may be reviewed any time the best interest of the child requires it. For this reason, it is important to conduct yourself according to the court's wishes even if you are not currently involved in litigation. In other words, if you are a non-custodial parent, be sure to exercise your visitation rights fully. If you are the obligor of child support payments, keep the payments current. If you do decide to ask for expanded visitation or custody at a later date, the court likely will examine how you handled your parental responsibilities to that point. Did you make the effort to see your children? Did you pay their support in a timely fashion? If the answer to these questions is "no," it may come back to haunt you when a judge is evaluating your request. More importantly, you should fulfill your obligation as a parent to give financial and emotional support simply because it is the right thing to do.

Glossary

A

affidavit. Written testimony that is given under oath, signed, and notarized.

annotation. A summary of a relevant case provided to show how courts have applied a particular statutory provision to a set of facts.

appeal. The process by which an unsatisfactory trial court decision may be considered by a higher court.

appellant. The litigant who files an appeal.

appellee. The litigant who must respond to an appeal after it has been filed.

B

bar association. A professional organization for attorneys offering various services, including referrals for the public to attorneys practicing in a particular area of law.

best interest of the child. The standard according to which courts make custody, visitation, and support rulings, whereby the main consideration is what is of the greatest benefit to the child in question.

C

case reporter. A volume of printed court decisions, organized by, for example, state or region.

citation. An abbreviated form of a case opinion, statute, or other reference to legal material.

citation to discover assets. A court order requiring a judgment debtor to appear and provide a creditor with information about the debtor's income and assets.

confidential information. Communications between a client and his or her attorney that the attorney may not disclose to third parties.

conflict of interest. Situation where an attorney may not represent two different parties because of a past or present relationship between the two parties that could give rise to the possibility that confidential information of one or both parties will be disclosed.

contempt of court. A ruling that a party has willfully disobeyed an order of a court, with the possibility of civil or criminal penalties.

contingent basis. A fee arrangement for an attorney's services where the attorney receives a percentage of whatever moneys he or she recovers on behalf of the client.

custody. The right to physical possession of or legal decision-making authority over another person, usually a minor or disabled person.

D

default. A court ruling that the responding party to a legal action has failed to make an appearance in or response to the action, often resulting in the respondent's being prohibited from defending himself or herself in the action.

deposition. Out-of-court testimony, given under oath and transcribed by a court reporter in response to questions asked by the attorney for one of the parties to a legal action.

discovery. The process of gathering information from the other party to a legal action, using methods provided for by statute.

docketing statement. A document filed with an appellate court, giving background information about a case on appeal.

E

emancipation. The manner by which a minor child legally becomes an adult; for example, by marriage, joining the military, or becoming financially independent and living on one's own.

emergency order of protection. An order of protection that may be granted without notice to the defendant and lasts between fourteen and twenty-one days.

ex parte. Without giving notice and opportunity to another party; usually used only in emergency situations.

G

garnishment. A method of satisfying a money judgment by obtaining a court order allowing seizure of certain property of a judgment debtor; for example, the debtor's bank accounts.

guardian ad litem. A person appointed by the court in a custody case to represent the child's best interest.

H

home state. The state in which a child lived with his or her parent or parents, or guardian, for the preceeding six consecutive months.

I

initial consultation. The first meeting between an attorney and a potential client.

interim order of protection. An order of protection that may be effective, pending a full hearing, for up to thirty days.

interrogatories. A method of discovery where a number of written questions are served upon a party to a legal action to be answered in writing within a certain period of time; the subject matter of the interrogatories must be relevant to the legal action at hand.

J

joint custody. A court ruling where both parents are given shared physical and/or legal custody of a child.

judgment. A final ruling by a court in a legal action.

jurisdiction. The authority of a court to hear a particular case.

L

legal custody. The right of a parent to make major life decisions on behalf of a child.

levy and sale. The placing of an order allowing confiscation and sale of a debtor's personal property in order to satisfy a money judgment against the debtor.

M

mediation. A method of alternative dispute resolution where the parties meet with a neutral third party—often an attorney or social worker—to reach a mutually satisfactory resolution on various issues.

motion. A formal request for court action by a litigant, relating to the current legal proceedings, which the court will either grant or deny.

N

notice of appeal. A document filed by a litigant in order to initiate an appeal.

notice to appear. A document that is served upon a party demanding that the party appear, usually for deposition, at a certain date, time, and place.

O

order of protection. A court order formulated in response to allegations of domestic violence that sets out various requirements and prohibitions to be followed by the alleged abuser.

P

parentage. The establishment of the identity of a child's parents.

parental alienation syndrome. Repeated, intentional acts by one parent to sabotage a child's relationship with the other parent.

paternity. The establishment of the identity of a child's father.

petitioner. The party who initiates a legal action regarding custody, visitation, or support.

physical custody. The right of a parent to actual residential possession of a child.

pleading. Generally, a document that sets forth assertions of fact and/or law, submitted to the court by a litigant in support of the litigant's claims.

plenary order of protection. An order of protection based on a full evidentiary hearing, effective for up to two years.

precedent. Prior case law relied upon by parties in making a legal argument and by judges in ruling on a legal action.

pretrial. A conference between the parties and the judge in a legal action, prior to trial, in order to resolve outstanding procedural issues and possibly to reach settlement of the case.

primary caregiver. The person who is the main provider of basic necessities for a child; not necessarily the main wage-earner or the person with whom the child spends the most time, but the person who does the most to actually care for the child.

primary source. Statutory or legislative law, considered to be the most authoritative source of legal principles.

pro se. Representing oneself without the assistance of an attorney.

R

request to admit facts. A discovery device whereby a litigant sets out facts that he or she wishes the other party to admit without having to elicit actual testimony at trial, in order to save time and reduce the number of issues in dispute between the parties.

request to produce. A discovery device whereby one litigant asks the other party to provide copies of documents that are relevant to the facts of the case.

respondent. A person who is served with notice that another party has initiated a legal action against the person.

retainer. A lump-sum advance payment to an attorney in order to secure the attorney's representation.

rule to show cause. A court order requiring a party to respond and show why he or she should not be held in contempt of court for failing to obey a prior order.

S

service of process. The means by which a party is given notice of a legal proceeding affecting the rights of the party; generally, by either delivering written notice of the proceeding to the party, delivering notice to a member of the party's household who is over the age of thirteen, or, in appropriate cases, by publishing notice in the newspaper.

spousal support. Court-ordered financial support given by a party to the ex-spouse in a divorce.

standard visiation. A typical custody or visitation arrangement; generally, alternating weekends and alternating holidays.

standing. The right of a person or organization to be a party to a certain legal action.

statute of limiations. The time period within which a legal action must be brought or else it is barred.

subpoena. A document, usually served upon a non-party either by a process server or by certified mail, requiring the recipient to comply, typically used to compel either appearance in court or the production of items to be used as evidence in a case.

summons. Formal notice of a legal proceeding that must be served upon the respondent by a sheriff or other authorized third party.

T

temporary custody. A court ruling setting out non-permanent living arrangements for a child until a final custody determination is made.

trial. Proceeding during which factual evidence and legal arguments are presented to a judge (or jury, although generally not in custody, visitation, or support cases), who then makes final determinations on the various issues in the case.

V

venue. The location of the proper court in which to file a custody, visitation, or support action.

visitation. The right of a person to have access to and spend time with a child.

W

wage deduction. A method of satisfying a money judgment by serving the employer of the judgment debtor with an order requiring the employer to deduct a certain amount from the debtor's paycheck to be disbursed to the party to whom the money is owed.

Appendix A: State Statutory Provisions

720 ILCS 5/10-5.5 Unlawful visitation interference.

(a) As used in this Section, the terms "child", "detain", and "lawful custodian" shall have the meanings ascribed to them in Section 10.5 of this Code.

(b) Every person who, in violation of the visitation provisions of a court order relating to child custody, detains or conceals a child with the intent to deprive another person of his or her rights to visitation shall be guilty of unlawful visitation interference.

(c) A person committing unlawful visitation interference is guilty of a petty offense. However, any person violating this Section after 2 prior convictions of unlawful visitation interference is guilty of a Class A misdemeanor.

(d) Any law enforcement officer who has probable cause to believe that a person has committed or is committing an act in violation of this Section shall issue to that person a notice to appear.

(e) The notice shall:
   (1) be in writing;
   (2) state the name of the person and his address, if known;
   (3) set forth the nature of the offense;
   (4) be signed by the officer issuing the notice; and
   (5) request the person to appear before a court at a certain time and place.

(f) Upon failure of the person to appear, a summons or warrant of arrest may be issued.

(g) It is an affirmative defense that:
   (1) a person or lawful custodian committed the act to protect the child from imminent physical harm, provided that the defendant's belief that there was physical harm imminent was reasonable and that the defendant's conduct in withholding visitation rights was a reasonable response to the harm believed imminent;
   (2) the act was committed with the mutual consent of all parties having a right to custody and visitation of the child; or
   (3) the act was otherwise authorized by law.

(h) A person convicted of unlawful visitation interference shall not be subject to a civil contempt citation for the same conduct for violating visitation provisions of a court order issued under the Illinois Marriage and Dissolution of Marriage Act.

   *   *   *

750 ILCS 5/502

Agreement. (a) To promote amicable settlement of disputes between parties to a marriage attendant upon the dissolution of their marriage, the parties may enter into a written or oral agreement containing provisions for disposition of any property owned by either of them, maintenance of either of them and support, custody and visitation of their children.

(b) The terms of the agreement, except those providing for the support, custody and visitation of children, are binding upon the court unless it finds, after considering the economic circumstances of the parties and any other relevant evidence produced by the parties, on their own motion or on request of the court, that the agreement is unconscionable.

(c) If the court finds the agreement unconscionable, it may request the parties to submit a revised agreement or upon hearing, may make orders for the disposition of property, maintenance, child support and other matters.

(d) Unless the agreement provides to the contrary, its terms shall be set forth in the judgment, and the parties shall be ordered to perform under such terms, or if the agreement provides that its terms shall not be set forth in the judgment, the judgment shall identify the agreement and state that the court has approved its terms.

(e) Terms of the agreement set forth in the judgment are enforceable by all remedies available for enforcement of a judgment, including contempt, and are enforceable as contract terms.

(f) Except for terms concerning the support, custody or visitation of children, the judgment may expressly preclude or limit modification of terms set forth in the judgment if the agreement so provides. Otherwise, terms of an agreement set forth in the judgment are automatically modified by modification of the judgment.

750 ILCS 5/505

Child support; contempt; penalties.

(a) In a proceeding for dissolution of marriage, legal separation, declaration of invalidity of marriage, a proceeding for child support following dissolution of the marriage by a court which lacked personal jurisdiction over the absent spouse, a proceeding for modification of a previous order for child support under Section 510 of this Act, or any proceeding authorized under Section 501 or 601 of this Act, the court may order either or both parents owing a duty of support to a child of the marriage to pay an amount reasonable and necessary for his support, without regard to marital misconduct. The duty of support owed to a child includes the obligation to provide for the reasonable and necessary physical, mental and emotional health needs of the child. For purposes of this Section, the term "child" shall include any child under age 18 and any child under age 19 who is still attending high school.

(1) The Court shall determine the minimum amount of support by using the following guidelines:

Number of Children Percent of Supporting Party's Net Income
1 20%
2 28%
3 32%
4 40%
5 45%
6 or more 50%

(2) The above guidelines shall be applied in each case unless the court makes a finding that application of the guidelines would be inappropriate, after considering the best interests of the child in light of evidence including but not limited to one or more of the following relevant factors:

(a) the financial resources and needs of the child;

(b) the financial resources and needs of the custodial parent;

(c) the standard of living the child would have enjoyed had the marriage not been dissolved;

(d) the physical and emotional condition of the child, and his educational needs; and

(e) the financial resources and needs of the non-custodial parent.

If the court deviates from the guidelines, the court's finding shall state the amount of support that would have been required under the guidelines, if determinable. The court shall include the reason or reasons for the variance from the guidelines.

(3) "Net income" is defined as the total of all income from all sources, minus the following deductions:

(a) Federal income tax (properly calculated withholding or estimated payments);

(b) State income tax (properly calculated withholding or estimated payments);

(c) Social Security (FICA payments);

(d) Mandatory retirement contributions required by law or as a condition of employment;

(e) Union dues;

(f) Dependent and individual health/hospitalization insurance premiums;

(g) Prior obligations of support or maintenance actually paid pursuant to a court order;

(h) Expenditures for repayment of debts that represent reasonable and necessary expenses for the production of income, medical expenditures necessary to preserve life or health, reasonable expenditures for the benefit of the child and the other parent, exclusive of gifts. The court shall reduce net income in determining the minimum amount of support to be ordered only for the period that such payments are due and shall enter an order containing provisions for its self-executing modification upon termination of such payment period.

(4) In cases where the court order provides for health/hospitalization insurance coverage pursuant to Section 505.2 of this Act, the premiums for that insurance, or that portion of the premiums for which the supporting party is responsible in the case of insurance provided through an employer's health insurance plan where the employer pays a portion of the premiums, shall be subtracted from net income in determining the minimum amount of support to be ordered.

(4.5) In a proceeding for child support following dissolution of the marriage by a court that lacked personal jurisdiction over the absent spouse, and in which the court is requiring payment of support for the period before the date an order for current support is entered, there is a rebuttable presumption that the supporting party's net income for the prior period was the same as his or her net income at the time the order for current support is entered.

(5) If the net income cannot be determined because of default or any other reason, the court shall order support in an amount considered reasonable in the particular case. The final order in all cases shall state the support level in dollar amounts. However, if the court finds that the child support amount cannot be expressed exclusively as a dollar amount because all or a portion of the payor's net income is uncertain

as to source, time of payment, or amount, the court may order a percentage amount of support in addition to a specific dollar amount and enter such other orders as may be necessary to determine and enforce, on a timely basis, the applicable support ordered.

(6) If (i) the non-custodial parent was properly served with a request for discovery of financial information relating to the non-custodial parent's ability to provide child support, (ii) the non-custodial parent failed to comply with the request, despite having been ordered to do so by the court, and (iii) the non-custodial parent is not present at the hearing to determine support despite having received proper notice, then any relevant financial information concerning the non-custodial parent's ability to provide child support that was obtained pursuant to subpoena and proper notice shall be admitted into evidence without the need to establish any further foundation for its admission.

(a-5) In an action to enforce an order for support based on the respondent's failure to make support payments as required by the order, notice of proceedings to hold the respondent in contempt for that failure may be served on the respondent by personal service or by regular mail addressed to the respondent's last known address. The respondent's last known address may be determined from records of the clerk of the court, from the Federal Case Registry of Child Support Orders, or by any other reasonable means.

(b) Failure of either parent to comply with an order to pay support shall be punishable as in other cases of contempt. In addition to other penalties provided by law the Court may, after finding the parent guilty of contempt, order that the parent be:

(1) placed on probation with such conditions of probation as the Court deems advisable;

(2) sentenced to periodic imprisonment for a period not to exceed 6 months; provided, however, that the Court may permit the parent to be released for periods of time during the day or night to:

(A) work; or

(B) conduct a business or other self-employed occupation.

The Court may further order any part or all of the earnings of a parent during a sentence of periodic imprisonment paid to the Clerk of the Circuit Court or to the parent having custody or to the guardian having custody of the children of the sentenced parent for the support of said children until further order of the Court.

If there is a unity of interest and ownership sufficient to render no financial separation between a non-custodial parent and another person or persons or business entity, the court may pierce the ownership veil of the person, persons, or business entity to discover assets of the non-custodial parent held in the name of that person, those persons, or that business entity. The following circumstances are sufficient to authorize a court to order discovery of the assets of a person, persons, or business entity and to compel the application of any discovered assets toward payment on the judgment for support:

(1) the non-custodial parent and the person, persons, or

business entity maintain records together.

(2) the non-custodial parent and the person, persons, or business entity fail to maintain an arms length relationship between themselves with regard to any assets.

(3) the non-custodial parent transfers assets to the person, persons, or business entity with the intent to perpetrate a fraud on the custodial parent.

With respect to assets which are real property, no order entered under this paragraph shall affect the rights of bona fide purchasers, mortgagees, judgment creditors, or other lien holders who acquire their interests in the property prior to the time a notice of lis pendens pursuant to the Code of Civil Procedure or a copy of the order is placed of record in the office of the recorder of deeds for the county in which the real property is located.

The court may also order in cases where the parent is 90 days or more delinquent in payment of support or has been adjudicated in arrears in an amount equal to 90 days obligation or more, that the parent's Illinois driving privileges be suspended until the court determines that the parent is in compliance with the order of support. The court may also order that the parent be issued a family financial responsibility driving permit that would allow limited driving privileges for employment and medical purposes in accordance with Section 7-702.1 of the Illinois Vehicle Code. The clerk of the circuit court shall certify the order suspending the driving privileges of the parent or granting the issuance of a family financial responsibility driving permit to the Secretary of State on forms prescribed by the Secretary. Upon receipt of the authenticated documents, the Secretary of State shall suspend the parent's driving privileges until further order of the court and shall, if ordered by the court, subject to the provisions of Section 7-702.1 of the Illinois Vehicle Code, issue a family financial responsibility driving permit to the parent.

In addition to the penalties or punishment that may be imposed under this Section, any person whose conduct constitutes a violation of Section 15 of the Non-Support Punishment Act may be prosecuted under that Act, and a person convicted under that Act may be sentenced in accordance with that Act. The sentence may include but need not be limited to a requirement that the person perform community service under Section 50 of that Act or participate in a work alternative program under Section 50 of that Act. A person may not be required to participate in a work alternative program under Section 50 of that Act if the person is currently participating in a work program pursuant to Section 505.1 of this Act.

A support obligation, or any portion of a support obligation, which becomes due and remains unpaid as of the end of each month, excluding the child support that was due for that month to the extent that it was not paid in that month, shall accrue simple interest as set forth in Section 12-109 of the Code of Civil Procedure. An order for support entered or modified on or after January 1, 2006 shall contain a statement that a support obligation required under the order, or any portion of a support obligation required under the order, that becomes due and remains unpaid as of the end of each month, excluding the child support that was due for that month to the extent that it was not paid in that month, shall accrue simple interest as set forth in Section 12-109 of the Code of Civil Procedure. Failure to include the statement in the order for support does not affect the validity of the order or the accrual of interest as provided in this Section.

(c) A one-time charge of 20% is imposable upon the amount of past-due child support owed on July 1, 1988 which has accrued under a support order entered by the court. The charge shall be imposed in accordance with the provisions of Section 10-21 of the Illinois Public Aid Code and shall be enforced by the court upon petition.

(d) Any new or existing support order entered by the court under this Section shall be deemed to be a series of judgments against the person obligated to pay support thereunder, each such judgment to be in the amount of each payment or installment of support and each such judgment to be deemed entered as of the date the corresponding payment or installment becomes due under the terms of the support order. Each such judgment shall have the full force, effect and attributes of any other judgment of this State, including the ability to be enforced. A lien arises by operation of law against the real and personal property of the noncustodial parent for each installment of overdue support owed by the noncustodial parent.

(e) When child support is to be paid through the clerk of the court in a county of 1,000,000 inhabitants or less, the order shall direct the obligor to pay to the clerk, in addition to the child support payments, all fees imposed by the county board under paragraph (3) of subsection (u) of Section 27.1 of the Clerks of Courts Act. Unless paid in cash or pursuant to an order for withholding, the payment of the fee shall be by a separate instrument from the support payment and shall be made to the order of the Clerk.

(f) All orders for support, when entered or modified, shall include a provision requiring the obligor to notify the court and, in cases in which a party is receiving child and spouse services under Article X of the Illinois Public Aid Code, the Illinois Department of Public Aid, within 7 days, (i) of the name and address of any new employer of the obligor, (ii) whether the obligor has access to health insurance coverage through the employer or other group coverage and, if so, the policy name and number and the names of persons covered under the policy, and (iii) of any new residential or mailing address or telephone number of the non-custodial parent. In any subsequent action to enforce a support order, upon a sufficient showing that a diligent effort has been made to ascertain the location of the non-custodial parent, service of process or provision of notice necessary in the case may be made at the last known address of the non-custodial parent in any manner expressly provided by the Code of Civil Procedure or this Act, which service shall be sufficient for purposes of due process.

(g) An order for support shall include a date on which the current support obligation terminates. The termination date shall be no earlier than the date on which the child covered by the order will attain the age of 18. However, if the child will not graduate from high school until after attaining the age of 18,

then the termination date shall be no earlier than the earlier of the date on which the child's high school graduation will occur or the date on which the child will attain the age of 19. The order for support shall state that the termination date does not apply to any arrearage that may remain unpaid on that date. Nothing in this subsection shall be construed to prevent the court from modifying the order or terminating the order in the event the child is otherwise emancipated.

(g-5) If there is an unpaid arrearage or delinquency (as those terms are defined in the Income Withholding for Support Act) equal to at least one month's support obligation on the termination date stated in the order for support or, if there is no termination date stated in the order, on the date the child attains the age of majority or is otherwise emancipated, the periodic amount required to be paid for current support of that child immediately prior to that date shall automatically continue to be an obligation, not as current support but as periodic payment toward satisfaction of the unpaid arrearage or delinquency. That periodic payment shall be in addition to any periodic payment previously required for satisfaction of the arrearage or delinquency. The total periodic amount to be paid toward satisfaction of the arrearage or delinquency may be enforced and collected by any method provided by law for enforcement and collection of child support, including but not limited to income withholding under the Income Withholding for Support Act. Each order for support entered or modified on or after the effective date of this amendatory Act of the 93rd General Assembly must contain a statement notifying the parties of the requirements of this subsection. Failure to include the statement in the order for support does not affect the validity or the operation of the provisions of this subsection with regard to the order. This subsection shall not be construed to prevent or affect the establishment or modification of an order for support of a minor child or the establishment or modification of an order for support of a non-minor child or educational expenses under Section 513 of this Act.

(h) An order entered under this Section shall include a provision requiring the obligor to report to the obligee and to the clerk of court within 10 days each time the obligor obtains new employment, and each time the obligor's employment is terminated for any reason. The report shall be in writing and shall, in the case of new employment, include the name and address of the new employer. Failure to report new employment or the termination of current employment, if coupled with nonpayment of support for a period in excess of 60 days, is indirect criminal contempt. For any obligor arrested for failure to report new employment bond shall be set in the amount of the child support that should have been paid during the period of unreported employment. An order entered under this Section shall also include a provision requiring the obligor and obligee parents to advise each other of a change in residence within 5 days of the change except when the court finds that the physical, mental, or emotional health of a party or that of a child, or both, would be seriously endangered by disclosure of the party's address.

(i) The court does not lose the powers of contempt, driver's license suspension, or other child support enforcement mechanisms, including, but not limited to, criminal prosecution as set forth in this Act, upon the emancipation of the minor child or children.

750 ILCS 5/505.1

(a) Whenever it is determined in a proceeding to establish or enforce a child support or maintenance obligation that the person owing a duty of support is unemployed, the court may order the person to seek employment and report periodically to the court with a diary, listing or other memorandum of his or her efforts in accordance with such order. Additionally, the court may order the unemployed person to report to the Department of Employment Security for job search services or to make application with the local Job Training Partnership Act provider for participation in job search, training or work programs and where the duty of support is owed to a child receiving child support enforcement services under Article X of the Illinois Public Aid Code, as amended, the court may order the unemployed person to report to the Illinois Department of Public Aid for participation in job search, training or work programs established under Section 9-6 and Article IXA of that Code.

(b) Whenever it is determined that a person owes past-due support for a child or for a child and the parent with whom the child is living, and the child is receiving assistance under the Illinois Public Aid Code, the court shall order at the request of the Illinois Department of Public Aid:

(1) that the person pay the past-due support in accordance with a plan approved by the court; or

(2) if the person owing past-due support is unemployed, is subject to such a plan, and is not incapacitated, that the person participate in such job search, training, or work programs established under Section 9-6 and Article IXA of the Illinois Public Aid Code as the court deems appropriate.

*   *   *

750 ILCS 5/506 Representation of child.

(a) Duties. In any proceedings involving the support, custody, visitation, education, parentage, property interest, or general welfare of a minor or dependent child, the court may, on its own motion or that of any party, appoint an attorney to serve in one of the following capacities to address the issues the court delineates:

(1) Attorney. The attorney shall provide independent legal counsel for the child and shall owe the same duties of undivided loyalty, confidentiality, and competent representation as are due an adult client.

(2) Guardian ad litem. The guardian ad litem shall testify or submit a written report to the court regarding his or her recommendations in accordance with the best interest of the child. The report shall be made available to all parties. The guardian ad litem may be called as a witness for purposes of cross-examination regarding the guardian ad litem's report or recommendations. The guardian ad litem shall investigate the facts of the case and interview the child and the parties.

(3) Child representative. The child representative shall advocate what the child representative finds to be in the best interests of the child after reviewing the facts and circumstances of the case. The child representative shall meet with the child and the parties, investigate the facts of the case, and encourage settlement and the use of alternative forms of dispute resolution. The child representative shall have the same authority and obligation to participate in the litigation as does an attorney for a party and shall possess all the powers of investigation as does a guardian ad litem. The child representative shall consider, but not be bound by, the expressed wishes of the child. A child representative shall have received training in child advocacy or shall possess such experience as determined to be equivalent to such training by the chief judge of the circuit where the child representative has been appointed. The child representative shall not disclose confidential communications made by the child, except as required by law or by the Rules of Professional Conduct. The child representative shall not render an opinion, recommendation, or report to the court and shall not be called as a witness, but shall offer evidence-based legal arguments. The child representative shall disclose the position as to what the child representative intends to advocate in a pre-trial memorandum that shall be served upon all counsel of record prior to the trial. The position disclosed in the pre-trial memorandum shall not be considered evidence. The court and the parties may consider the position of the child representative for purposes of a settlement conference.

(a-3) Additional appointments. During the proceedings the court may appoint an additional attorney to serve in the capacity described in subdivision (a)(1) or an additional attorney to serve in another of the capacities described in subdivision (a)(2) or (a)(3) on the court's own motion or that of a party only for good cause shown and when the reasons for the additional appointment are set forth in specific findings.

(a-5) Appointment considerations. In deciding whether to make an appointment of an attorney for the minor child, a guardian ad litem, or a child representative, the court shall consider the nature and adequacy of the evidence to be presented by the parties and the availability of other methods of obtaining information, including social service organizations and evaluations by mental health professions, as well as resources for payment.

In no event is this Section intended to or designed to abrogate the decision making power of the trier of fact. Any appointment made under this Section is not intended to nor should it serve to place any appointed individual in the role of a surrogate judge.

(b) Fees and costs. The court shall enter an order as appropriate for costs, fees, and disbursements, including a retainer, when the attorney, guardian ad litem, or child's representative is appointed. Any person appointed under this Section shall file with the court within 90 days of his or her appointment, and every subsequent 90-day period thereafter during the course of his or her representation, a detailed invoice for services rendered with a copy being sent to each party. The court shall review the invoice submitted and approve the fees, if they are reasonable and necessary. Any order approving the fees shall require payment by either or both parents, by any other party or source, or from the marital estate or the child's separate estate. The court may not order payment by the Illinois Department of Public Aid in cases in which the Department is providing child support enforcement services under Article X of the Illinois Public Aid Code. Unless otherwise ordered by the court at the time fees and costs are approved, all fees and costs payable to an attorney, guardian ad litem, or child representative under this Section are by implication deemed to be in the nature of support of the child and are within the exceptions to discharge in bankruptcy under 11 U.S.C.A. 523. The provisions of Sections 501 and 508 of this Act shall apply to fees and costs for attorneys appointed under this Section.

750 ILCS 5/507

Payment of maintenance or support to court.

(a) In actions instituted under this Act, the court shall order that maintenance and support payments be made to the clerk of court as trustee for remittance to the person entitled to receive the payments. However, the court in its discretion may direct otherwise where circumstances so warrant.

(b) The clerk of court shall maintain records listing the amount of payments, the date payments are required to be made and the names and addresses of the parties affected by the order. For those cases in which support is payable to the clerk of the circuit court for transmittal to the Illinois Department of Public Aid by order of the court or upon notification of the Illinois Department of Public Aid, and the Illinois Department of Public Aid collects support by assignment, offset, withholding, deduction or other process permitted by law, the Illinois Department shall notify the clerk of the date and amount of such collection. Upon notification, the clerk shall record the collection on the payment record for the case.

(c) The parties affected by the order shall inform the clerk of court of any change of address or of other condition that may affect the administration of the order.

(d) The provisions of this Section shall not apply to cases that come under the provisions of Sections 709 through 712.

(e) To the extent the provisions of this Section are inconsistent with the requirements pertaining to the State Disbursement Unit under Section 507.1 of this Act and Section 10-26 of the Illinois Public Aid Code, the requirements pertaining to the State Disbursement Unit shall apply.

750 ILCS 5/507.1

Payment of Support to State Disbursement Unit.

(a) As used in this Section:

"Order for support", "obligor", "obligee", and "payor" mean those terms as defined in the Income Withholding for Support Act, except that "order for support" shall not mean orders providing for spousal maintenance under which there is no child support obligation.

(b) Notwithstanding any other provision of this Act to the contrary, each order for support entered or modified on or after October 1, 1999 shall require that support payments be made to the State Disbursement Unit established under Section 10-26 of the Illinois Public Aid Code if:

(1) a party to the order is receiving child support enforcement services under Article X of the Illinois Public Aid Code; or

(2) no party to the order is receiving child support enforcement services, but the support payments are made through income withholding.

(c) Support payments shall be made to the State Disbursement Unit if:

(1) the order for support was entered before October 1, 1999, and a party to the order is receiving child support enforcement services under Article X of the Illinois Public Aid Code; or

(2) no party to the order is receiving child support enforcement services, and the support payments are being made through income withholding.

(c-5) If no party to the order is receiving child support enforcement services under Article X of the Illinois Public Aid Code, and the support payments are not made through income withholding, then support payments shall be made as directed by the order for support.

(c-10) At any time, and notwithstanding the existence of an order directing payments to be made elsewhere, the Department of Public Aid may provide notice to the obligor and, where applicable, to the obligor's payor:

(1) to make support payments to the State Disbursement Unit if:

(A) a party to the order for support is receiving child support enforcement services under Article X of the Illinois Public Aid Code; or

(B) no party to the order for support is receiving child support enforcement services under Article X of the Illinois Public Aid Code, but the support payments are made through income withholding; or

(2) to make support payments to the State Disbursement Unit of another state upon request of another state's Title IV-D child support enforcement agency, in accordance with the requirements of Title IV, Part D of the Social Security Act and regulations promulgated under that Part D.

The Department of Public Aid shall provide a copy of the notice to the obligee and to the clerk of the circuit court.

(c-15) Within 15 days after the effective date of this amendatory Act of the 91st General Assembly, the clerk of the circuit court shall provide written notice to the obligor to make payments directly to the clerk of the circuit court if no party to the order is receiving child support enforcement services under Article X of the Illinois Public Aid Code, the support payments are not made through income withholding, and the order for support requires support payments to be made directly to the clerk of the circuit court. The clerk shall provide a copy of the notice to the obligee.

(c-20) If the State Disbursement Unit receives a support payment that was not appropriately made to the Unit under this Section, the Unit shall immediately return the payment to the sender, including, if possible, instructions detailing where to send the support payment.

(d) The notices under subsections (c-10) and (c-15) may be sent by ordinary mail, certified mail, return receipt requested, facsimile transmission, or other electronic process, or may be served upon the obligor or payor using any method provided by law for service of a summons.

750 ILCS 5/508

Attorney's Fees; Client's Rights and Responsibilities Respecting Fees and Costs.

(a) The court from time to time, after due notice and hearing, and after considering the financial resources of the parties, may order any party to pay a reasonable amount for his own or the other party's costs and attorney's fees. Interim attorney's fees and costs may be awarded from the opposing party, in accordance with subsection (c-1) of Section 501. At the conclusion of the case, contribution to attorney's fees and costs may be awarded from the opposing party in accordance with subsection (j) of Section 503. Fees and costs may be awarded to counsel from a former client in accordance with subsection (c) of this Section. Awards may be made in connection with the following:

(1) The maintenance or defense of any proceeding under this Act.

(2) The enforcement or modification of any order or judgment under this Act.

(3) The defense of an appeal of any order or judgment under this Act, including the defense of appeals of post-judgment orders.

(3.1) The prosecution of any claim on appeal (if the prosecuting party has substantially prevailed).

(4) The maintenance or defense of a petition brought under Section 2-1401 of the Code of Civil Procedure seeking relief from a final order or judgment under this Act.

(5) The costs and legal services of an attorney rendered in preparation of the commencement of the proceeding brought under this Act.

(6) Ancillary litigation incident to, or reasonably connected with, a proceeding under this Act.

The court may order that the award of attorney's fees and costs (including an interim or contribution award) shall be paid directly to the attorney, who may enforce the order in his or her name, or that it shall be paid to the appropriate party. Judgment may be entered and enforcement had accordingly. Except as otherwise provided in subdivision (e)(1) of this Section, subsection (c) of this Section is exclusive as to the right of any counsel (or former counsel) of record to petition a court for an award and judgment for final fees and costs during the pendency of a proceeding under this Act.

(b) In every proceeding for the enforcement of an order or judgment when the court finds that the failure to comply with the order or judgment was without compelling cause or justification, the court shall order the party against whom the proceeding is brought to pay promptly the costs and reasonable attorney's fees of the prevailing party. If non-compliance is with respect to a discovery order, the non-compliance is presumptively without compelling cause or justification, and the presumption may only be rebutted by clear and convincing evidence. If at any time a court finds that a hearing under this Section was precipitated or conducted for any improper pur-

pose, the court shall allocate fees and costs of all parties for the hearing to the party or counsel found to have acted improperly. Improper purposes include, but are not limited to, harassment, unnecessary delay, or other acts needlessly increasing the cost of litigation.

(c) Final hearings for attorney's fees and costs against an attorney's own client, pursuant to a Petition for Setting Final Fees and Costs of either a counsel or a client, shall be governed by the following:

(1) No petition of a counsel of record may be filed against a client unless the filing counsel previously has been granted leave to withdraw as counsel of record or has filed a motion for leave to withdraw as counsel. On receipt of a petition of a client under this subsection (c), the counsel of record shall promptly file a motion for leave to withdraw as counsel. If the client and the counsel of record agree, however, a hearing on the motion for leave to withdraw as counsel filed pursuant to this subdivision (c)(1) may be deferred until completion of any alternative dispute resolution procedure under subdivision (c)(4). As to any Petition for Setting Final Fees and Costs against a client or counsel over whom the court has not obtained jurisdiction, a separate summons shall issue. Whenever a separate summons is not required, original notice as to a Petition for Setting Final Fees and Costs may be given, and documents served, in accordance with Illinois Supreme Court Rules 11 and 12.

(2) No final hearing under this subsection (c) is permitted unless: (i) the counsel and the client had entered into a written engagement agreement at the time the client retained the counsel (or reasonably soon thereafter) and the agreement meets the requirements of subsection (f); (ii) the written engagement agreement is attached to an affidavit of counsel that is filed with the petition or with the counsel's response to a client's petition; (iii) judgment in any contribution hearing on behalf of the client has been entered or the right to a contribution hearing under subsection (j) of Section 503 has been waived; (iv) the counsel has withdrawn as counsel of record; and (v) the petition seeks adjudication of all unresolved claims for fees and costs between the counsel and the client. Irrespective of a Petition for Setting Final Fees and Costs being heard in conjunction with an original proceeding under this Act, the relief requested under a Petition for Setting Final Fees and Costs constitutes a distinct cause of action. A pending but undetermined Petition for Setting Final Fees and Costs shall not affect appealability of any judgment or other adjudication in the original proceeding.

(3) The determination of reasonable attorney's fees and costs either under this subsection (c), whether initiated by a counsel or a client, or in an independent proceeding for services within the scope of subdivisions (1) through (5) of subsection (a), is within the sound discretion of the trial court. The court shall first consider the written engagement agreement and, if the court finds that the former client and the filing counsel, pursuant to their written engagement agreement, entered into a contract which meets applicable requirements of court rules and addresses all material terms, then the contract

shall be enforceable in accordance with its terms, subject to the further requirements of this subdivision (c)(3). Before ordering enforcement, however, the court shall consider the performance pursuant to the contract. Any amount awarded by the court must be found to be fair compensation for the services, pursuant to the contract, that the court finds were reasonable and necessary. Quantum meruit principles shall govern any award for legal services performed that is not based on the terms of the written engagement agreement (except that, if a court expressly finds in a particular case that aggregate billings to a client were unconscionably excessive, the court in its discretion may reduce the award otherwise determined appropriate or deny fees altogether).

(4) No final hearing under this subsection (c) is permitted unless any controversy over fees and costs (that is not otherwise subject to some form of alternative dispute resolution) has first been submitted to mediation, arbitration, or any other court approved alternative dispute resolution procedure, except as follows:

(A) In any circuit court for a single county with a population in excess of 1,000,000, the requirement of the controversy being submitted to an alternative dispute resolution procedure is mandatory unless the client and the counsel both affirmatively opt out of such procedures; or

(B) In any other circuit court, the requirement of the controversy being submitted to an alternative dispute resolution procedure is mandatory only if neither the client nor the counsel affirmatively opts out of such procedures.

After completion of any such procedure (or after one or both sides has opted out of such procedures), if the dispute is unresolved, any pending motion for leave to withdraw as counsel shall be promptly granted and a final hearing under this subsection (c) shall be expeditiously set and completed.

(5) A petition (or a praecipe for fee hearing without the petition) shall be filed no later than the end of the period in which it is permissible to file a motion pursuant to Section 2-1203 of the Code of Civil Procedure. A praecipe for fee hearing shall be dismissed if a Petition for Setting Final Fees and Costs is not filed within 60 days after the filing of the praecipe. A counsel who becomes a party by filing a Petition for Setting Final Fees and Costs, or as a result of the client filing a Petition for Setting Final Fees and Costs, shall not be entitled to exercise the right to a substitution of a judge without cause under subdivision (a)(2) of Section 2-1001 of the Code of Civil Procedure.

(d) A consent judgment, in favor of a current counsel of record against his or her own client for a specific amount in a marital settlement agreement, dissolution judgment, or any other instrument involving the other litigant, is prohibited. A consent judgment between client and counsel, however, is permissible if it is entered pursuant to a verified petition for entry of consent judgment, supported by an affidavit of the counsel of record that incorporates an itemization of the billing or billings to the client, detailing hourly costs, time spent, and tasks performed, and by an affidavit of the client acknowledg-

ing receipt of that documentation, awareness of the right to a hearing, the right to be represented by counsel (other than counsel to whom the consent judgment is in favor), and the right to be present at the time of presentation of the petition, and agreement to the terms of the judgment. The petition may be filed at any time during which it is permissible for counsel of record to file a petition (or a praecipe) for a final fee hearing, except that no such petition for entry of consent judgment may be filed before adjudication (or waiver) of the client's right to contribution under subsection (j) of Section 503 or filed after the filing of a petition (or a praecipe) by counsel of record for a fee hearing under subsection (c) if the petition (or praecipe) remains pending. No consent security arrangement between a client and a counsel of record, pursuant to which assets of a client are collateralized to secure payment of legal fees or costs, is permissible unless approved in advance by the court as being reasonable under the circumstances.

(e) Counsel may pursue an award and judgment against a former client for legal fees and costs in an independent proceeding in the following circumstances:

(1) While a case under this Act is still pending, a former counsel may pursue such an award and judgment at any time subsequent to 90 days after the entry of an order granting counsel leave to withdraw; and

(2) After the close of the period during which a petition (or praecipe) may be filed under subdivision (c)(5), if no such petition (or praecipe) for the counsel remains pending, any counsel or former counsel may pursue such an award and judgment in an independent proceeding.

In an independent proceeding, the prior applicability of this Section shall in no way be deemed to have diminished any other right of any counsel (or former counsel) to pursue an award and judgment for legal fees and costs on the basis of remedies that may otherwise exist under applicable law; and the limitations period for breach of contract shall apply. In an independent proceeding under subdivision (e)(1) in which the former counsel had represented a former client in a dissolution case that is still pending, the former client may bring in his or her spouse as a third-party defendant, provided on or before the final date for filing a petition (or praecipe) under subsection (c), the party files an appropriate third-party complaint under Section 2-406 of the Code of Civil Procedure. In any such case, any judgment later obtained by the former counsel shall be against both spouses or ex-spouses, jointly and severally (except that, if a hearing under subsection (j) of Section 503 has already been concluded and the court hearing the contribution issue has imposed a percentage allocation between the parties as to fees and costs otherwise being adjudicated in the independent proceeding, the allocation shall be applied without deviation by the court in the independent proceeding and a separate judgment shall be entered against each spouse for the appropriate amount). After the period for the commencement of a proceeding under subsection (c), the provisions of this Section (other than the standard set forth in subdivision (c)(3) and the terms respecting consent security arrangements in subsection (d) of this Section 508) shall be inapplicable.

The changes made by this amendatory Act of the 94th General Assembly are declarative of existing law.

(f) Unless the Supreme Court by rule addresses the matters set out in this subsection (f), a written engagement agreement within the scope of subdivision (c)(2) shall have appended to it verbatim the following Statement:

"STATEMENT OF CLIENT'S RIGHTS AND RESPONSIBILITIES

(1) WRITTEN ENGAGEMENT AGREEMENT. The written engagement agreement, prepared by the counsel, shall clearly address the objectives of representation and detail the fee arrangement, including all material terms. If fees are to be based on criteria apart from, or in addition to, hourly rates, such criteria (e.g., unique time demands and/or utilization of unique expertise) shall be delineated. The client shall receive a copy of the written engagement agreement and any additional clarification requested and is advised not to sign any such agreement which the client finds to be unsatisfactory or does not understand.

(2) REPRESENTATION. Representation will commence upon the signing of the written engagement agreement. The counsel will provide competent representation, which requires legal knowledge, skill, thoroughness and preparation to handle those matters set forth in the written engagement agreement. Once employed, the counsel will act with reasonable diligence and promptness, as well as use his best efforts on behalf of the client, but he cannot guarantee results. The counsel will abide by the client's decision concerning the objectives of representation, including whether or not to accept an offer of settlement, and will endeavor to explain any matter to the extent reasonably necessary to permit the client to make informed decisions regarding representation. During the course of representation and afterwards, the counsel may not use or reveal a client's confidence or secrets, except as required or permitted by law.

(3) COMMUNICATION. The counsel will keep the client reasonably informed about the status of representation and will promptly respond to reasonable requests for information, including any reasonable request for an estimate respecting future costs of the representation or an appropriate portion of it. The client shall be truthful in all discussions with the counsel and provide all information or documentation required to enable the counsel to provide competent representation. During representation, the client is entitled to receive all pleadings and substantive documents prepared on behalf of the client and every document received from any other counsel of record. At the end of the representation and on written request from the client, the counsel will return to the client all original documents and exhibits. In the event that the counsel withdraws from representation, or is discharged by the client, the counsel will turn over to the substituting counsel (or, if no substitutions, to the client) all original documents and exhibits together with complete copies of all pleadings and discovery within thirty (30) days of the counsel's withdrawal or discharge.

(4) ETHICAL CONDUCT. The counsel cannot be required to engage in conduct which is illegal, unethical, or fraudulent. In matters involving minor children, the counsel may refuse to

engage in conduct which, in the counsel's professional judgment, would be contrary to the best interest of the client's minor child or children. A counsel who cannot ethically abide by his client's directions shall be allowed to withdraw from representation.

(5) FEES. The counsel's fee for services may not be contingent upon the securing of a dissolution of marriage, upon obtaining custody, or be based upon the amount of maintenance, child support, or property settlement received, except as specifically permitted under Supreme Court rules. The counsel may not require a non-refundable retainer fee, but must remit back any overpayment at the end of the representation. The counsel may enter into a consensual security arrangement with the client whereby assets of the client are pledged to secure payment of legal fees or costs, but only if the counsel first obtains approval of the Court. The counsel will prepare and provide the client with an itemized billing statement detailing hourly rates (and/or other criteria), time spent, tasks performed, and costs incurred on a regular basis, at least quarterly. The client should review each billing statement promptly and address any objection or error in a timely manner. The client will not be billed for time spent to explain or correct a billing statement. If an appropriately detailed written estimate is submitted to a client as to future costs for a counsel's representation or a portion of the contemplated services (i.e., relative to specific steps recommended by the counsel in the estimate) and, without objection from the client, the counsel then performs the contemplated services, all such services are presumptively reasonable and necessary, as well as to be deemed pursuant to the client's direction. In an appropriate case, the client may pursue contribution to his or her fees and costs from the other party.

(6) DISPUTES. The counsel-client relationship is regulated by the Illinois Rules of Professional Conduct (Article VIII of the Illinois Supreme Court Rules), and any dispute shall be reviewed under the terms of such Rules."

(g) The changes to this Section 508 made by this amendatory Act of 1996 apply to cases pending on or after June 1, 1997, except as follows:

(1) Subdivisions (c)(1) and (c)(2) of this Section 508, as well as provisions of subdivision (c)(3) of this Section 508 pertaining to written engagement agreements, apply only to cases filed on or after June 1, 1997.

(2) The following do not apply in the case of a hearing under this Section that began before June 1, 1997:

(A) Subsection (c-1) of Section 501.

(B) Subsection (j) of Section 503.

(C) The changes to this Section 508 made by this amendatory Act of 1996 pertaining to the final setting of fees.

(750 ILCS 5/510) (from Ch. 40, par. 510)

Sec. 510. Modification and termination of provisions for maintenance, support, educational expenses, and property disposition.

(a) Except as otherwise provided in paragraph (f) of Section 502 and in subsection (b), clause (3) of Section 505.2, the provisions of any judgment respecting maintenance or support may be modified only as to installments accruing subsequent to due notice by the moving party of the filing of the motion for modification. An order for child support may be modified as follows:

(1) upon a showing of a substantial change in circumstances; and

(2) without the necessity of showing a substantial change in circumstances, as follows:

(A) upon a showing of an inconsistency of at least 20%, but no less than $10 per month, between the amount of the existing order and the amount of child support that results from application of the guidelines specified in Section 505 of this Act unless the inconsistency is due to the fact that the amount of the existing order resulted from a deviation from the guideline amount and there has not been a change in the circumstances that resulted in that deviation; or

(B) Upon a showing of a need to provide for the health care needs of the child under the order through health insurance or other means. In no event shall the eligibility for or receipt of medical assistance be considered to meet the need to provide for the child's health care needs.

The provisions of subparagraph (a)(2)(A) shall apply only in cases in which a party is receiving child support enforcement services from the Illinois Department of Public Aid under Article X of the Illinois Public Aid Code, and only when at least 36 months have elapsed since the order for child support was entered or last modified.

(a-5) An order for maintenance may be modified or terminated only upon a showing of a substantial change in circumstances. In all such proceedings, as well as in proceedings in which maintenance is being reviewed, the court shall consider the applicable factors set forth in subsection (a) of Section 504 and the following factors:

(1) any change in the employment status of either party and whether the change has been made in good faith;

(2) the efforts, if any, made by the party receiving maintenance to become self-supporting, and the reasonableness of the efforts where they are appropriate;

(3) any impairment of the present and future earning capacity of either party;

(4) the tax consequences of the maintenance payments upon the respective economic circumstances of the parties;

(5) the duration of the maintenance payments previously paid (and remaining to be paid) relative to the length of the marriage;

(6) the property, including retirement benefits, awarded to each party under the judgment of dissolution of marriage, judgment of legal separation, or judgment of declaration of invalidity of marriage and the present status of the property;

(7) the increase or decrease in each party's income since the prior judgment or order from which a review, modification, or termination is being sought;

(8) the property acquired and currently owned by each party after the entry of the judgment of dissolution of marriage, judgment of legal separation, or judgment of declaration of invalidity of marriage; and

(9) any other factor that the court expressly finds to be just and equitable.

(b) The provisions as to property disposition may not be revoked or modified, unless the court finds the existence of conditions that justify the reopening of a judgment under the laws of this State.

(c) Unless otherwise agreed by the parties in a written agreement set forth in the judgment or otherwise approved by the court, the obligation to pay future maintenance is terminated upon the death of either party, or the remarriage of the party receiving maintenance, or if the party receiving maintenance cohabits with another person on a resident, continuing conjugal basis.

(d) Unless otherwise provided in this Act, or as agreed in writing or expressly provided in the judgment, provisions for the support of a child are terminated by emancipation of the child, or if the child has attained the age of 18 and is still attending high school, provisions for the support of the child are terminated upon the date that the child graduates from high school or the date the child attains the age of 19, whichever is earlier, but not by the death of a parent obligated to support or educate the child. An existing obligation to pay for support or educational expenses, or both, is not terminated by the death of a parent. When a parent obligated to pay support or educational expenses, or both, dies, the amount of support or educational expenses, or both, may be enforced, modified, revoked or commuted to a lump sum payment, as equity may require, and that determination may be provided for at the time of the dissolution of the marriage or thereafter.

(e) The right to petition for support or educational expenses, or both, under Sections 505 and 513 is not extinguished by the death of a parent. Upon a petition filed before or after a parent's death, the court may award sums of money out of the decedent's estate for the child's support or educational expenses, or both, as equity may require. The time within which a claim may be filed against the estate of a decedent under Sections 505 and 513 and subsection (d) and this subsection shall be governed by the provisions of the Probate Act of 1975, as a barrable, noncontingent claim.

(f) A petition to modify or terminate child support, custody, or visitation shall not delay any child support enforcement litigation or supplementary proceeding on behalf of the obligee, including, but not limited to, a petition for a rule to show cause, for non-wage garnishment, or for a restraining order.

750 ILCS 5/513

Support for Non-minor Children and Educational Expenses.

(a) The court may award sums of money out of the property and income of either or both parties or the estate of a deceased parent, as equity may require, for the support of the child or children of the parties who have attained majority in the following instances:

(1) When the child is mentally or physically disabled and not otherwise emancipated, an application for support may

be made before or after the child has attained majority.

(2) The court may also make provision for the educational expenses of the child or children of the parties, whether of minor or majority age, and an application for educational expenses may be made before or after the child has attained majority, or after the death of either parent. The authority under this Section to make provision for educational expenses extends not only to periods of college education or professional or other training after graduation from high school, but also to any period during which the child of the parties is still attending high school, even though he or she attained the age of 19. The educational expenses may include, but shall not be limited to, room, board, dues, tuition, transportation, books, fees, registration and application costs, medical expenses including medical insurance, dental expenses, and living expenses during the school year and periods of recess, which sums may be ordered payable to the child, to either parent, or to the educational institution, directly or through a special account or trust created for that purpose, as the court sees fit.

If educational expenses are ordered payable, each parent and the child shall sign any consents necessary for the educational institution to provide the supporting parent with access to the child's academic transcripts, records, and grade reports. The consents shall not apply to any non-academic records. Failure to execute the required consent may be a basis for a modification or termination of any order entered under this Section.

The authority under this Section to make provision for educational expenses, except where the child is mentally or physically disabled and not otherwise emancipated, terminates when the child receives a baccalaureate degree

(b) In making awards under paragraph (1) or (2) of subsection (a), or pursuant to a petition or motion to decrease, modify, or terminate any such award, the court shall consider all relevant factors that appear reasonable and necessary, including:

(1) The financial resources of both parents.

(2) The standard of living the child would have enjoyed had the marriage not been dissolved.

(3) The financial resources of the child.

(4) The child's academic performance.

750 ILCS 5/601

Jurisdiction; Commencement of Proceeding.

(a) A court of this State competent to decide child custody matters has jurisdiction to make a child custody determination in original or modification proceedings as provided in Section 201 of the Uniform Child-Custody Jurisdiction and Enforcement Act as adopted by this State.

(b) A child custody proceeding is commenced in the court:

(1) by a parent, by filing a petition:

(i) for dissolution of marriage or legal separation or declaration of invalidity of marriage; or

(ii) for custody of the child, in the county in which he is permanently resident or found;

(2) by a person other than a parent, by filing a petition for custody of the child in the county in which he is permanently resident or found, but only if he is not in the physical custody of one of his parents; or

(3) by a stepparent, by filing a petition, if all of the following circumstances are met:

(A) the child is at least 12 years old;

(B) the custodial parent and stepparent were married for at least 5 years during which the child resided with the parent and stepparent;

(C) the custodial parent is deceased or is disabled and cannot perform the duties of a parent to the child;

(D) the stepparent provided for the care, control, and welfare to the child prior to the initiation of custody proceedings;

(E) the child wishes to live with the stepparent; and

(F) it is alleged to be in the best interests

and welfare of the child to live with the stepparent as provided in Section 602 of this Act.

(4) When one of the parents is deceased, by a grandparent who is a parent or stepparent of a deceased parent, by filing a petition, if one or more of the following existed at the time of the parent's death:

(A) the surviving parent had been absent from the marital abode for more than one month without the deceased spouse knowing his or her whereabouts;

(B) the surviving parent was in State or federal custody; or

(C) the surviving parent had: (i) received supervision for or been convicted of any violation of Article 12 of the Criminal Code of 1961 directed towards the deceased parent or the child; or (ii) received supervision or been convicted of violating an order of protection entered under Section 217, 218, or 219 of the Illinois Domestic Violence Act of 1986 for the protection of the deceased parent or the child. </DIV"

(c) Notice of a child custody proceeding, including an action for modification of a previous custody order, shall be given to the child's parents, guardian and custodian, who may appear, be heard, and file a responsive pleading. The court, upon showing of good cause, may permit intervention of other interested parties.

(d) Proceedings for modification of a previous custody order commenced more than 30 days following the entry of a previous custody order must be initiated by serving a written notice and a copy of the petition for modification upon the child's parent, guardian and custodian at least 30 days prior to hearing on the petition. Nothing in this Section shall preclude a party in custody modification proceedings from moving for a temporary order under Section 603 of this Act.

(e) (Blank).

(f) The court shall, at the court's discretion or upon the request of any party entitled to petition for custody of the child, appoint a guardian ad litem to represent the best interest of the child for the duration of the custody proceeding or for any modifications of any custody orders entered. Nothing in this Section shall be construed to prevent the court from appointing the same guardian ad litem for 2 or more children that are siblings or half-siblings.

750 ILCS 5/602

Best Interest of Child.

(a) The court shall determine custody in accordance with the best interest of the child. The court shall consider all relevant factors including:

(1) the wishes of the child's parent or parents as to his custody;

(2) the wishes of the child as to his custodian;

(3) the interaction and interrelationship of the child with his parent or parents, his siblings and any other person who may significantly affect the child's best interest;

(4) the child's adjustment to his home, school and community;

(5) the mental and physical health of all individuals involved;

(6) the physical violence or threat of physical violence by the child's potential custodian, whether directed against the child or directed against another person;

(7) the occurrence of ongoing abuse as defined in Section 103 of the Illinois Domestic Violence Act of 1986, whether directed against the child or directed against another person;

(8) the willingness and ability of each parent to facilitate and encourage a close and continuing relationship between the other parent and the child; and

(9) whether one of the parents is a sex offender. In the case of a custody proceeding in which a stepparent has standing under Section 601, it is presumed to be in the best interest of the minor child that the natural parent have the custody of the minor child unless the presumption is rebutted by the stepparent.

(b) The court shall not consider conduct of a present or proposed custodian that does not affect his relationship to the child.

(c) Unless the court finds the occurrence of ongoing abuse as defined in Section 103 of the Illinois Domestic Violence Act of 1986, the court shall presume that the maximum involvement and cooperation of both parents regarding the physical, mental, moral, and emotional well-being of their child is in the best interest of the child. There shall be no presumption in favor of or against joint custody.

750 ILCS 5/604.5 Evaluation of child's best interest.

(a) In a proceeding for custody, visitation, or removal of a child from Illinois, upon notice and motion made within a reasonable time before trial, the court may order an evaluation concerning the best interest of the child as it relates to custody, visitation, or removal. The motion may be made by a party, a parent, the child's custodian, the attorney for the child, the child's guardian ad litem, or the child's representative. The requested evaluation may be in place of or in addition to an evaluation conducted under subsection (b) of Section 604.

The motion shall state the identity of the proposed evaluator and set forth the evaluator's specialty or discipline. The court

may refuse to order an evaluation by the proposed evaluator, but in that event, the court may permit the party seeking the evaluation to propose one or more other evaluators.

(b) An order for an evaluation shall fix the time, place, conditions, and scope of the evaluation and shall designate the evaluator. A party or person shall not be required to travel an unreasonable distance for the evaluation.

(c) The person requesting an evaluator shall pay the fee for the evaluation unless otherwise ordered by the court.

(d) Within 21 days after the completion of the evaluation, if the moving party or person intends to call the evaluator as a witness, the evaluator shall prepare and mail or deliver to the attorneys of record duplicate originals of the written evaluation. The evaluation shall set forth the evaluator's findings, the results of all tests administered, and the evaluator's conclusions and recommendations. If the written evaluation is not delivered or mailed to the attorneys within 21 days or within any extensions or modifications granted by the court, the written evaluation and the evaluator's testimony, conclusions, and recommendations may not be received into evidence.

(e) The person calling an evaluator to testify at trial shall disclose the evaluator as an opinion witness in accordance with the Supreme Court Rules.

(f) Subject to compliance with the Supreme Court Rules, nothing in this Section bars a person who did not request the evaluation from calling the evaluator as a witness. In that case, however, that person shall pay the evaluator's fee for testifying unless otherwise ordered by the court.

750 ILCS 5/607 Visitation.

(a) A parent not granted custody of the child is entitled to reasonable visitation rights unless the court finds, after a hearing, that visitation would endanger seriously the child's physical, mental, moral or emotional health. If the custodian's street address is not identified, pursuant to Section 708, the court shall require the parties to identify reasonable alternative arrangements for visitation by a non-custodial parent, including but not limited to visitation of the minor child at the residence of another person or at a local public or private facility.

(a-3) Grandparents, great-grandparents, and siblings of a minor child, who is one year old or older, have standing to bring an action in circuit court by petition, requesting visitation in accordance with this Section. The term "sibling" in this Section means a brother, sister, stepbrother, or stepsister of the minor child. Grandparents, great-grandparents, and siblings also have standing to file a petition for visitation rights in a pending dissolution proceeding or any other proceeding that involves custody or visitation issues, requesting visitation in accordance with this Section. A petition for visitation with a child by a person other than a parent must be filed in the county in which the child resides. Nothing in this subsection (a-3) and subsection (a-5) of this Section shall apply to a child in whose interests a petition is pending under Section 2-13 of the Juvenile Court Act of 1987 or a petition to adopt an unrelated child is pending under the Adoption Act.

(a-5)(1) Except as otherwise provided in this subsection (a-5), any grandparent, great-grandparent, or sibling may file a petition for visitation rights to a minor child if there is an unreasonable denial of visitation by a parent and at least one of the following conditions exists:

(A) (Blank);

(A-5) the child's other parent is deceased or has been missing for at least 3 months. For the purposes of this Section a parent is considered to be missing if the parent's location has not been determined and the parent has been reported as missing to a law enforcement agency;

(A-10) a parent of the child is incompetent as a matter of law;

(A-15) a parent has been incarcerated in jail or prison during the 3 month period preceding the filing of the petition;

(B) the child's mother and father are divorced or have been legally separated from each other or there is pending a dissolution proceeding involving a parent of the child or another court proceeding involving custody or visitation of the child (other than any adoption proceeding of an unrelated child) and at least one parent does not object to the grandparent, great-grandparent, or sibling having visitation with the child. The visitation of the grandparent, great-grandparent, or sibling must not diminish the visitation of the parent who is not related to the grandparent, great-grandparent, or sibling seeking visitation;

(C) (Blank);

(D) the child is born out of wedlock, the parents are not living together, and the petitioner is a maternal grandparent, great-grandparent, or sibling of the child born out of wedlock; or

(E) the child is born out of wedlock, the parents are not living together, the petitioner is a paternal grandparent, great-grandparent, or sibling, and the paternity has been established by a court of competent jurisdiction.

(2) Any visitation rights granted pursuant to this Section before the filing of a petition for adoption of a child shall automatically terminate by operation of law upon the entry of an order terminating parental rights or granting the adoption of the child, whichever is earlier. If the person or persons who adopted the child are related to the child, as defined by Section 1 of the Adoption Act, any person who was related to the child as grandparent, great-grandparent, or sibling prior to the adoption shall have standing to bring an action pursuant to this Section requesting visitation with the child.

(3) In making a determination under this subsection (a-5), there is a rebuttable presumption that a fit parent's actions and decisions regarding grandparent, great-grandparent, or sibling visitation are not harmful to the child's mental, physical, or emotional health. The burden is on the party filing a petition under this Section to prove that the parent's actions and decisions regarding visitation times are harmful to the child's mental, physical, or emotional health.

(4) In determining whether to grant visitation, the court shall consider the following:

(A) the preference of the child if the child is determined to be of sufficient maturity to express a preference;

(B) the mental and physical health of the child;

(C) the mental and physical health of the grandparent, great-grandparent, or sibling;

(D) the length and quality of the prior relationship between the child and the grandparent, great-grandparent, or sibling;

(E) the good faith of the party in filing the petition;

(F) the good faith of the person denying visitation;

(G) the quantity of the visitation time requested and the potential adverse impact that visitation would have on the child's customary activities;

(H) whether the child resided with the petitioner for at least 6 consecutive months with or without the current custodian present;

(I) whether the petitioner had frequent or regular contact or visitation with the child for at least 12 consecutive months;

(J) any other fact that establishes that the loss of the relationship between the petitioner and the child is likely to harm the child's mental, physical, or emotional health; and

(K) whether the grandparent, great-grandparent, or sibling was a primary caretaker of the child for a period of not less than 6 consecutive months.

(5) The court may order visitation rights for the grandparent, great-grandparent, or sibling that include reasonable access without requiring overnight or possessory visitation.

(a-7)(1) Unless by stipulation of the parties, no motion to modify a grandparent, great-grandparent, or sibling visitation order may be made earlier than 2 years after the date the order was filed, unless the court permits it to be made on the basis of affidavits that there is reason to believe the child's present environment may endanger seriously the child's mental, physical, or emotional health.

(2) The court shall not modify an order that grants visitation to a grandparent, great-grandparent, or sibling unless it finds by clear and convincing evidence, upon the basis of facts that have arisen since the prior visitation order or that were unknown to the court at the time of entry of the prior visitation, that a change has occurred in the circumstances of the child or his or her custodian, and that the modification is necessary to protect the mental, physical, or emotional health of the child. The court shall state in its decision specific findings of fact in support of its modification or termination of the grandparent, great-grandparent, or sibling visitation. A child's parent may always petition to modify visitation upon changed circumstances when necessary to promote the child's best interest.

(3) Attorney fees and costs shall be assessed against a party seeking modification of the visitation order if the court finds that the modification action is vexatious and constitutes harassment.

(4) Notice under this subsection (a-7) shall be given as provided in subsections (c) and (d) of Section 601.

(b) (1) (Blank.)

(1.5) The Court may grant reasonable visitation privileges to a stepparent upon petition to the court by the stepparent, with notice to the parties required to be notified under Section 601 of this Act, if the court determines that it is in the best interests and welfare of the child, and may issue any necessary orders to enforce those visitation privileges. A petition for visitation privileges may be filed under this paragraph (1.5) whether or not a petition pursuant to this Act has been previously filed or is currently pending if the following circumstances are met:

(A) the child is at least 12 years old;

(B) the child resided continuously with the parent and stepparent for at least 5 years;

(C) the parent is deceased or is disabled and is unable to care for the child;

(D) the child wishes to have reasonable visitation with the stepparent; and

(E) the stepparent was providing for the care, control, and welfare to the child prior to the initiation of the petition for visitation.

(2)(A) A petition for visitation privileges shall not be filed pursuant to this subsection (b) by the parents or grandparents of a putative father if the paternity of the putative father has not been legally established.

(B) A petition for visitation privileges may not be filed under this subsection (b) if the child who is the subject of the grand-parents' or great-grandparents' petition has been voluntarily surrendered by the parent or parents, except for a surrender to the Illinois Department of Children and Family Services or a foster care facility, or has been previously adopted by an individual or individuals who are not related to the biological parents of the child or is the subject of a pending adoption petition by an individual or individuals who are not related to the biological parents of the child.

(3) (Blank).

(c) The court may modify an order granting or denying visitation rights of a parent whenever modification would serve the best interest of the child; but the court shall not restrict a parent's visitation rights unless it finds that the visitation would endanger seriously the child's physical, mental, moral or emotional health.

(d) If any court has entered an order prohibiting a non-custodial parent of a child from any contact with a child or restricting the non-custodial parent's contact with the child, the following provisions shall apply:

(1) If an order has been entered granting visitation privileges with the child to a grandparent or great-grandparent who is related to the child through the non-custodial parent, the visitation privileges of the grandparent or great-grandparent may be revoked if:

(i) a court has entered an order prohibiting the non-custodial parent from any contact with the child, and the grandparent or great-grandparent is found to have used his or her visitation privileges to facilitate contact between the child and the non-custodial parent; or

(ii) a court has entered an order restricting the non-custodial parent's contact with the child, and the grandparent or great-grandparent is found to have used his or her visitation privileges to facilitate contact between the child and the non-custodial parent in a manner that violates the terms of the order restricting the non-custodial parent's contact with the child.

Nothing in this subdivision (1) limits the authority of the court to enforce its orders in any manner permitted by law.

(2) Any order granting visitation privileges with the child to a grandparent or great-grandparent who is related to the child through the non-custodial parent shall contain the following provision:

"If the (grandparent or great-grandparent, whichever is applicable) who has been granted visitation privileges under this order uses the visitation privileges to facilitate contact between the child and the child's non-custodial parent, the visitation privileges granted under this order shall be permanently revoked."

(e) No parent, not granted custody of the child, or grand-parent, or great-grandparent, or stepparent, or sibling of any minor child, convicted of any offense involving an illegal sex act perpetrated upon a victim less than 18 years of age including but not limited to offenses for violations of Article 12 of the Criminal Code of 1961, is entitled to visitation rights while incarcerated or while on parole, probation, conditional discharge, periodic imprisonment, or mandatory supervised release for that offense, and upon discharge from incarceration for a misdemeanor offense or upon discharge from parole, probation, conditional discharge, periodic imprisonment, or mandatory supervised release for a felony offense, visitation shall be denied until the person successfully completes a treatment program approved by the court.

(f) Unless the court determines, after considering all relevant factors, including but not limited to those set forth in Section 602(a), that it would be in the best interests of the child to allow visitation, the court shall not enter an order providing visitation rights and pursuant to a motion to modify visitation shall revoke visitation rights previously granted to any person who would otherwise be entitled to petition for visitation rights under this Section who has been convicted of first degree murder of the parent, grandparent, great-grandparent, or sibling of the child who is the subject of the order. Until an order is entered pursuant to this subsection, no person shall visit, with the child present, a person who has been convicted of first degree murder of the parent, grandparent, great-grandparent, or sibling of the child without the consent of the child's parent, other than a parent convicted of first degree murder as set forth herein, or legal guardian.

(g) (Blank).

750 ILCS 5/607.1 Enforcement of visitation orders; visitation abuse.

(a) The circuit court shall provide an expedited procedure for enforcement of court ordered visitation in cases of visitation abuse. Visitation abuse occurs when a party has willfully and without justification: (1) denied another party visitation as set forth by the court; or (2) exercised his or her visitation rights in a manner that is harmful to the child or child's custodian.

(b) An Action may be commenced by filing a petition setting forth: (i) the petitioner's name, residence address or mailing address, and telephone number; (ii) respondent's name and place of residence, place of employment, or mailing address; (iii) the nature of the visitation abuse, giving dates and other relevant information; (iv) that a reasonable attempt was made to resolve the dispute; and (v) the relief sought.

Notice of the filing of the petitions shall be given as provided in Section 511.

(c) After hearing all of the evidence, the court may order one or more of the following:

(1) Modification of the visitation order to specifically outline periods of visitation or restrict visitation as provided by law.

(2) Supervised visitation with a third party or public agency.

(3) Make up visitation of the same time period, such as weekend for weekend, holiday for holiday.

(4) Counseling or mediation, except in cases where there is evidence of domestic violence, as defined in Section 1 of the Domestic Violence Shelters Act, occurring between the parties.

(5) Other appropriate relief deemed equitable.

(d) Nothing contained in this Section shall be construed to limit the court's contempt power, except as provided in subsection (g) of this Section.

(e) When the court issues an order holding a party in contempt of court for violation of a visitation order, the clerk shall transmit a copy of the contempt order to the sheriff of the county. The sheriff shall furnish a copy of each contempt order to the Department of State Police on a daily basis in the form and manner required by the Department. The Department shall maintain a complete record and index of the contempt orders and make this data available to all local law enforcement agencies.

(f) Attorney fees and costs shall be assessed against a party if the court finds that the enforcement action is vexatious and constitutes harassment.

(g) A person convicted of unlawful visitation interference under Section 10-5.5 of the Criminal Code of 1961 shall not be subject to the provisions of this Section and the court may not enter a contempt order for visitation abuse against any person for the same conduct for which the person was convicted of unlawful visitation interference or subject that person to the sanctions provided for in this Section.

*   *   *

750 ILCS 5/610
Modification.
(a) Unless by stipulation of the parties or except as provided in subsection (a-5), no motion to modify a custody judgment may be made earlier than 2 years after its date, unless the court permits it to be made on the basis of affidavits that there is reason to believe the child's present environment may endanger seriously his physical, mental, moral or emotional health.

(a-5) A motion to modify a custody judgment may be made at any time by a party who has been informed of the existence of facts requiring notice to be given under Section 609.5.
(b) The court shall not modify a prior custody judgment unless it finds by clear and convincing evidence, upon the basis of facts that have arisen since the prior judgment or that were unknown to the court at the time of entry of the prior judgment, that a change has occurred in the circumstances of the child or his custodian, or in the case of a joint custody arrangement that a change has occurred in the circumstances of the child or either or both parties having custody, and that the modification is necessary to serve the best interest of the child. The existence of facts requiring notice to be given under Section 609.5 of this Act shall be considered a change in circumstance. In the case of joint custody, if the parties agree to a termination of a joint custody arrangement, the court shall so terminate the joint custody and make any modification which is in the child's best interest. The court shall state in its decision specific findings of fact in support of its modification or termination of joint custody if either parent opposes the modification or termination.
(c) Attorney fees and costs shall be assessed against a party seeking modification if the court finds that the modification action is vexatious and constitutes harassment.
(d) Notice under this Section shall be given as provided in subsections (c) and (d) of Section 601.
750 ILCS 5/611
Enforcement of custody order or order prohibiting removal of child from the jurisdiction of the court.
(a) The court may enter a judgment to enforce a custody order or a court order prohibiting removal of the child from the jurisdiction of the court if it finds that the respondent has violated the terms of the court order by having improperly removed the child from the physical custody of the petitioner or another person entitled to custody or by having improperly retained the child after a visit or other temporary relinquishment of physical custody.
If the general whereabouts of the child are known, the judgment shall direct any sheriff or law enforcement officer to provide assistance to the petitioner in apprehending the child and shall further authorize any child care personnel, babysitter, teacher or any person having physical custody of the child to surrender the child to such sheriff or law enforcement officer.
(b) The court may enter a judgment pursuant to subsection (a) of this Section without prior notice to the respondent if the court finds that prior notice would be likely to cause the respondent's flight from the jurisdiction or cause further removal or concealment of the child. If an ex parte order is entered pursuant to this subsection, the respondent may, upon 2 days notice to the petitioner or upon such shorter notice as the court may prescribe, appear and move for the dissolution or modification of the judgment and in that event the court shall proceed to hear and determine such motion as expeditiously as possible.
(c) Nothing contained in this Section shall be construed to limit the court's contempt power.

*   *   *

750 ILCS 5/706.3
Information concerning obligors.
(a) In this Section:
"Arrearage", "delinquency", "obligor", and "order for support" have the meanings attributed to those terms in the Income Withholding for Support Act.
"Consumer reporting agency" has the meaning attributed to that term in Section 603(f) of the Fair Credit Reporting Act, 15 U.S.C. 1681a(f).
(b) Whenever a court of competent jurisdiction finds that an obligor either owes an arrearage of more than $10,000, is delinquent in payment of an amount equal to at least 3 months' support obligation pursuant to an order for support, or fails to pay the child support annual fee for a period of 3 years, the court shall direct the clerk of the court to make information concerning the obligor available to consumer reporting agencies.
(c) Whenever a court of competent jurisdiction finds that an obligor either owes an arrearage of more than $10,000 or is delinquent in payment of an amount equal to at least 3 months' support obligation pursuant to an order for support, the court shall direct the clerk of the court to cause the obligor's name and address to be published in a newspaper of general circulation in the area in which the obligor resides. The clerk shall cause the obligor's name and address to be published only after sending to the obligor at the obligor's last known address, by certified mail, return receipt requested, a notice of intent to publish the information. This subsection (c) applies only if the obligor resides in the county in which the clerk of the court holds office.

*   *   *

750 ILCS 5/709
Mandatory child support payments to clerk.
(a) As of January 1, 1982, child support orders entered in any county covered by this subsection shall be made pursuant to the provisions of Sections 709 through 712 of this Act. For purposes of these Sections, the term "child support payment" or "payment" shall include any payment ordered to be made solely for the purpose of the support of a child or children or any payment ordered for general support which includes any amount for support of any child or children.
The provisions of Sections 709 through 712 shall be applicable to any county with a population of 2 million or more and to any other county which notifies the Supreme Court of its desire to be included within the coverage of these Sections and is certified pursuant to Supreme Court Rules.
The effective date of inclusion, however, shall be subject to approval of the application for reimbursement of the costs of the support program by the Department of Public Aid as provided in Section 712.
(b) In any proceeding for a dissolution of marriage, legal separation, or declaration of invalidity of marriage, or in any supplementary proceedings in which a judgment or modification thereof for the payment of child support is entered on or after January 1, 1982, in any county covered by Sections 709

through 712, and the person entitled to payment is receiving a grant of financial aid under Article IV of the Illinois Public Aid Code or has applied and qualified for child support enforcement services under Section 10-1 of that Code, the court shall direct: (1) that such payments be made to the clerk of the court and (2) that the parties affected shall each thereafter notify the clerk of any change of address or change in other conditions that may affect the administration of the order, including the fact that a party who was previously not on public aid has become a recipient of public aid, within 10 days of such change. All notices sent to the obligor's last known address on file with the clerk shall be deemed sufficient to proceed with enforcement pursuant to the provisions of Sections 709 through 712.
In all other cases, the court may direct that payments be made to the clerk of the court.
(c) Except as provided in subsection (d) of this Section, the clerk shall disburse the payments to the person or persons entitled thereto under the terms of the order or judgment.
(d) The court shall determine, prior to the entry of the support order, if the party who is to receive the support is presently receiving public aid or has a current application for public aid pending and shall enter the finding on the record.
If the person entitled to payment is a recipient of aid under the Illinois Public Aid Code, the clerk, upon being informed of this fact by finding of the court, by notification by the party entitled to payment, by the Illinois Department of Public Aid or by the local governmental unit, shall make all payments to: (1) the Illinois Department of Public Aid if the person is a recipient under Article III, IV, or V of the Code or (2) the local governmental unit responsible for his or her support if the person is a recipient under Article VI or VII of the Code. In accordance with federal law and regulations, the Illinois Department of Public Aid may continue to collect current maintenance payments or child support payments, or both, after those persons cease to receive public assistance and until termination of services under Article X of the Illinois Public Aid Code. The Illinois Department of Public Aid shall pay the net amount collected to those persons after deducting any costs incurred in making the collection or any collection fee from the amount of any recovery made. Upon termination of public aid payments to such a recipient or termination of services under Article X of the Illinois Public Aid Code, the Illinois Department of Public Aid or the appropriate local governmental unit shall notify the clerk in writing or by electronic transmission that all subsequent payments are to be sent directly to the person entitled thereto.
Payments under this Section to the Illinois Department of Public Aid pursuant to the Child Support Enforcement Program established by Title IV-D of the Social Security Act shall be paid into the Child Support Enforcement Trust Fund. All payments under this Section to the Illinois Department of Human Services shall be deposited in the DHS Recoveries Trust Fund. Disbursements from these funds shall be as provided in the Illinois Public Aid Code. Payments received by a local governmental unit shall be deposited in that unit's General Assistance Fund.

(e) Any order or judgment may be amended by the court, upon its own motion or upon the motion of either party, to conform with the provisions of Sections 709 through 712, either as to the requirement of making payments to the clerk or, where payments are already being made to the clerk, as to the statutory fees provided for under Section 711.

(f) The clerk may invest in any interest bearing account or in any securities, monies collected for the benefit of a payee, where such payee cannot be found; however, the investment may be only for the period until the clerk is able to locate and present the payee with such monies. The clerk may invest in any interest bearing account, or in any securities, monies collected for the benefit of any other payee; however, this does not alter the clerk's obligation to make payments to the payee in a timely manner. Any interest or capital gains accrued shall be for the benefit of the county and shall be paid into the special fund established in subsection (b) of Section 711.

(g) The clerk shall establish and maintain a payment record of all monies received and disbursed and such record shall constitute prima facie evidence of such payment and non-payment, as the case may be.

(h) For those cases in which child support is payable to the clerk of the circuit court for transmittal to the Illinois Department of Public Aid by order of court or upon notification by the Illinois Department of Public Aid, the clerk shall transmit all such payments, within 4 working days of receipt, to insure that funds are available for immediate distribution by the Department to the person or entity entitled thereto in accordance with standards of the Child Support Enforcement Program established under Title IV-D of the Social Security Act. The clerk shall notify the Department of the date of receipt and amount thereof at the time of transmittal. Where the clerk has entered into an agreement of cooperation with the Department to record the terms of child support orders and payments made thereunder directly into the Department's automated data processing system, the clerk shall account for, transmit and otherwise distribute child support payments in accordance with such agreement in lieu of the requirements contained herein.

(i) To the extent the provisions of this Section are inconsistent with the requirements pertaining to the State Disbursement Unit under Section 507.1 of this Act and Section 10-26 of the Illinois Public Aid Code, the requirements pertaining to the State Disbursement Unit shall apply.

750 ILCS 5/710. Enforcement; Penalties.

(a) In counties certified as included under the provisions of Sections 709 through 712 and whose application for reimbursement is approved, there shall be instituted a child support enforcement program to be conducted by the clerk of the circuit court and the state's attorney of the county. The program is to be limited to enforcement of child support orders entered pursuant to this Act.

The child support enforcement program is to be conducted only on behalf of dependent children included in a grant of financial aid under Article IV of The Illinois Public Aid Code and parties who apply and qualify for child support enforcement services pursuant to Section 10-1 of such Code.

Nothing in this Section shall be construed to prohibit the establishment of a child support enforcement program by the clerk of the circuit court in cooperation with the State's Attorney of the county.

(b) In the event of a delinquency in payment, as determined from the record maintained by the clerk in a county covered by the child support enforcement program, such clerk shall notify both the party obligated to make the payment, hereinafter called the payor, and the recipient of such payment, hereinafter called the payee, of such delinquency and that if the amount then due and owing is not remitted in the time period required by circuit court rules, the matter will be referred to the state's attorney for enforcement proceedings. Upon failure of the payor to remit as required, the clerk shall refer the matter to the state's attorney, except as provided by rule of the circuit court.

(c) Upon referral from the clerk, the state's attorney shall promptly initiate enforcement proceedings against the payor. Legal representation by the state's attorney shall be limited to child support and shall not extend to visitation, custody, property or other matters; however, if the payor properly files pleadings raising such matters during the course of the child support hearing and the court finds that it has jurisdiction of such matters, the payee shall be granted the opportunity to obtain a continuance in order to secure representation for those other matters, and the court shall not delay entry of an appropriate support order pending the disposition of such other matters. If the state's attorney does not commence enforcement proceedings within 30 days, the clerk shall inform the court which, upon its own motion, shall appoint counsel for purposes of enforcement. The fees and expenses of such counsel shall be paid by the payor and shall not be paid by the State.

Nothing in this Section shall be construed to prevent a payee from instituting independent enforcement proceedings or limit the remedies available to payee in such proceedings. However, absent the exercise under this provision of a private right of enforcement, enforcement shall be as otherwise provided in this Section.

(d) At the time any support order is entered, the payee shall be informed of the procedure used for enforcement and shall be given the address and telephone number both of the clerk and of the Child and Spouse Support Unit as provided in Section 712.

The payee shall be informed that, if no action is taken within 2 months of any complaint to the clerk, payee may contact the Unit to seek assistance in obtaining enforcement.

(e) Upon a finding that payor is in default and that such non-payment is for a period of two months and that such non-payment is without good cause, the court shall order the payor to pay a sum equal to 2% of the arrearage as a penalty along with his payment.

The court may further assess against the payor any fees and expenses incurred in the enforcement of any order or the reasonable value thereof and may impose any penalty otherwise available to it in a case of contempt.

All penalties, fees and expenses assessed against the payor

pursuant to this subsection are to cover the expenses of enforcement, are to be paid to the clerk and are to be placed by him in the special fund provided for in Section 711.

(f) Any person not covered by the child support enforcement program may institute private and independent proceedings to enforce payment of support.

*   *   *

750 ILCS 5/712

(a) The Supreme Court may make Rules concerning the certification of counties for inclusion in the child support enforcement program and the application of the procedures created by Sections 709 through 712 in the various counties.

The Supreme Court shall inform each circuit court and clerk of the court of the availability of the program to reimburse counties desiring to participate in the program of enforcement of child support payments.

The Supreme Court shall also distribute to each circuit court and clerk of the court any materials prepared by the Child and Spouse Support Unit comparing child support enforcement in counties included and not included in this program.

(b) The Illinois Department of Public Aid, through the Child and Spouse Support Unit provided for by Section 10-3.1 of The Illinois Public Aid Code, shall have general supervision of the child support programs created by Sections 709 through 712 and shall have the powers and duties provided in this Section, including the following:

(1) to make advance payments to any county included in the program for expenses in preparing programs to enforce payment of child support to the clerk from appropriations made for such purposes by the General Assembly;

(2) to make payments to each covered county to pay for its reasonable expenses actually necessary to maintain a continuing program not paid for by fees, penalties, or other monies; provided that, with respect to that portion of the program on behalf of dependent children included in a grant of financial aid under Article IV of The Illinois Public Aid Code the Unit shall pay only such expenses as is its current practice or as it may deem appropriate; provided further that the Unit shall only pay expenses of the entire program subject to the availability of federal monies to pay the majority of expenses of the entire child support enforcement program; provided further that the Unit or Department may set standards relating to enforcement which have to be met by any county seeking to enter a contract with the Department for reimbursement of expenses of the entire enforcement program prior to an application for reimbursement being approved and the contract granted; and provided further that such standards may relate to, but are not limited to the following factors: maintenance of the payment record, the definition of delinquency; the period of time in which a delinquency must be determined, the payor notified, the remittance received, the referral to the state's attorney made, and the payment remitted by the clerk to the payee or other party entitled to the payment; the conditions under which referral will not be made to the state's attorney; and the definitions and procedures for other matters necessary for the conduct and operation of the program;

(3) to monitor the various local programs for enforcement of child support payments to the clerk;

(4) to act to encourage enforcement whenever local enforcement procedures are inadequate;

(5) to receive monies from any source for assistance in enforcement of child support; and

(6) to assist any county desirous of assistance in establishing and maintaining a child support enforcement program.

(c) Any county may apply for financial assistance to the Unit to initiate or maintain a program of child support enforcement. Every county which desires such assistance shall apply according to procedures established by the Unit. In its application, it shall state the following: financial needs, personnel requirements, anticipated caseloads, any amounts collected or anticipated in fees or penalties, and any other information required by the Unit.

(d) In the case that any advance money is given to any county under this Section to initiate an enforcement system, the county shall reimburse the state within 2 years from the date such monies are given to it. The Unit may establish an appropriate schedule of reimbursement for any county.

(e) In the event of the unavailability of federal monies to pay for the greater part of the costs to a county of the child support enforcement program under Sections 709 through 712 and the resulting cessation of state participation, the operation of the child support enforcement program under Sections 709 through 712 shall terminate. The date and the method of termination shall be determined by Supreme Court Rule.

*   *   *

750 ILCS 16/15 Failure to support.

(a) A person commits the offense of failure to support when he or she:

(1) willfully, without any lawful excuse, refuses to provide for the support or maintenance of his or her spouse, with the knowledge that the spouse is in need of such support or maintenance, or, without lawful excuse, deserts or willfully refuses to provide for the support or maintenance of his or her child or children in need of support or maintenance and the person has the ability to provide the support; or

(2) willfully fails to pay a support obligation required under a court or administrative order for support, if the obligation has remained unpaid for a period longer than 6 months, or is in arrears in an amount greater than $5,000, and the person has the ability to provide the support; or

(3) leaves the State with the intent to evade a support obligation required under a court or administrative order for support, if the obligation, regardless of when it accrued, has remained unpaid for a period longer than 6 months, or is in arrears in an amount greater than $10,000; or

(4) willfully fails to pay a support obligation required under a court or administrative order for support, if the obligation has remained unpaid for a period longer than one year, or is in arrears in an amount greater than $20,000, and the person has the ability to provide the support.

(a-5) Presumption of ability to pay support. The existence of a court or administrative order of support that was not based on a default judgment and was in effect for the time period charged in the indictment or information creates a rebuttable presumption that the obligor has the ability to pay the support obligation for that time period.

(b) Sentence. A person convicted of a first offense under subdivision (a)(1) or (a)(2) is guilty of a Class A misdemeanor. A person convicted of an offense under subdivision (a)(3) or (a)(4) or a second or subsequent offense under subdivision (a)(1) or (a)(2) is guilty of a Class 4 felony.

(c) Expungement. A person convicted of a first offense under subdivision (a)(1) or (a)(2) who is eligible for the Earnfare program, shall, in lieu of the sentence prescribed in subsection (b), be referred to the Earnfare program. Upon certification of completion of the Earnfare program, the conviction shall be expunged. If the person fails to successfully complete the Earnfare program, he or she shall be sentenced in accordance with subsection (b).

(d) Fine. Sentences of imprisonment and fines for offenses committed under this Act shall be as provided under Articles 8 and 9 of Chapter V of the Unified Code of Corrections, except that the court shall order restitution of all unpaid support payments and may impose the following fines, alone, or in addition to a sentence of imprisonment under the following circumstances:

(1) from $1,000 to $5,000 if the support obligation has remained unpaid for a period longer than 2 years, or is in arrears in an amount greater than $1,000 and not exceeding $10,000;

(2) from $5,000 to $10,000 if the support obligation has remained unpaid for a period longer than 5 years, or is in arrears in an amount greater than $10,000 and not exceeding $20,000; or

(3) from $10,000 to $25,000 if the support obligation has remained unpaid for a period longer than 8 years, or is in arrears in an amount greater than $20,000.

(e) Restitution shall be ordered in an amount equal to the total unpaid support obligation as it existed at the time of sentencing. Any amounts paid by the obligor shall be allocated first to current support and then to restitution ordered and then to fines imposed under this Section.

(f) For purposes of this Act, the term "child" shall have the meaning ascribed to it in Section 505 of the Illinois Marriage and Dissolution of Marriage Act.

750 ILCS 16/20 Entry of order for support; income withholding.

(a) In a case in which no court or administrative order for support is in effect against the defendant:

(1) at any time before the trial, upon motion of the State's Attorney, or of the Attorney General if the action has been instituted by his office, and upon notice to the defendant, or at the time of arraignment or as a condition of postponement of arraignment, the court may enter such temporary order for support as may seem just, providing for the support or maintenance of the spouse or child or children of the defendant, or both, pendente lite; or

(2) before trial with the consent of the defendant,

or at the trial on entry of a plea of guilty, or after conviction, instead of imposing the penalty provided in this Act, or in addition thereto, the court may enter an order for support, subject to modification by the court from time to time as circumstances may require, directing the defendant to pay a certain sum for maintenance of the spouse, or for support of the child or children, or both.

(b) The court shall determine the amount of child support by using the guidelines and standards set forth in subsection (a) of Section 505 and in Section 505.2 of the Illinois Marriage and Dissolution of Marriage Act.

If (i) the non-custodial parent was properly served with a request for discovery of financial information relating to the non-custodial parent's ability to provide child support, (ii) the non-custodial parent failed to comply with the request, despite having been ordered to do so by the court, and (iii) the non-custodial parent is not present at the hearing to determine support despite having received proper notice, then any relevant financial information concerning the non-custodial parent's ability to provide support that was obtained pursuant to subpoena and proper notice shall be admitted into evidence without the need to establish any further foundation for its admission.

(c) The court shall determine the amount of maintenance using the standards set forth in Section 504 of the Illinois Marriage and Dissolution of Marriage Act.

(d) The court may, for violation of any order under this Section, punish the offender as for a contempt of court, but no pendente lite order shall remain in effect longer than 4 months, or after the discharge of any panel of jurors summoned for service thereafter in such court, whichever is sooner.

(e) Any order for support entered by the court under this Section shall be deemed to be a series of judgments against the person obligated to pay support under the judgments, each such judgment to be in the amount of each payment or installment of support and each judgment to be deemed entered as of the date the corresponding payment or installment becomes due under the terms of the support order. Each judgment shall have the full force, effect, and attributes of any other judgment of this State, including the ability to be enforced. Each judgment is subject to modification or termination only in accordance with Section 510 of the Illinois Marriage and Dissolution of Marriage Act. A lien arises by operation of law against the real and personal property of the noncustodial parent for each installment of overdue support owed by the noncustodial parent.

(f) An order for support entered under this Section shall include a provision requiring the obligor to report to the obligee and to the clerk of the court within 10 days each time the obligor obtains new employment, and each time the obligor's employment is terminated for any reason. The report shall be in writing and shall, in the case of new employment, include the name and address of the new employer.

Failure to report new employment or the termination of current employment, if coupled with nonpayment of support for a period in excess of 60 days, is indirect criminal contempt. For any obligor arrested for failure to report new employment, bond shall be set in the amount of the child support that should have been paid during the period of unreported employment.

An order for support entered under this Section shall also include a provision requiring the obligor and obligee parents to advise each other of a change in residence within 5 days of the change except when the court finds that the physical, mental, or emotional health of a party or of a minor child, or both, would be seriously endangered by disclosure of the party's address.

(g) An order for support entered or modified in a case in which a party is receiving child support enforcement services under Article X of the Illinois Public Aid Code shall include a provision requiring the noncustodial parent to notify the Illinois Department of Public Aid, within 7 days, of the name and address of any new employer of the noncustodial parent, whether the noncustodial parent has access to health insurance coverage through the employer or other group coverage and, if so, the policy name and number and the names of persons covered under the policy.

(h) In any subsequent action to enforce an order for support entered under this Act, upon sufficient showing that diligent effort has been made to ascertain the location of the noncustodial parent, service of process or provision of notice necessary in that action may be made at the last known address of the noncustodial parent, in any manner expressly provided by the Code of Civil Procedure or in this Act, which service shall be sufficient for purposes of due process.

(i) An order for support shall include a date on which the current support obligation terminates. The termination date shall be no earlier than the date on which the child covered by the order will attain the age of 18. However, if the child will not graduate from high school until after attaining the age of 18, then the termination date shall be no earlier than the earlier of the date on which the child's high school graduation will occur or the date on which the child will attain the age of 19. The order for support shall state that the termination date does not apply to any arrearage that may remain unpaid on that date. Nothing in this subsection shall be construed to prevent the court from modifying the order or terminating the order in the event the child is otherwise emancipated.

(i-5) If there is an unpaid arrearage or delinquency (as those terms are defined in the Income Withholding for Support Act) equal to at least one month's support obligation on the termination date stated in the order for support or, if there is no termination date stated in the order, on the date the child attains the age of majority or is otherwise emancipated, the periodic amount required to be paid for current support of that child immediately prior to that date shall automatically continue to be an obligation, not as current support but as periodic payment toward satisfaction of the unpaid arrearage or delinquency. That periodic payment shall be in addition to any periodic payment previously required for satisfaction of the arrearage or delinquency. The total periodic amount to be paid toward satisfaction of the arrearage or delinquency may be

enforced and collected by any method provided by law for enforcement and collection of child support, including but not limited to income withholding under the Income Withholding for Support Act. Each order for support entered or modified on or after the effective date of this amendatory Act of the 93rd General Assembly must contain a statement notifying the parties of the requirements of this subsection. Failure to include the statement in the order for support does not affect the validity of the order or the operation of the provisions of this subsection with regard to the order. This subsection shall not be construed to prevent or affect the establishment or modification of an order for support of a minor child or the establishment or modification of an order for support of a non-minor child or educational expenses under Section 513 of the Illinois Marriage and Dissolution of Marriage Act.

(j) A support obligation, or any portion of a support obligation, which becomes due and remains unpaid as of the end of each month, excluding the child support that was due for that month to the extent that it was not paid in that month, shall accrue simple interest as set forth in Section 12-109 of the Code of Civil Procedure. An order for support entered or modified on or after January 1, 2006 shall contain a statement that a support obligation required under the order, or any portion of a support obligation required under the order, that becomes due and remains unpaid as of the end of each month, excluding the child support that was due for that month to the extent that it was not paid in that month, shall accrue simple interest as set forth in Section 12-109 of the Code of Civil Procedure. Failure to include the statement in the order for support does not affect the validity of the order or the accrual of interest as provided in this Section.

750 ILCS 16/22 Withholding of income to secure payment of support. An order for support entered or modified under this Act is subject to the Income Withholding for Support Act.

750 ILCS 16/23 Interest on support obligations. A support obligation, or any portion of a support obligation, which becomes due and remains unpaid as of the end of each month, excluding the child support that was due for that month to the extent that it was not paid in that month, shall accrue interest as set forth in Section 12-109 of the Code of Civil Procedure.

750 ILCS 16/25 Payment of support to State Disbursement Unit; clerk of the court.

(a) As used in this Section, "order for support", "obligor", "obligee", and "payor" mean those terms as defined in the Income Withholding for Support Act.

(b) Each order for support entered or modified under Section 20 of this Act shall require that support payments be made to the State Disbursement Unit established under the Illinois Public Aid Code, under the following circumstances:

(1) when a party to the order is receiving child support enforcement services under Article X of the Illinois Public Aid Code; or

(2) when no party to the order is receiving child support enforcement services, but the support payments are made through income withholding.

(c) When no party to the order is receiving child support

enforcement services, and payments are not being made through income withholding, the court shall order the obligor to make support payments to the clerk of the court.

(d) At any time, and notwithstanding the existence of an order directing payments to be made elsewhere, the Department of Public Aid may provide notice to the obligor and, where applicable, to the obligor's payor:

(1) to make support payments to the State Disbursement Unit if:

(A) a party to the order for support is receiving child support enforcement services under Article X of the Illinois Public Aid Code; or

(B) no party to the order for support is receiving child support enforcement services under Article X of the Illinois Public Aid Code, but the support payments are made through income withholding; or

(2) to make support payments to the State Disbursement Unit of another state upon request of another state's Title IV-D child support enforcement agency, in accordance with the requirements of Title IV, Part D of the Social Security Act and regulations promulgated under that Part D.

The Department of Public Aid shall provide a copy of the notice to the obligee and to the clerk of the circuit court.

(e) If a State Disbursement Unit as specified by federal law has not been created in Illinois upon the effective date of this Act, then, until the creation of a State Disbursement Unit as specified by federal law, the following provisions regarding payment and disbursement of support payments shall control and the provisions in subsections (a), (b), (c), and (d) shall be inoperative. Upon the creation of a State Disbursement Unit as specified by federal law, the payment and disbursement provisions of subsections (a), (b), (c), and (d) shall control, and this subsection (e) shall be inoperative to the extent that it conflicts with those subsections.

(1) In cases in which an order for support is entered under Section 20 of this Act, the court shall order that maintenance and support payments be made to the clerk of the court for remittance to the person or agency entitled to receive the payments. However, the court in its discretion may direct otherwise where exceptional circumstances so warrant.

(2) The court shall direct that support payments be sent by the clerk to (i) the Illinois Department of Public Aid if the person in whose behalf payments are made is receiving aid under Articles III, IV, or V of the Illinois Public Aid Code, or child support enforcement services under Article X of the Code, or (ii) to the local governmental unit responsible for the support of the person if he or she is a recipient under Article VI of the Code. In accordance with federal law and regulations, the Illinois Department of Public Aid may continue to collect current maintenance payments or child support payments, or both, after those persons cease to receive public assistance and until termination of services under Article X of the Illinois Public Aid Code. The Illinois Department shall pay the net amount collected to those persons after deducting any costs incurred in making the collection or any collection fee from the amount of any recovery made. The order shall permit the

Illinois Department of Public Aid or the local governmental unit, as the case may be, to direct that support payments be made directly to the spouse, children, or both, or to some person or agency in their behalf, upon removal of the spouse or children from the public aid rolls or upon termination of services under Article X of the Illinois Public Aid Code; and upon such direction, the Illinois Department or the local governmental unit, as the case requires, shall give notice of such action to the court in writing or by electronic transmission.

(3) The clerk of the court shall establish and maintain current records of all moneys received and disbursed and of delinquencies and defaults in required payments. The court, by order or rule, shall make provision for the carrying out of these duties.

(4) (Blank).

(5) Payments under this Section to the Illinois Department of Public Aid pursuant to the Child Support Enforcement Program established by Title IV-D of the Social Security Act shall be paid into the Child Support Enforcement Trust Fund. All other payments under this Section to the Illinois Department of Public Aid shall be deposited in the Public Assistance Recoveries Trust Fund. Disbursements from these funds shall be as provided in the Illinois Public Aid Code. Payments received by a local governmental unit shall be deposited in that unit's General Assistance Fund.

(6) For those cases in which child support is payable to the clerk of the circuit court for transmittal to the Illinois Department of Public Aid by order of court or upon notification by the Illinois Department of Public Aid, the clerk shall transmit all such payments, within 4 working days of receipt, to insure that funds are available for immediate distribution by the Department to the person or entity entitled thereto in accordance with standards of the Child Support Enforcement Program established under Title IV-D of the Social Security Act. The clerk shall notify the Department of the date of receipt and amount thereof at the time of transmittal. Where the clerk has entered into an agreement of cooperation with the Department to record the terms of child support orders and payments made thereunder directly into the Department's automated data processing system, the clerk shall account for, transmit and otherwise distribute child support payments in accordance with such agreement in lieu of the requirements contained herein. 750 ILCS 16/30 Information to State Case Registry.

(a) In this Section:

"Order for support", "obligor", "obligee", and "business day" are defined as set forth in the Income Withholding for Support Act.

"State Case Registry" means the State Case Registry established under Section 10-27 of the Illinois Public Aid Code.

(b) Each order for support entered or modified by the circuit court under this Act shall require that the obligor and obligee (i) file with the clerk of the circuit court the information required by this Section (and any other information required under Title IV, Part D of the Social Security Act or by the federal Department of Health and Human Services) at the time of entry or modification of the order for support and (ii) file updated information with the clerk within 5 business days of any change. Failure of the obligor or obligee to file or update the required information shall be punishable as in cases of contempt. The failure shall not prevent the court from entering or modifying the order for support, however.

(c) The obligor shall file the following information: the obligor's name, date of birth, social security number, and mailing address.

If either the obligor or the obligee receives child support enforcement services from the Illinois Department of Public Aid under Article X of the Illinois Public Aid Code, the obligor shall also file the following information: the obligor's telephone number, driver's license number, and residential address (if different from the obligor's mailing address), and the name, address, and telephone number of the obligor's employer or employers.

(d) The obligee shall file the following information:

(1) The names of the obligee and the child or children covered by the order for support.

(2) The dates of birth of the obligee and the child or children covered by the order for support.

(3) The social security numbers of the obligee and the child or children covered by the order for support.

(4) The obligee's mailing address.

(e) In cases in which the obligee receives child support enforcement services from the Illinois Department of Public Aid under Article X of the Illinois Public Aid Code, the order for support shall (i) require that the obligee file the information required under subsection (d) with the Illinois Department of Public Aid for inclusion in the State Case Registry, rather than file the information with the clerk, and (ii) require that the obligee include the following additional information:

(1) The obligee's telephone and driver's license numbers.

(2) The obligee's residential address, if different from the obligee's mailing address.

(3) The name, address, and telephone number of the obligee's employer or employers.

The order for support shall also require that the obligee update the information filed with the Illinois Department of Public Aid within 5 business days of any change.

(f) The clerk shall provide the information filed under this Section, together with the court docket number and county in which the order for support was entered, to the State Case Registry within 5 business days after receipt of the information.

(g) In a case in which a party is receiving child support enforcement services under Article X of the Illinois Public Aid Code, the clerk shall provide the following additional information to the State Case Registry within 5 business days after entry or modification of an order for support or request from the Illinois Department of Public Aid:

(1) The amount of monthly or other periodic support owed under the order for support and other amounts, including arrearage, interest, or late payment penalties and fees, due or overdue under the order.

(2) Any such amounts that have been received by the clerk, and the distribution of those amounts by the clerk.

(h) Information filed by the obligor and obligee under this Section that is not specifically required to be included in the body of an order for support under other laws is not a public record and shall be treated as confidential and subject to disclosure only in accordance with the provisions of this Section, Section 10-27 of the Illinois Public Aid Code, and Title IV, Part D of the Social Security Act.

750 ILCS 16/33 Information to locate putative fathers and noncustodial parents.

(a) Upon request by a public office, employers, labor unions, and telephone companies shall provide location information concerning putative fathers and noncustodial parents for the purpose of establishing a child's paternity or establishing, enforcing, or modifying a child support obligation. The term "public office" is defined as set forth in the Income Withholding for Support Act. In this Section, "location information" means information about (i) the physical whereabouts of a putative father or noncustodial parent, (ii) the employer of the putative father or noncustodial parent, or (iii) the salary, wages, and other compensation paid and the health insurance coverage provided to the putative father or noncustodial parent by the employer of the putative father or noncustodial parent or by a labor union of which the putative father or noncustodial parent is a member. An employer, labor union, or telephone company shall respond to the request of the public office within 15 days after receiving the request. Any employer, labor union, or telephone company that willfully fails to fully respond within the 15-day period shall be subject to a penalty of $100 for each day that the response is not provided to the public office after the 15-day period has expired. The penalty may be collected in a civil action, which may be brought against the employer, labor union, or telephone company in favor of the public office.

(b) Upon being served with a subpoena (including an administrative subpoena as authorized by law), a utility company or cable television company must provide location information to a public office for the purpose of establishing a child's paternity or establishing, enforcing, or modifying a child support obligation.

(c) Notwithstanding the provisions of any other State or local law to the contrary, an employer, labor union, telephone company, utility company, or cable television company shall not be liable to any person for disclosure of location information under the requirements of this Section, except for willful and wanton misconduct.

750 ILCS 16/35 Fine; release of defendant on probation; violation of order for support; forfeiture of recognizance.

(a) Whenever a fine is imposed it may be directed by the court to be paid, in whole or in part, to the spouse, ex-spouse, or if the support of a child or children is involved, to the custodial parent, to the clerk, probation officer, or to the Illinois Department of Public Aid if a recipient of child support enforcement services under Article X of the Illinois Public Aid Code is involved as the case requires, to be disbursed by such officers or agency under the terms of the order.

(b) The court may also relieve the defendant from custody on probation for the period fixed in the order or judgment upon his or her entering into a recognizance, with or without surety, in the sum as the court orders and approves. The condition of the recognizance shall be such that if the defendant makes his or her personal appearance in court whenever ordered to do so by the court, during such period as may be so fixed, and further complies with the terms of the order for support, or any subsequent modification of the order, then the recognizance shall be void; otherwise it will remain in full force and effect.

(c) If the court is satisfied by testimony in open court, that at any time during the period of one year the defendant has violated the terms of the order for support, it may proceed with the trial of the defendant under the original charge, or sentence him or her under the original conviction, or enforce the suspended sentence, as the case may be. In case of forfeiture of recognizance, and enforcement of recognizance by execution, the sum so recovered may, in the discretion of the court, be paid, in whole or in part, to the spouse, ex-spouse, or if the support of a child or children is involved, to the custodial parent, to the clerk, or to the Illinois Department of Public Aid if a recipient of child support enforcement services under Article X of the Illinois Public Aid Code is involved as the case requires, to be disbursed by the clerk or the Department under the terms of the order.

*   *   *

750 ILCS 16/60
Unemployed persons owing duty of support.
(a) Whenever it is determined in a proceeding to establish or enforce a child support or maintenance obligation that the person owing a duty of support is unemployed, the court may order the person to seek employment and report periodically to the court with a diary, listing or other memorandum of his or her efforts in accordance with such order. Additionally, the court may order the unemployed person to report to the Department of Employment Security for job search services or to make application with the local Job Training Partnership Act provider for participation in job search, training, or work programs and where the duty of support is owed to a child receiving child support enforcement services under Article X of the Illinois Public Aid Code the court may order the unemployed person to report to the Illinois Department of Public Aid for participation in job search, training, or work programs established under Section 9-6 and Article IXA of that Code.
(b) Whenever it is determined that a person owes past due support for a child or for a child and the parent with whom the child is living, and the child is receiving assistance under the Illinois Public Aid Code, the court shall order at the request of the Illinois Department of Public Aid:

(1) that the person pay the past-due support in accordance with a plan approved by the court; or

(2) if the person owing past-due support is unemployed, is subject to such a plan, and is not incapacitated, that the person participate in such job search, training, or work programs established under Section 9-6 and Article IXA of the Illinois Public Aid Code as the court deems appropriate.

*   *   *

750 ILCS 22/101 Short title. This Act may be cited as the Uniform Interstate Family Support Act.
750 ILCS 22/201 Bases for jurisdiction over nonresident.
(a) In a proceeding to establish or enforce a support order or to determine parentage, a tribunal of this State may exercise personal jurisdiction over a nonresident individual or the individual's guardian or conservator if:

(1) the individual is personally served with notice within this State;

(2) the individual submits to the jurisdiction of this State by consent, by entering a general appearance, or by filing a responsive document having the effect of waiving any contest to personal jurisdiction;

(3) the individual resided with the child in this State;

(4) the individual resided in this State and provided prenatal expenses or support for the child;

(5) the child resides in this State as a result of the acts or directives of the individual;

(6) the individual engaged in sexual intercourse in this State and the child may have been conceived by that act of intercourse;

(7) (blank); or

(8) there is any other basis consistent with the constitutions of this State and the United States for the exercise of personal jurisdiction.

(b) The bases of personal jurisdiction set forth in subsection (a) or in any other law of this State may not be used to acquire personal jurisdiction for a tribunal of the State to modify a child support order of another state unless the requirements of Section 611 or 615 are met.
750 ILCS 22/204 Simultaneous proceedings.
(a) A tribunal of this State may exercise jurisdiction to establish a support order if the petition is filed after a petition or comparable pleading is filed in another state only if:

(1) the petition in this State is filed before the expiration of the time allowed in the other state for filing a responsive pleading challenging the exercise of jurisdiction by the other state;

(2) the contesting party timely challenges the exercise of jurisdiction in the other state; and

(3) if relevant, this State is the home state of the child.

(b) A tribunal of this State may not exercise jurisdiction to establish a support order if the petition is filed before a petition or comparable pleading is filed in another state if:

(1) the petition or comparable pleading in the other state is filed before the expiration of the time allowed in this State for filing a responsive pleading challenging the exercise of jurisdiction by this State;

(2) the contesting party timely challenges the exercise of jurisdiction in this State; and

(3) if relevant, the other state is the home state of the child.

750 ILCS 22/205 Continuing, exclusive jurisdiction to modify child-support order.

(a) A tribunal of this State that has issued a support order consistent with the law of this State has and shall exercise continuing, exclusive jurisdiction to modify its child-support order if the order is the controlling order and:

    (1) at the time of the filing of a request for modification this State is the residence of the obligor, the individual obligee, or the child for whose benefit the support order is issued; or

    (2) even if this State is not the residence of the obligor, the individual obligee, or the child for whose benefit the support order is issued, the parties consent in a record or in open court that the tribunal of this State may continue to exercise the jurisdiction to modify its order.

(b) A tribunal of this State that has issued a child-support order consistent with the law of this State may not exercise continuing exclusive jurisdiction to modify the order if:

    (1) all of the parties who are individuals file consent in a record with the tribunal of this State that a tribunal of another state that has jurisdiction over at least one of the parties who is an individual or that is located in the state of residence of the child may modify the order and assume continuing, exclusive jurisdiction; or

    (2) its order is not the controlling order.

(c) If a tribunal of another state has issued a child-support order pursuant to the Uniform Interstate Family Support Act or a law substantially similar to that Act which modifies a child-support order of a tribunal of this State, tribunals of this State shall recognize the continuing, exclusive jurisdiction of the tribunal of the other state.

(d) A tribunal of this State that lacks continuing, exclusive jurisdiction to modify a child-support order may serve as an initiating tribunal to request a tribunal of another state to modify a support order issued in that state.

(e) A temporary support order issued ex parte or pending resolution of a jurisdictional conflict does not create continuing, exclusive jurisdiction in the issuing tribunal.

750 ILCS 22/206 Continuing jurisdiction to enforce child-support order.

(a) A tribunal of this State that has issued a child-support order consistent with the law of this State may serve as an initiating tribunal to request a tribunal of another state to enforce:

    (1) the order if the order is the controlling order and has not been modified by a tribunal of another state that assumed jurisdiction pursuant to the Uniform Interstate Family Support Act; or

    (2) a money judgment for arrears of support and interest on the order accrued before a determination that an order of another state is the controlling order.

(b) A tribunal of this State having continuing jurisdiction over a support order may act as a responding tribunal to enforce the order.

750 ILCS 22/207 Determination of controlling child-support order.

(a) If a proceeding is brought under this Act and only one tribunal has issued a child-support order, the order of that tribunal controls and must be so recognized.

(b) If a proceeding is brought under this Act, and two or more child-support orders have been issued by tribunals of this State or another state with regard to the same obligor and same child, a tribunal of this State having personal jurisdiction over both the obligor and individual obligee shall apply the following rules and by order shall determine which order controls:

    (1) If only one of the tribunals would have continuing, exclusive jurisdiction under this Act, the order of that tribunal controls and must be so recognized.

    (2) If more than one of the tribunals would have continuing, exclusive jurisdiction under this Act:

        (A) an order issued by a tribunal in the current home state of the child controls; but

        (B) if an order has not been issued in the current home state of the child, the order most recently issued controls.

    (3) If none of the tribunals would have continuing, exclusive jurisdiction under this Act, the tribunal of this State shall issue a child-support order, which controls.

(c) If two or more child-support orders have been issued for the same obligor and same child, upon request of a party who is an individual or a support enforcement agency, a tribunal of this State having personal jurisdiction over both the obligor and the obligee who is an individual shall determine which order controls under subsection (b). The request may be filed with a registration for enforcement or registration for modification pursuant to Article 6, or may be filed as a separate proceeding.

(d) A request to determine which is the controlling order must be accompanied by a copy of every child-support order in effect and the applicable record of payments. The requesting party shall give notice of the request to each party whose rights may be affected by the determination.

(e) The tribunal that issued the controlling order under subsection (a), (b), or (c) has continuing jurisdiction to the extent provided in Section 205 or 206.

(f) A tribunal of this State that determines by order which is the controlling order under subsection (b)(1) or (2) or (c), or that issues a new controlling order under subsection (b)(3), shall state in that order:

    (1) the basis upon which the tribunal made its determination;

    (2) the amount of prospective support, if any; and

    (3) the total amount of consolidated arrears and accrued interest, if any, under all of the orders after all payments made are credited as provided by Section 209.

(g) Within 30 days after issuance of an order determining which is the controlling order, the party obtaining the order shall file a certified copy of it in each tribunal that issued or registered an earlier order of child support. A party or support enforcement agency obtaining the order that fails to file a certified copy is subject to appropriate sanctions by a tribunal in which the issue of failure to file arises. The failure to file does not affect the validity or enforceability of the controlling order.

(h) An order that has been determined to be the controlling order, or a judgment for consolidated arrears of support and interest, if any, made pursuant to this Section must be recognized in proceedings under this Act.

*　　　*　　　*

750 ILCS 22/501 Employer's receipt of income-withholding order of another state. An income-withholding order issued in another state may be sent by or on behalf of the obligee, or by the support enforcement agency, to the person defined as the obligor's employer under the income-withholding law of this State without first filing a petition or comparable pleading or registering the order with a tribunal of this State.

750 ILCS 22/613 Jurisdiction to modify child-support order of another state when individual parties reside in this State.

(a) If all of the parties who are individuals reside in this State and the child does not reside in the issuing state, a tribunal of this State has jurisdiction to enforce and to modify the issuing state's child-support order in a proceeding to register that order.

(b) A tribunal of this State exercising jurisdiction under this Section shall apply the provisions of Articles 1 and 2, this Article, and the procedural and substantive law of this State to the proceeding for enforcement or modification. Articles 3, 4, 5, 7, and 8 do not apply.

*　　　*　　　*

750 ILCS 36/101 Short Title. This Act may be cited as the Uniform Child-Custody Jurisdiction and Enforcement Act.

750 ILCS 36/102 Definitions. In this Act:

(1) "Abandoned" means left without provision for reasonable and necessary care or supervision.

(2) "Child" means an individual who has not attained 18 years of age.

(3) "Child-custody determination" means a judgment, decree, or other order of a court providing for the legal custody, physical custody, or visitation with respect to a child. The term includes a permanent, temporary, initial, and modification order. The term does not include an order relating to child support or other monetary obligation of an individual.

(4) "Child-custody proceeding" means a proceeding in which legal custody, physical custody, or visitation with respect to a child is an issue. The term includes a proceeding for divorce, separation, neglect, abuse, dependency, guardianship, paternity, termination of parental rights, and protection from domestic violence, in which the issue may appear. The term does not include a proceeding involving juvenile delinquency, contractual emancipation, or enforcement under Article 3.

(5) "Commencement" means the filing of the first pleading in a proceeding.

(6) "Court" means an entity authorized under the law of a state to establish, enforce, or modify a child-custody determination.

(7) "Home state" means the state in which a child lived with a parent or a person acting as a parent for at least six consecutive months immediately before the commencement of a child-custody proceeding. In the case of a child less than six months of age, the term means the state in which the child lived from birth with any of the persons mentioned. A period of temporary absence of any of the mentioned persons is part of the period.

(8) "Initial determination" means the first child-custody determination concerning a particular child.

(9) "Issuing court" means the court that makes a child-custody determination for which enforcement is sought under this Act.

(10) "Issuing state" means the state in which a child-custody determination is made.

(11) "Modification" means a child-custody determination that changes, replaces, supersedes, or is otherwise made after a previous determination concerning the same child, whether or not it is made by the court that made the previous determination.

(12) "Person" means an individual, corporation, business trust, estate, trust, partnership, limited liability company, association, joint venture, government; governmental subdivision, agency, or instrumentality; public corporation; or any other legal or commercial entity.

(13) "Person acting as a parent" means a person, other than a parent, who:

(A) has physical custody of the child or has had physical custody for a period of six consecutive months, including any temporary absence, within one year immediately before the commencement of a child-custody proceeding; and

(B) has been awarded legal custody by a court or claims a right to legal custody under the law of this State.

(14) "Physical custody" means the physical care and supervision of a child.

(15) "State" means a state of the United States, the District of Columbia, Puerto Rico, the United States Virgin Islands, or any territory or insular possession subject to the jurisdiction of the United States.

(16) "Tribe" means an Indian tribe or band, or Alaskan Native village, which is recognized by federal law or formally acknowledged by a state.

(17) "Warrant" means an order issued by a court authorizing law enforcement officers to take physical custody of a child.

750 ILCS 36/103 Proceedings Governed By Other Law. This Act does not govern an adoption proceeding or a proceeding pertaining to the authorization of emergency medical care for a child.

750 ILCS 36/104 Application To Indian Tribes.

(a) A child-custody proceeding that pertains to an Indian child as defined in the Indian Child Welfare Act, 25 U.S.C. 1901 et seq., is not subject to this Act to the extent that it is governed by the Indian Child Welfare Act.

(b) A court of this State shall treat a tribe as if it were a state of the United States for the purpose of applying Articles 1 and 2.

(c) A child-custody determination made by a tribe under factual circumstances in substantial conformity with the jurisdictional standards of this Act must be recognized and enforced under Article 3.

750 ILCS 36/105 International Application Of Act.

(a) A court of this State shall treat a foreign country as if it were a state of the United States for the purpose of applying Articles 1 and 2.

(b) Except as otherwise provided in subsection (c), a child-custody determination made in a foreign country under factual circumstances in substantial conformity with the jurisdictional standards of this Act must be recognized and enforced under Article 3.

(c) A court of this State need not apply this Act if the child custody law of a foreign country violates fundamental principles of human rights.

750 ILCS 36/106 Effect Of Child-Custody Determination. A child-custody determination made by a court of this State that had jurisdiction under this Act binds all persons who have been served in accordance with the laws of this State or notified in accordance with Section 108 or who have submitted to the jurisdiction of the court, and who have been given an opportunity to be heard. As to those persons, the determination is conclusive as to all decided issues of law and fact except to the extent the determination is modified.

750 ILCS 36/107

Priority. If a question of existence or exercise of jurisdiction under this Act is raised in a child-custody proceeding, the question, upon request of a party, must be given priority on the calendar and handled expeditiously.

750 ILCS 36/108. Notice To Persons Outside State.

(a) Notice required for the exercise of jurisdiction when a person is outside this State may be given in a manner prescribed by the law of this State for service of process or by the law of the state in which the service is made. Notice must be given in a manner reasonably calculated to give actual notice but may be by publication if other means are not effective.

(b) Proof of service may be made in the manner prescribed by the law of this State or by the law of the state in which the service is made.

(c) Notice is not required for the exercise of jurisdiction with respect to a person who submits to the jurisdiction of the court.

750 ILCS 36/109 Appearance And Limited Immunity.

(a) A party to a child-custody proceeding, including a modification proceeding, or a petitioner or respondent in a proceeding to enforce or register a child-custody determination, is not subject to personal jurisdiction in this State for another proceeding or purpose solely by reason of having participated, or of having been physically present for the purpose of participating, in the proceeding.

(b) A person who is subject to personal jurisdiction in this State on a basis other than physical presence is not immune from service of process in this State. A party present in this State who is subject to the jurisdiction of another state is not immune from service of process allowable under the laws of that state.

(c) The immunity granted by subsection (a) does not extend to civil litigation based on acts unrelated to the participation in a proceeding under this Act committed by an individual while present in this State.

750 ILCS 36/110 Communication Between Courts.

(a) A court of this State may communicate with a court in another state concerning a proceeding arising under this Act.

(b) The court may allow the parties to participate in the communication. If the parties are not able to participate in the communication, they must be given the opportunity to present facts and legal arguments before a decision on jurisdiction is made.

(c) Communication between courts on schedules, calendars, court records, and similar matters may occur without informing the parties. A record need not be made of the communication.

(d) Except as otherwise provided in subsection (c), a record must be made of a communication under this Section. The parties must be informed promptly of the communication and granted access to the record.

(e) For the purposes of this Section, "record" means information that is inscribed on a tangible medium or that is stored in an electronic or other medium and is retrievable in perceivable form.

750 ILCS 36/111 Taking Testimony In Another State.

(a) In addition to other procedures available to a party, a party to a child-custody proceeding may offer testimony of witnesses who are located in another state, including testimony of the parties and the child, by deposition or other means allowable in this State for testimony taken in another state. The court on its own motion may order that the testimony of a person be taken in another state and may prescribe the manner in which and the terms upon which the testimony is taken.

(b) A court of this State may permit an individual residing in another state to be deposed or to testify by telephone, audiovisual means, or other electronic means before a designated court or at another location in that state. A court of this State shall cooperate with courts of other states in designating an appropriate location for the deposition or testimony.

(c) Documentary evidence transmitted from another state to a court of this State by technological means that do not produce an original writing may not be excluded from evidence on an objection based on the means of transmission.

750 ILCS 36/112 Cooperation Between Courts; Preservation Of Records.

(a) A court of this State may request the appropriate court of another state to:

(1) hold an evidentiary hearing;

(2) order a person to produce or give evidence pursuant to procedures of that state;

(3) order that an evaluation be made with respect to the custody of a child involved in a pending proceeding;

(4) forward to the court of this State a certified copy of the transcript of the record of the hearing, the evidence otherwise presented, and any evaluation prepared in compliance with the request; and

(5) order a party to a child-custody proceeding or any person having physical custody of the child to appear in the proceeding with or without the child.

(b) Upon request of a court of another state, a court of this State may hold a hearing or enter an order described in subsection (a).

(c) Travel and other necessary and reasonable expenses

incurred under subsections (a) and (b) may be assessed against the parties according to the law of this State.

(d) A court of this State shall preserve the pleadings, orders, decrees, records of hearings, evaluations, and other pertinent records with respect to a child-custody proceeding until the child attains 18 years of age. Upon appropriate request by a court or law enforcement official of another state, the court shall forward a certified copy of those records.

750 ILCS 36/201 Initial Child-Custody Jurisdiction.

(a) Except as otherwise provided in Section 204, a court of this State has jurisdiction to make an initial child-custody determination only if:

(1) this State is the home state of the child on the date of the commencement of the proceeding, or was the home state of the child within six months before the commencement of the proceeding and the child is absent from this State but a parent or person acting as a parent continues to live in this State;

(2) a court of another state does not have jurisdiction under paragraph (1), or a court of the home state of the child has declined to exercise jurisdiction on the ground that this State is the more appropriate forum under Section 207 or 208, and:

(A) the child and the child's parents, or the child and at least one parent or a person acting as a parent, have a significant connection with this State other than mere physical presence; and

(B) substantial evidence is available in this State concerning the child's care, protection, training, and personal relationships;

(3) all courts having jurisdiction under paragraph (1) or (2) have declined to exercise jurisdiction on the ground that a court of this State is the more appropriate forum to determine the custody of the child under Section 207 or 208; or

(4) no court of any other state would have jurisdiction under the criteria specified in paragraph (1), (2), or (3).

(b) Subsection (a) is the exclusive jurisdictional basis for making a child-custody determination by a court of this State.

(c) Physical presence of, or personal jurisdiction over, a party or a child is not necessary or sufficient to make a child-custody determination.

750 ILCS 36/202 Exclusive, Continuing Jurisdiction.

(a) Except as otherwise provided in Section 204, a court of this State which has made a child-custody determination consistent with Section 201 or 203 has exclusive, continuing jurisdiction over the determination until:

(1) a court of this State determines that neither the child, the child's parents, and any person acting as a parent do not have a significant connection with this State and that substantial evidence is no longer available in this State concerning the child's care, protection, training, and personal relationships; or

(2) a court of this State or a court of another state determines that the child, the child's parents, and any

person acting as a parent do not presently reside in this State.

(b) A court of this State which has made a child-custody determination and does not have exclusive, continuing jurisdiction under this Section may modify that determination only if it has jurisdiction to make an initial determination under Section 201.

750 ILCS 36/203 Jurisdiction To Modify Determination. Except as otherwise provided in Section 204, a court of this State may not modify a child-custody determination made by a court of another state unless a court of this State has jurisdiction to make an initial determination under Section 201(a)(1) or (2) and:

(1) the court of the other state determines it no longer has exclusive, continuing jurisdiction under Section 202 or that a court of this State would be a more convenient forum under Section 207; or

(2) a court of this State or a court of the other state determines that the child, the child's parents, and any person acting as a parent do not presently reside in the other state.

750 ILCS 36/204 Temporary Emergency Jurisdiction.

(a) A court of this State has temporary emergency jurisdiction if the child is present in this State and the child has been abandoned or it is necessary in an emergency to protect the child because the child, or a sibling or parent of the child, is subjected to or threatened with mistreatment or abuse.

(b) If there is no previous child-custody determination that is entitled to be enforced under this Act and a child-custody proceeding has not been commenced in a court of a state having jurisdiction under Sections 201 through 203, a child-custody determination made under this Section remains in effect until an order is obtained from a court of a state having jurisdiction under Sections 201 through 203. If a child-custody proceeding has not been or is not commenced in a court of a state having jurisdiction under Sections 201 through 203, a child-custody determination made under this Section becomes a final determination, if it so provides and this State becomes the home state of the child.

(c) If there is a previous child-custody determination that is entitled to be enforced under this Act, or a child-custody proceeding has been commenced in a court of a state having jurisdiction under Sections 201 through 203, any order issued by a court of this State under this Section must specify in the order a period that the court considers adequate to allow the person seeking an order to obtain an order from the state having jurisdiction under Sections 201 through 203. The order issued in this State remains in effect until an order is obtained from the other state within the period specified or the period expires.

(d) A court of this State which has been asked to make a child-custody determination under this Section, upon being informed that a child-custody proceeding has been commenced in, or a child-custody determination has been made by, a court of a state having jurisdiction under Sections 201 through 203, shall immediately communicate with the other court. A court of this State which is exercising jurisdiction pursuant to Sections 201 through 203, upon being informed that a child-custody proceeding has been commenced in, or a child-custody determination has been made by, a court of another state under a statute similar to this Section shall immediately communicate with the court of that state to resolve the emergency, protect the safety of the parties and the child, and determine a period for the duration of the temporary order.

750 ILCS 36/205 Notice; Opportunity To Be Heard; Joinder.

(a) Before a child-custody determination is made under this Act, notice and an opportunity to be heard in accordance with the standards of Section 108 must be given to all persons entitled to notice under the law of this State as in child-custody proceedings between residents of this State, any parent whose parental rights have not been previously terminated, and any person having physical custody of the child.

(b) This Act does not govern the enforceability of a child-custody determination made without notice or an opportunity to be heard.

(c) The obligation to join a party and the right to intervene as a party in a child-custody proceeding under this Act are governed by the law of this State as in child-custody proceedings between residents of this State.

750 ILCS 36/206 Simultaneous Proceedings.

(a) Except as otherwise provided in Section 204, a court of this State may not exercise its jurisdiction under this Article if, at the time of the commencement of the proceeding, a proceeding concerning the custody of the child has been commenced in a court of another state having jurisdiction substantially in conformity with this Act, unless the proceeding has been terminated or is stayed by the court of the other state because a court of this State is a more convenient forum under Section 207.

(b) Except as otherwise provided in Section 204, a court of this State, before hearing a child-custody proceeding, shall examine the court documents and other information supplied by the parties pursuant to Section 209. If the court determines that a child-custody proceeding has been commenced in a court in another state having jurisdiction substantially in accordance with this Act, the court of this State shall stay its proceeding and communicate with the court of the other state. If the court of the state having jurisdiction substantially in accordance with this Act does not determine that the court of this State is a more appropriate forum, the court of this State shall dismiss the proceeding.

(c) In a proceeding to modify a child-custody determination, a court of this State shall determine whether a proceeding to enforce the determination has been commenced in another state. If a proceeding to enforce a child-custody determination has been commenced in another state, the court may:

(1) stay the proceeding for modification pending the entry of an order of a court of the other state enforcing, staying, denying, or dismissing the proceeding for enforcement;

(2) enjoin the parties from continuing with the proceeding for enforcement; or

(3) proceed with the modification under conditions it considers appropriate.

750 ILCS 36/207 Inconvenient Forum.

(a) A court of this State which has jurisdiction under this Act to make a child-custody determination may decline to exercise its jurisdiction at any time if it determines that it is an inconvenient forum under the circumstances and that a court of another state is a more appropriate forum. The issue of inconvenient forum may be raised upon motion of a party, the court's own motion, or request of another court.

(b) Before determining whether it is an inconvenient forum, a court of this State shall consider whether it is appropriate for a court of another state to exercise jurisdiction. For this purpose, the court shall allow the parties to submit information and shall consider all relevant factors, including:

(1) whether domestic violence has occurred and is likely to continue in the future and which state could best protect the parties and the child;

(2) the length of time the child has resided outside this State;

(3) the distance between the court in this State and the court in the state that would assume jurisdiction;

(4) the relative financial circumstances of the parties;

(5) any agreement of the parties as to which state should assume jurisdiction;

(6) the nature and location of the evidence required to resolve the pending litigation, including testimony of the child;

(7) the ability of the court of each state to decide the issue expeditiously and the procedures necessary to present the evidence; and

(8) the familiarity of the court of each state with the facts and issues in the pending litigation.

(c) If a court of this State determines that it is an inconvenient forum and that a court of another state is a more appropriate forum, it shall stay the proceedings upon condition that a child-custody proceeding be promptly commenced in another designated state and may impose any other condition the court considers just and proper.

(d) A court of this State may decline to exercise its jurisdiction under this Act if a child-custody determination is incidental to an action for divorce or another proceeding while still retaining jurisdiction over the divorce or other proceeding.

750 ILCS 36/208 Jurisdiction Declined By Reason Of Conduct.

(a) Except as otherwise provided in Section 204 or by other law of this State, if a court of this State has jurisdiction under this Act because a person seeking to invoke its jurisdiction has engaged in unjustifiable conduct, the court shall decline to exercise its jurisdiction unless:

(1) the parents and all persons acting as parents have acquiesced in the exercise of jurisdiction;

(2) a court of the state otherwise having jurisdiction under Sections 201 through 203 determines that this State is a more appropriate forum under Section 207; or

(3) no court of any other state would have

jurisdiction under the criteria specified in Sections 201 through 203.

(b) If a court of this State declines to exercise its jurisdiction pursuant to subsection (a), it may fashion an appropriate remedy to ensure the safety of the child and prevent a repetition of the unjustifiable conduct, including staying the proceeding until a child-custody proceeding is commenced in a court having jurisdiction under Sections 201 through 203.

(c) If a court dismisses a petition or stays a proceeding because it declines to exercise its jurisdiction pursuant to subsection (a), it shall assess against the party seeking to invoke its jurisdiction necessary and reasonable expenses including costs, communication expenses, attorney's fees, investigative fees, expenses for witnesses, travel expenses, and child care during the course of the proceedings, unless the party from whom fees are sought establishes that the assessment would be clearly inappropriate. The court may not assess fees, costs, or expenses against this State unless authorized by law other than this Act.

750 ILCS 36/209 Information To Be Submitted To Court.

(a) Subject to any other law providing for the confidentiality of procedures, addresses, and other identifying information, in a child-custody proceeding, each party, in its first pleading or in an attached affidavit, shall give information, if reasonably ascertainable, under oath as to the child's present address or whereabouts, the places where the child has lived during the last five years, and the names and present addresses of the persons with whom the child has lived during that period. The pleading or affidavit must state whether the party:

(1) has participated, as a party or witness or in any other capacity, in any other proceeding concerning the custody of or visitation with the child and, if so, identify the court, the case number, and the date of the child-custody determination, if any;

(2) knows of any proceeding that could affect the current proceeding, including proceedings for enforcement and proceedings relating to domestic violence, protective orders, termination of parental rights, and adoptions and, if so, identify the court, the case number, and the nature of the proceeding; and

(3) knows the names and addresses of any person not a party to the proceeding who has physical custody of the child or claims rights of legal custody or physical custody of, or visitation with, the child and, if so, the names and addresses of those persons.

(b) If the information required by subsection (a) is not furnished, the court, upon motion of a party or its own motion, may stay the proceeding until the information is furnished.

(c) If the declaration as to any of the items described in subsection (a)(1) through (3) is in the affirmative, the declarant shall give additional information under oath as required by the court. The court may examine the parties under oath as to details of the information furnished and other matters pertinent to the court's jurisdiction and the disposition of the case.

(d) Each party has a continuing duty to inform the court of any proceeding in this or any other state that could affect the current proceeding.

(e) (Blank).

750 ILCS 36/210 Appearance Of Parties And Child.

(a) In a child-custody proceeding in this State, the court may order a party to the proceeding who is in this State to appear before the court in person with or without the child. The court may order any person who is in this State and who has physical custody or control of the child to appear in person with the child.

(b) If a party to a child-custody proceeding whose presence is desired by the court is outside this State, the court may order that a notice given pursuant to Section 108 include a statement directing the party to appear in person with or without the child and informing the party that failure to appear may result in a decision adverse to the party.

(c) The court may enter any orders necessary to ensure the safety of the child and of any person ordered to appear under this Section.

(d) If a party to a child-custody proceeding who is outside this State is directed to appear under subsection (b) or desires to appear personally before the court with or without the child, the court may require another party to pay reasonable and necessary travel and other expenses of the party so appearing and of the child.

750 ILCS 36/301 Definitions. In this Article:

(1) "Petitioner" means a person who seeks enforcement of an order for return of a child under the Hague Convention on the Civil Aspects of International Child Abduction or enforcement of a child-custody determination.

(2) "Respondent" means a person against whom a proceeding has been commenced for enforcement of an order for return of a child under the Hague Convention on the Civil Aspects of International Child Abduction or enforcement of a child-custody determination.

750 ILCS 36/302 Enforcement Under Hague Convention. Under this Article a court of this State may enforce an order for the return of the child made under the Hague Convention on the Civil Aspects of International Child Abduction as if it were a child-custody determination.

750 ILCS 36/303 Duty To Enforce.

(a) A court of this State shall recognize and enforce a child-custody determination of a court of another state if the latter court exercised jurisdiction in substantial conformity with this Act or the determination was made under factual circumstances meeting the jurisdictional standards of this Act and the determination has not been modified in accordance with this Act.

(b) A court of this State may utilize any remedy available under other law of this State to enforce a child-custody determination made by a court of another state. The remedies provided in this Article are cumulative and do not affect the availability of other remedies to enforce a child-custody determination.

750 ILCS 36/304 Temporary Visitation.

(a) A court of this State which does not have jurisdiction to modify a child-custody determination, may issue a temporary order enforcing:

(1) a visitation schedule made by a court of another state; or

(2) the visitation provisions of a child-custody determination of another state that does not provide for a specific visitation schedule.

(b) If a court of this State makes an order under subsection (a)(2), it shall specify in the order a period that it considers adequate to allow the petitioner to obtain an order from a court having jurisdiction under the criteria specified in Article 2. The order remains in effect until an order is obtained from the other court or the period expires.

750 ILCS 36/305 Registration Of Child-Custody Determination.

(a) A child-custody determination issued by a court of another state may be registered in this State, with or without a simultaneous request for enforcement, by sending to the circuit court in this State:

(1) a letter or other document requesting registration;

(2) two copies, including one certified copy, of the determination sought to be registered, and a statement under penalty of perjury that to the best of the knowledge and belief of the person seeking registration the order has not been modified; and

(3) except as otherwise provided in Section 209, the name and address of the person seeking registration and any parent or person acting as a parent who has been awarded custody or visitation in the child-custody determination sought to be registered.

(b) On receipt of the documents required by subsection (a), the registering court shall:

(1) cause the determination to be filed as a foreign judgment, together with one copy of any accompanying documents and information, regardless of their form; and

(2) serve notice upon the persons named pursuant to subsection (a)(3) and provide them with an opportunity to contest the registration in accordance with this Section.

(c) The notice required by subsection (b)(2) must state that:

(1) a registered determination is enforceable as of the date of the registration in the same manner as a determination issued by a court of this State;

(2) a hearing to contest the validity of the registered determination must be requested within 20 days after service of notice; and

(3) failure to contest the registration will result in confirmation of the child-custody determination and preclude further contest of that determination with respect to any matter that could have been asserted.

(d) A person seeking to contest the validity of a registered order must request a hearing within 20 days after service of the notice. At that hearing, the court shall confirm the registered order unless the person contesting registration establishes that:

(1) the issuing court did not have jurisdiction

under Article 2;

(2) the child-custody determination sought to be registered has been vacated, stayed, or modified by a court having jurisdiction to do so under Article 2; or

(3) the person contesting registration was entitled to notice, but notice was not given in accordance with the standards of Section 108, in the proceedings before the court that issued the order for which registration is sought.

(e) If a timely request for a hearing to contest the validity of the registration is not made, the registration is confirmed as a matter of law and the person requesting registration and all persons served must be notified of the confirmation.

(f) Confirmation of a registered order, whether by operation of law or after notice and hearing, precludes further contest of the order with respect to any matter that could have been asserted at the time of registration.

750 ILCS 36/306 Enforcement Of Registered Determination.

(a) A court of this State may grant any relief normally available under the law of this State to enforce a registered child-custody determination made by a court of another state.

(b) A court of this State shall recognize and enforce, but may not modify, except in accordance with Article 2, a registered child-custody determination of a court of another state.

750 ILCS 36/307

Sec. 307. Simultaneous Proceedings. If a proceeding for enforcement under this Article is commenced in a court of this State and the court determines that a proceeding to modify the determination is pending in a court of another state having jurisdiction to modify the determination under Article 2, the enforcing court shall immediately communicate with the modifying court. The proceeding for enforcement continues unless the enforcing court, after consultation with the modifying court, stays or dismisses the proceeding.

750 ILCS 36/308 Expedited Enforcement Of Child-Custody Determination.

(a) A petition under this Article must be verified. Certified copies of all orders sought to be enforced and of any order confirming registration must be attached to the petition. A copy of a certified copy of an order may be attached instead of the original.

(b) A petition for enforcement of a child-custody determination must state:

(1) whether the court that issued the determination identified the jurisdictional basis it relied upon in exercising jurisdiction and, if so, what the basis was;

(2) whether the determination for which enforcement is sought has been vacated, stayed, or modified by a court whose decision must be enforced under this Act and, if so, identify the court, the case number, and the nature of the proceeding;

(3) whether any proceeding has been commenced that could affect the current proceeding, including proceedings relating to domestic violence, protective orders, termination of parental rights, and adoptions and, if so, identify the court, the case number, and the nature of the proceeding;

(4) the present physical address of the child and

the respondent, if known;

(5) whether relief in addition to the immediate physical custody of the child and attorney's fees is sought, including a request for assistance from law enforcement officials and, if so, the relief sought; and

(6) if the child-custody determination has been registered and confirmed under Section 305, the date and place of registration.

(c) Upon the filing of a petition, the court shall issue an order directing the respondent to appear in person with or without the child at a hearing and may enter any order necessary to ensure the safety of the parties and the child. The hearing must be held on the next judicial day after service of the order unless that date is impossible. In that event, the court shall hold the hearing on the first judicial day possible. The court may extend the date of hearing at the request of the petitioner.

(d) An order issued under subsection (c) must state the time and place of the hearing and advise the respondent that at the hearing the court will order that the petitioner may take immediate physical custody of the child and the payment of fees, costs, and expenses under Section 312, and may schedule a hearing to determine whether further relief is appropriate, unless the respondent appears and establishes that:

(1) the child-custody determination has not been registered and confirmed under Section 305 and that:

(A) the issuing court did not have jurisdiction under Article 2;

(B) the child-custody determination for which enforcement is sought has been vacated, stayed, or modified by a court having jurisdiction to do so under Article 2;

(C) the respondent was entitled to notice, but notice was not given in accordance with the standards of Section 108, in the proceedings before the court that issued the order for which enforcement is sought; or

(2) the child-custody determination for which enforcement is sought was registered and confirmed under Section 304, but has been vacated, stayed, or modified by a court of a state having jurisdiction to do so under Article 2.

750 ILCS 36/309 Service Of Petition And Order. Except as otherwise provided in Section 311, the petition and order must be served, by any method authorized by the law of this State, upon respondent and any person who has physical custody of the child.

750 ILCS 36/310 Hearing And Order.

(a) Unless the court issues a temporary emergency order pursuant to Section 204, upon a finding that a petitioner is entitled to immediate physical custody of the child, the court shall order that the petitioner may take immediate physical custody of the child unless the respondent establishes that:

(1) the child-custody determination has not been registered and confirmed under Section 305 and that:

(A) the issuing court did not have jurisdiction under Article 2;

(B) the child-custody determination for which enforcement is sought has been vacated, stayed, or

modified by a court of a state having jurisdiction to do so under Article 2; or

(C) the respondent was entitled to notice, but notice was not given in accordance with the standards of Section 108, in the proceedings before the court that issued the order for which enforcement is sought; or

(2) the child-custody determination for which enforcement is sought was registered and confirmed under Section 305 but has been vacated, stayed, or modified by a court of a state having jurisdiction to do so under Article 2.

(b) The court shall award the fees, costs, and expenses authorized under Section 312 and may grant additional relief, including a request for the assistance of law enforcement officials, and set a further hearing to determine whether additional relief is appropriate.

(c) If a party called to testify refuses to answer on the ground that the testimony may be self-incriminating, the court may draw an adverse inference from the refusal.

(d) A privilege against disclosure of communications between spouses and a defense of immunity based on the relationship of husband and wife or parent and child may not be invoked in a proceeding under this Article.

750 ILCS 36/311 Warrant To Take Physical Custody Of Child.

(a) Upon the filing of a petition seeking enforcement of a child-custody determination, the petitioner may file a verified application for the issuance of a warrant to take physical custody of the child if the child is immediately likely to suffer serious physical harm or be removed from this State.

(b) If the court, upon the testimony of the petitioner or other witness, finds that the child is imminently likely to suffer serious physical harm or be removed from this State, it may issue a warrant to take physical custody of the child. The petition must be heard on the next judicial day after the warrant is executed unless that date is impossible. In that event, the court shall hold the hearing on the first judicial day possible. The application for the warrant must include the statements required by Section 308(b).

(c) A warrant to take physical custody of a child must:

(1) recite the facts upon which a conclusion of imminent serious physical harm or removal from the jurisdiction is based;

(2) direct law enforcement officers to take physical custody of the child immediately; and

(3) provide for the placement of the child pending final relief.

(d) The respondent must be served with the petition, warrant, and order immediately after the child is taken into physical custody.

(e) A warrant to take physical custody of a child is enforceable throughout this State. If the court finds on the basis of the testimony of the petitioner or other witness that a less intrusive remedy is not effective, it may authorize law enforcement officers to enter private property to take physical custody of the child. If required by exigent circumstances of the case, the court may authorize law enforcement officers to make a forcible entry at any hour.

(f) The court may impose conditions upon placement of a child to ensure the appearance of the child and the child's custodian.

750 ILCS 36/312 Costs, Fees, And Expenses.

(a) The court shall award the prevailing party, including a state, necessary and reasonable expenses incurred by or on behalf of the party, including costs, communication expenses, attorney's fees, investigative fees, expenses for witnesses, travel expenses, and child care during the course of the proceedings, unless the party from whom fees or expenses are sought establishes that the award would be clearly inappropriate.

(b) The court may not assess fees, costs, or expenses against a state unless authorized by law other than this Act.

750 ILCS 36/313 Recognition And Enforcement. A court of this State shall accord full faith and credit to an order issued by another state and consistent with this Act which enforces a child-custody determination by a court of another state unless the order has been vacated, stayed, or modified by a court having jurisdiction to do so under Article 2.

750 ILCS 36/314 Appeals. An appeal may be taken from a final order in a proceeding under this Article in accordance with expedited appellate procedures which are or may be established by Supreme Court Rule. Unless the court enters a temporary emergency order under Section 204, the enforcing court may not stay an order enforcing a child-custody determination pending appeal.

750 ILCS 36/315 Role Of State's Attorney.

(a) In a case arising under this Act or involving the Hague Convention on the Civil Aspects of International Child Abduction, the State's Attorney or other appropriate public official may take any lawful action, including resort to a proceeding under this Article or any other available civil proceeding to locate a child, obtain the return of a child, or enforce a child-custody determination if there is:

(1) an existing child-custody determination;

(2) a request to do so from a court in a pending child-custody proceeding;

(3) a reasonable belief that a criminal statute has been violated; or

(4) a reasonable belief that the child has been wrongfully removed or retained in violation of the Hague Convention on the Civil Aspects of International Child Abduction.

(b) A State's Attorney or appropriate public official acting under this Section acts on behalf of the court and may not represent any party.

750 ILCS 36/316 Role Of Law Enforcement. At the request of a State's Attorney or other appropriate public official acting under Section 315, a law enforcement officer may take any lawful action reasonably necessary to locate a child or a party and assist a State's Attorney or appropriate public official with responsibilities under Section 315.

750 ILCS 36/317 Costs And Expenses. If the respondent is not the prevailing party, the court may assess against the respondent all direct expenses and costs incurred by the State's Attorney or other appropriate public official and law enforcement officers under Section 315 or 316.

*   *   *

750 ILCS 45/1 Short Title. This Act shall be known and may be cited as the "Illinois Parentage Act of 1984".

750 ILCS 45/1.1 Public Policy. Illinois recognizes the right of every child to the physical, mental, emotional and monetary support of his or her parents under this Act.

750 ILCS 45/2 Parent and Child Relationship Defined. As used in this Act, "parent and child relationship" means the legal relationship existing between a child and his natural or adoptive parents incident to which the law confers or imposes rights, privileges, duties, and obligations. It includes the mother and child relationship and the father and child relationship.

750 ILCS 45/2.5 Definitions. As used in this Act, the terms "gestational surrogacy", "gestational surrogate", and "intended parent" have the same meanings as the terms are defined in Section 10 of the Gestational Surrogacy Act.

750 ILCS 45/3 Relationship and Support Not Dependent on Marriage. The parent and child relationship, including support obligations, extends equally to every child and to every parent, regardless of the marital status of the parents.

750 ILCS 45/3.1 A child's mother or a person found to be the father of a child under this Act, is not relieved of support and maintenance obligations to the child because he or she is a minor.

750 ILCS 45/4 How Parent and Child Relationship Established. The parent and child relationship between a child and

(1) the natural mother may be established by proof of her having given birth to the child, or under this Act;

(2) the natural father may be established under this Act;

(3) an adoptive parent may be established by proof of adoption, or by records established pursuant to Section 16 of the "Vital Records Act", approved August 8, 1961, as amended.

750 ILCS 45/4.1 Administrative paternity determinations. Notwithstanding any other provision of this Act, the Illinois Department of Public Aid may make administrative determinations of paternity and nonpaternity in accordance with Section 10-17.7 of the Illinois Public Aid Code. These determinations of paternity or nonpaternity shall have the full force and effect of judgments entered under this Act.

750 ILCS 45/5 Presumption of Paternity.

(a) A man is presumed to be the natural father of a child if:

(1) he and the child's natural mother are or have been married to each other, even though the marriage is or could be declared invalid, and the child is born or conceived during such marriage;

(2) after the child's birth, he and the child's natural mother have married each other, even though the marriage is or could be declared invalid, and he is named, with his written consent, as the child's father on the child's birth certificate;

(3) he and the child's natural mother have signed an acknowledgment of paternity in accordance with rules adopted by the Illinois Department of Public Aid under Section

10-17.7 of the Illinois Public Aid Code; or

(4) he and the child's natural mother have signed an acknowledgment of parentage or, if the natural father is someone other than one presumed to be the father under this Section, an acknowledgment of parentage and denial of paternity in accordance with Section 12 of the Vital Records Act.

(b) A presumption under subdivision (a)(1) or (a)(2) of this Section may be rebutted only by clear and convincing evidence. A presumption under subdivision (a)(3) or (a)(4) is conclusive, unless the acknowledgment of parentage is rescinded under the process provided in Section 12 of the Vital Records Act, upon the earlier of:

(1) 60 days after the date the acknowledgment of parentage is signed, or

(2) the date of an administrative or judicial proceeding relating to the child (including a proceeding to establish a support order) in which the signatory is a party; except that if a minor has signed the acknowledgment of paternity or acknowledgment of parentage and denial of paternity, the presumption becomes conclusive 6 months after the minor reaches majority or is otherwise emancipated.

750 ILCS 45/6 Establishment of Parent and Child Relationship by Consent of the Parties.

(a) A parent and child relationship may be established voluntarily by the signing and witnessing of a voluntary acknowledgment of parentage in accordance with Section 12 of the Vital Records Act, Section 10-17.7 of the Illinois Public Aid Code, or the provisions of the Gestational Surrogacy Act. The voluntary acknowledgment of parentage shall contain the social security numbers of the persons signing the voluntary acknowledgment of parentage; however, failure to include the social security numbers of the persons signing a voluntary acknowledgment of parentage does not invalidate the voluntary acknowledgment of parentage.

(1) A parent-child relationship may be established in the event of gestational surrogacy if all of the following conditions are met prior to the birth of the child:

(A) The gestational surrogate certifies that she is not the biological mother of the child, and that she is carrying the child for the intended parents.

(B) The husband, if any, of the gestational surrogate certifies that he is not the biological father of the child.

(C) The intended mother certifies that she provided or an egg donor donated the egg from which the child being carried by the gestational surrogate was conceived.

(D) The intended father certifies that he provided or a sperm donor donated the sperm from which the child being carried by the gestational surrogate was conceived.

(E) A physician licensed to practice medicine in all its branches in the State of Illinois certifies that the child being carried by the gestational surrogate is the biological child of the intended mother or the intended father or both and that neither the gestational surrogate nor the gestational surrogate's husband, if any, is a biological parent of the child being carried by the gestational surrogate.

(E-5) The attorneys for the intended parents and the gestational surrogate each certifies that the parties entered into a gestational surrogacy contract intended to satisfy the requirements of Section 25 of the Gestational Surrogacy Act with respect to the child.

(F) All certifications shall be in writing and witnessed by 2 competent adults who are not the gestational surrogate, gestational surrogate's husband, if any, intended mother, or intended father. Certifications shall be on forms prescribed by the Illinois Department of Public Health, shall be executed prior to the birth of the child, and shall be placed in the medical records of the gestational surrogate prior to the birth of the child. Copies of all certifications shall be delivered to the Illinois Department of Public Health prior to the birth of the child.

(2) Unless otherwise determined by order of the Circuit Court, the child shall be presumed to be the child of the gestational surrogate and of the gestational surrogate's husband, if any, if all requirements of subdivision (a)(1) are not met prior to the birth of the child. This presumption may be rebutted by clear and convincing evidence. The circuit court may order the gestational surrogate, gestational surrogate's husband, intended mother, intended father, and child to submit to such medical examinations and testing as the court deems appropriate.

(b) Notwithstanding any other provisions of this Act, paternity established in accordance with subsection (a) has the full force and effect of a judgment entered under this Act and serves as a basis for seeking a child support order without any further proceedings to establish paternity.

(c) A judicial or administrative proceeding to ratify paternity established in accordance with subsection (a) is neither required nor permitted.

(d) A signed acknowledgment of paternity entered under this Act may be challenged in court only on the basis of fraud, duress, or material mistake of fact, with the burden of proof upon the challenging party. Pending outcome of the challenge to the acknowledgment of paternity, the legal responsibilities of the signatories shall remain in full force and effect, except upon order of the court upon a showing of good cause.

(e) Once a parent and child relationship is established in accordance with subsection (a), an order for support may be established pursuant to a petition to establish an order for support by consent filed with the clerk of the circuit court. A copy of the properly completed acknowledgment of parentage form shall be attached to the petition. The petition shall ask that the circuit court enter an order for support. The petition may ask that an order for visitation, custody, or guardianship be entered. The filing and appearance fees provided under the Clerks of Courts Act shall be waived for all cases in which an acknowledgment of parentage form has been properly completed by the parties and in which a petition to establish an order for support by consent has been filed with the clerk of the circuit court. This subsection shall not be construed to prohibit filing any petition for child support, visitation, or custody under this Act, the Illinois Marriage and Dissolution of Marriage Act, or the Non-Support Punishment Act. This subsection shall also not be construed to prevent the establishment of an administrative support order in cases involving persons receiving child support enforcement services under Article X of the Illinois Public Aid Code.

750 ILCS 45/6.5 Custody or visitation by sex offender prohibited. A person found to be the father of a child under this Act, and who has been convicted of or who has pled guilty to a violation of Section 11-11 (sexual relations within families), Section 12-13 (criminal sexual assault), Section 12-14 (aggravated criminal sexual assault), Section 12-14.1 (predatory criminal sexual assault of a child), Section 12-15 (criminal sexual abuse), or Section 12-16 (aggravated criminal sexual abuse) of the Criminal Code of 1961 for his conduct in fathering that child, shall not be entitled to custody of or visitation with that child without the consent of the mother or guardian, other than the father of the child who has been convicted of or pled guilty to one of the offenses listed in this Section, or, in cases where the mother is a minor, the guardian of the mother of the child. Notwithstanding any other provision of this Act, nothing in this Section shall be construed to relieve the father of any support and maintenance obligations to the child under this Act.

750 ILCS 45/7 Determination of Father and Child Relationship; Who May Bring Action; Parties.

(a) An action to determine the existence of the father and child relationship, whether or not such a relationship is already presumed under Section 5 of this Act, may be brought by the child; the mother; a pregnant woman; any person or public agency who has custody of, or is providing or has provided financial support to, the child; the Illinois Department of Public Aid if it is providing or has provided financial support to the child or if it is assisting with child support collection services; or a man presumed or alleging himself to be the father of the child or expected child. The complaint shall be verified and shall name the person or persons alleged to be the father of the child.

(b) An action to declare the non-existence of the parent and child relationship may be brought by the child, the natural mother, or a man presumed to be the father under subdivision (a)(1) or (a)(2) of Section 5 of this Act. Actions brought by the child, the natural mother or a presumed father shall be brought by verified complaint.

After the presumption that a man presumed to be the father under subdivision (a)(1) or (a)(2) of Section 5 has been rebutted, paternity of the child by another man may be determined in the same action, if he has been made a party.

(b-5) An action to declare the non-existence of the parent and child relationship may be brought subsequent to an adjudication of paternity in any judgment by the man adjudicated to be the father pursuant to the presumptions in Section 5 of this Act if, as a result of deoxyribonucleic acid (DNA) tests, it is discovered that the man adjudicated to be the father is not the natural father of the child. Actions brought by the adjudicated

father shall be brought by verified complaint. If, as a result of the deoxyribonucleic acid (DNA) tests, the plaintiff is determined not to be the father of the child, the adjudication of paternity and any orders regarding custody, visitation, and future payments of support may be vacated.

(c) If any party is a minor, he or she may be represented by his or her general guardian or a guardian ad litem appointed by the court, which may include an appropriate agency. The court may align the parties.

(d) Regardless of its terms, an agreement, other than a settlement approved by the court, between an alleged or presumed father and the mother or child, does not bar an action under this Section.

(e) If an action under this Section is brought before the birth of the child, all proceedings shall be stayed until after the birth, except for service or process, the taking of depositions to perpetuate testimony, and the ordering of blood tests under appropriate circumstances.

750 ILCS 45/8 Statute of limitations.

(a) (1) An action brought by or on behalf of a child, an action brought by a party alleging that he or she is the child's natural parent, or an action brought by the Illinois Department of Public Aid, if it is providing or has provided financial support to the child or if it is assisting with child support collection services, shall be barred if brought later than 2 years after the child reaches the age of majority; however, if the action on behalf of the child is brought by a public agency, other than the Illinois Department of Public Aid if it is providing or has provided financial support to the child or if it is assisting with child support collection services, it shall be barred 2 years after the agency has ceased to provide assistance to the child.

(2) Failure to bring an action within 2 years shall not bar any party from asserting a defense in any action to declare the non-existence of the parent and child relationship.

(3) An action to declare the non-existence of the parent and child relationship brought under subsection (b) of Section 7 of this Act shall be barred if brought later than 2 years after the petitioner obtains knowledge of relevant facts. The 2-year period for bringing an action to declare the nonexistence of the parent and child relationship shall not extend beyond the date on which the child reaches the age of 18 years. Failure to bring an action within 2 years shall not bar any party from asserting a defense in any action to declare the existence of the parent and child relationship.

(4) An action to declare the non-existence of the parent and child relationship brought under subsection (b-5) of Section 7 of this Act shall be barred if brought more than 6 months after the effective date of this amendatory Act of 1998 or more than 2 years after the petitioner obtains actual knowledge of relevant facts, whichever is later. The 2-year period shall not apply to periods of time where the natural mother or the child refuses to submit to deoxyribonucleic acid (DNA) tests. The 2-year period for bringing an action to declare the nonexistence of the parent and child relationship shall not extend beyond the date on which the child reaches the age of 18 years. Failure to bring an action within 2 years shall not bar

any party from asserting a defense in any action to declare the existence of the parent and child relationship.

(b) The time during which any party is not subject to service of process or is otherwise not subject to the jurisdiction of the courts of this State shall toll the aforementioned periods.

(c) This Act does not affect the time within which any rights under the Probate Act of 1975 may be asserted beyond the time provided by law relating to distribution and closing of decedent's estates or to the determination of heirship, or otherwise.

750 ILCS 45/9 Jurisdiction; Venue. (a) The circuit courts shall have jurisdiction of an action brought under this Act. In any civil action not brought under this Act, the provisions of this Act shall apply if parentage is at issue. The Court may join any action under this Act with any other civil action where applicable.

(b) The action may be brought in the county in which any party resides or is found or, if the father is deceased, in which proceedings for probate of his estate have been or could be commenced.

(c) The summons that is served on a defendant shall include the return date on or by which the defendant must appear and shall contain the following information, in a prominent place and in conspicuous language, in addition to the information required to be provided by the laws of this State: "If you do not appear as instructed in this summons, you may be required to support the child named in this petition until the child is at least 18 years old. You may also have to pay the pregnancy and delivery costs of the mother."

750 ILCS 45/9.1 Notice to Presumed Father.

(a) In any action brought under Section 6 or 7 of this Act where the man signing the petition for an order establishing the existence of the parent and child relationship by consent or the man alleged to be the father in a complaint is different from a man who is presumed to be father of the child under Section 5, a notice shall be served on the presumed father in the same manner as summonses are served in other civil proceedings or, in lieu of personal service, service may be made as follows:

(1) The person requesting notice shall pay to the Clerk of the Court a mailing fee of $1.50 and furnish to the Clerk an original and one copy of a notice together with an affidavit setting forth the presumed father's last known address. The original notice shall be retained by the Clerk.

(2) The Clerk shall promptly mail to the presumed father, at the address appearing in the affidavit, the copy of the notice, certified mail, return receipt requested. The envelope and return receipt shall bear the return address of the Clerk. The receipt for certified mail shall state the name and address of the addressee, and the date of mailing, and shall be attached to the original notice.

(3) The return receipt, when returned to the Clerk, shall be attached to the original notice, and shall constitute proof of service.

(4) The Clerk shall note the fact of service in a permanent record.

(b) The notice shall read as follows:

IN THE MATTER OF NOTICE TO .... PRESUMED FATHER.
You have been identified as the presumed father of .... born on ....

The mother of the child is ....

An action is being brought to establish the parent and child relationship between the named child and a man named by the mother, ...

Under the law, you are presumed to be the father if (1) you and the child's mother are or have been married to each other, and the child was born or conceived during the marriage; or if (2) upon the child's birth, you and the child's mother married each other and you were named, with your consent, as the child's father on the child's birth certificate.

As the presumed father, you have certain legal rights with respect to the named child, including the right to notice of the filing of proceedings instituted for the establishment of parentage of said child and if named as the father in a petition to establish parentage, the right to submit, along with the mother and child, to deoxyribonucleic acid (DNA) tests to determine inherited characteristics. If you wish to retain your rights with respect to said child, you must file with the Clerk of this Circuit Court of .... County, Illinois whose address is ...., Illinois, within 30 days after the date of receipt of this notice, a declaration of parentage stating that you are, in fact, the father of said child and that you intend to retain your legal rights with respect to said child, or request to be notified of any further proceedings with respect to the parentage of said child.

If you do not file such declaration of parentage, or a request for notice, then whatever legal rights you have with respect to the named child, including the right to notice of any future proceedings for the establishment of parentage of the child, may be terminated without any further notice to you. When your legal rights with respect to the named child are so terminated, you will not be entitled to notice of any future proceedings.

(c) The notice to presumed fathers provided for in this Section in any action brought by a public agency shall be prepared and mailed by such public agency and the mailing fee to the Clerk shall be waived.

750 ILCS 45/10 Pre-trial Proceedings. (a) As soon as practicable after an action to declare the existence or non-existence of the father and child relationship has been brought, and the parties are at issue, the court may conduct a pre-trial conference.

750 ILCS 45/11 Tests to determine inherited characteristics.

(a) As soon as practicable, the court or Administrative Hearing Officer in an Expedited Child Support System may, and upon request of a party shall, order or direct the mother, child and alleged father to submit to deoxyribonucleic acid (DNA) tests to determine inherited characteristics. If any party refuses to submit to the tests, the court may resolve the question of paternity against that party or enforce its order if the rights of others and the interests of justice so require.

(b) The tests shall be conducted by an expert qualified as an examiner of blood or tissue types and appointed by the court. The expert shall determine the testing procedures. However, any interested party, for good cause shown, in advance of the scheduled tests, may request a hearing to object to the qualifications of the expert or the testing procedures. The expert appointed by the court shall testify at the pre-test hearing at the expense of the party requesting the hearing, except as provided in subsection (h) of this Section for an indigent party. An expert not appointed by the court shall testify at the pre-test hearing at the expense of the party retaining the expert. Inquiry into an expert's qualifications at the pre-test hearing shall not affect either parties' right to have the expert qualified at trial.

(c) The expert shall prepare a written report of the test results. If the test results show that the alleged father is not excluded, the report shall contain a combined paternity index relating to the probability of paternity. The expert may be called by the court as a witness to testify to his or her findings and, if called, shall be subject to cross-examination by the parties. If the test results show that the alleged father is not excluded, any party may demand that other experts, qualified as examiners of blood or tissue types, perform independent tests under order of court, including, but not limited to, blood types or other tests of genetic markers such as those found by Human Leucocyte Antigen (HLA) tests. The results of the tests may be offered into evidence. The number and qualifications of the experts shall be determined by the court.

(d) Documentation of the chain of custody of the blood or tissue samples, accompanied by an affidavit or certification in accordance with Section 1-109 of the Code of Civil Procedure, is competent evidence to establish the chain of custody.

(e) The report of the test results prepared by the appointed expert shall be made by affidavit or by certification as provided in Section 1-109 of the Code of Civil Procedure and shall be mailed to all parties. A proof of service shall be filed with the court. The verified report shall be admitted into evidence at trial without foundation testimony or other proof of authenticity or accuracy, unless a written motion challenging the admissibility of the report is filed by either party within 28 days of receipt of the report, in which case expert testimony shall be required. A party may not file such a motion challenging the admissibility of the report later than 28 days before commencement of trial. Before trial, the court shall determine whether the motion is sufficient to deny admission of the report by verification. Failure to make that timely motion constitutes a waiver of the right to object to admission by verification and shall not be grounds for a continuance of the hearing to determine paternity.

(f) Tests taken pursuant to this Section shall have the following effect:

(1) If the court finds that the conclusion of the expert or experts, as disclosed by the evidence based upon the tests, is that the alleged father is not the parent of the child, the question of paternity shall be resolved accordingly.

(2) If the experts disagree in their findings or conclusions, the question shall be weighed with other competent evidence of paternity.

(3) If the tests show that the alleged father is not excluded and that the combined paternity index is less than 500 to 1, this evidence shall be admitted by the court and shall

be weighed with other competent evidence of paternity.

(4) If the tests show that the alleged father is not excluded and that the combined paternity index is at least 500 to 1, the alleged father is presumed to be the father, and this evidence shall be admitted. This presumption may be rebutted by clear and convincing evidence.

(g) Any presumption of parentage as set forth in Section 5 of this Act is rebutted if the court finds that the conclusion of the expert or experts excludes paternity of the presumed father.

(h) The expense of the tests shall be paid by the party who requests the tests. Where the tests are requested by the party seeking to establish paternity and that party is found to be indigent by the court, the expense shall be paid by the public agency providing representation; except that where a public agency is not providing representation, the expense shall be paid by the county in which the action is brought. Where the tests are ordered by the court on its own motion or are requested by the alleged or presumed father and that father is found to be indigent by the court, the expense shall be paid by the county in which the action is brought. Any part of the expense may be taxed as costs in the action, except that no costs may be taxed against a public agency that has not requested the tests.

(i) The compensation of each expert witness appointed by the court shall be paid as provided in subsection (h) of this Section. Any part of the payment may be taxed as costs in the action, except that no costs may be taxed against a public agency that has not requested the services of the expert witness.

(j) Nothing in this Section shall prevent any party from obtaining tests of his or her own blood or tissue independent of those ordered by the court or from presenting expert testimony interpreting those tests or any other blood tests ordered pursuant to this Section. Reports of all the independent tests, accompanied by affidavit or certification pursuant to Section 1-109 of the Code of Civil Procedure, and notice of any expert witnesses to be called to testify to the results of those tests shall be submitted to all parties at least 30 days before any hearing set to determine the issue of parentage.

750 ILCS 45/12 Pre-Trial Recommendations. (a) On the basis of the information produced at a pretrial conference, the court shall evaluate the probability of determining the existence or non-existence of the father and child relationship in a trial and whether a judicial declaration of the relationship would be in the best interest of the child. On the basis of the evaluation, an appropriate recommendation for settlement shall be made to the parties, which may include that the alleged father consent to a finding of his paternity of the child, or that the action be dismissed with or without prejudice.

(b) If the parties accept a recommendation made in accordance with subsection (a) of this Section, judgment shall be entered accordingly.

750 ILCS 45/12.1 Settlement Orders. In cases where the alleged father has not consented to a finding of paternity and where the parties have requested a settlement, the court shall review the proposed settlement in light of the allegations made,

the probable evidence and the circumstances of the parties. If the court is satisfied that the best interests of the child and of the parties will be served by entry of an order incorporating the settlement, and if the court is satisfied that the financial security of the child is adequately provided for and that the child and its mother are not likely to become public charges, it may enter an order so incorporating the settlement. The order may be directed to the defendant, or the mother, or both. Notwithstanding subsection (d) of Section 7 of this Act, neither the entry of a settlement order, nor the terms of a settlement order shall bar an action brought under this Act by a child to ascertain paternity.

750 ILCS 45/13 Civil Action.

(a) An action under this Act is a civil action governed by the provisions of the "Code of Civil Procedure", approved August 19, 1981, as amended, and the Supreme Court rules applicable thereto, except where otherwise specified in this Act.

(b) Trial by jury is not available under this Act.

(c) Certified copies of the bills for costs incurred for pregnancy and childbirth shall be admitted into evidence at judicial or administrative proceedings without foundation testimony or other proof of authenticity or accuracy.

750 ILCS 45/13.1 Temporary order for child support. Notwithstanding any other law to the contrary, pending the outcome of a judicial determination of parentage, the court shall issue a temporary order for child support, upon motion by a party and a showing of clear and convincing evidence of paternity. In determining the amount of the temporary child support award, the court shall use the guidelines and standards set forth in subsection (a) of Section 505 and in Section 505.2 of the Illinois Marriage and Dissolution of Marriage Act.

Any new or existing support order entered by the court under this Section shall be deemed to be a series of judgments against the person obligated to pay support thereunder, each such judgment to be in the amount of each payment or installment of support and each judgment to be deemed entered as of the date the corresponding payment or installment becomes due under the terms of the support order. Each such judgment shall have the full force, effect, and attributes of any other judgment of this State, including the ability to be enforced. Any such judgment is subject to modification or termination only in accordance with Section 510 of the Illinois Marriage and Dissolution of Marriage Act. A lien arises by operation of law against the real and personal property of the noncustodial parent for each installment of overdue support owed by the noncustodial parent.

All orders for support, when entered or modified, shall include a provision requiring the non-custodial parent to notify the court, and in cases in which a party is receiving child support enforcement services under Article X of the Illinois Public Aid Code, the Illinois Department of Public Aid, within 7 days, (i) of the name, address, and telephone number of any new employer of the non-custodial parent, (ii) whether the non-custodial parent has access to health insurance coverage through the employer or other group coverage, and, if so, the policy name and number and the names of persons covered under the policy, and (iii) of any new residential or mailing address or telephone number of the non-custodial parent.

In any subsequent action to enforce a support order, upon sufficient showing that diligent effort has been made to ascertain the location of the non-custodial parent, service of process or provision of notice necessary in that action may be made at the last known address of the non-custodial parent, in any manner expressly provided by the Code of Civil Procedure or in this Act, which service shall be sufficient for purposes of due process.

An order for support shall include a date on which the current support obligation terminates. The termination date shall be no earlier than the date on which the child covered by the order will attain the age of majority or is otherwise emancipated. The order for support shall state that the termination date does not apply to any arrearage that may remain unpaid on that date. Nothing in this paragraph shall be construed to prevent the court from modifying the order.

If there is an unpaid arrearage or delinquency (as those terms are defined in the Income Withholding for Support Act) equal to at least one month's support obligation on the termination date stated in the order for support or, if there is no termination date stated in the order, on the date the child attains the age of majority or is otherwise emancipated, then the periodic amount required to be paid for current support of that child immediately prior to that date shall automatically continue to be an obligation, not as current support but as periodic payment toward satisfaction of the unpaid arrearage or delinquency. That periodic payment shall be in addition to any periodic payment previously required for satisfaction of the arrearage or delinquency. The total periodic amount to be paid toward satisfaction of the arrearage or delinquency may be enforced and collected by any method provided by law for the enforcement and collection of child support, including but not limited to income withholding under the Income Withholding for Support Act. Each order for support entered or modified on or after the effective date of this amendatory Act of the 93rd General Assembly must contain a statement notifying the parties of the requirements of this paragraph. Failure to include the statement in the order for support does not affect the validity of the order or the operation of the provisions of this paragraph with regard to the order. This paragraph shall not be construed to prevent or affect the establishment or modification of an order for the support of a minor child or the establishment or modification of an order for the support of a nonminor child or educational expenses under Section 513 of the Illinois Marriage and Dissolution of Marriage Act.

750 ILCS 45/13.5 Injunctive relief.

(a) In any action brought under this Act for the initial determination of custody or visitation of a child or for modification of a prior custody or visitation order, the court, upon application of any party, may enjoin a party having physical possession or custody of a child from temporarily or permanently removing the child from Illinois pending the adjudication of the issues of custody and visitation. When deciding whether to enjoin removal of a child, the Court shall consider the following factors including, but not limited to:

(1) the extent of previous involvement with the child by the party seeking to enjoin removal;

(2) the likelihood that parentage will be established; and

(3) the impact on the financial, physical, and emotional health of the party being enjoined from removing the child.

(b) Injunctive relief under this Act shall be governed by the relevant provisions of the Code of Civil Procedure.

(c) Notwithstanding the provisions of subsection (a), the court may decline to enjoin a domestic violence victim having physical possession or custody of a child from temporarily or permanently removing the child from Illinois pending the adjudication of the issues of custody and visitation. In determining whether a person is a domestic violence victim, the court shall consider the following factors:

(1) a sworn statement by the person that the person has good reason to believe that he or she is the victim of domestic violence or stalking;

(2) a sworn statement that the person fears for his or her safety or the safety of his or her children;

(3) evidence from police, court or other government agency records or files;

(4) documentation from a domestic violence program if the person is alleged to be a victim of domestic violence;

(5) documentation from a legal, clerical, medical, or other professional from whom the person has sought assistance in dealing with the alleged domestic violence; and

(6) any other evidence that supports the sworn statements, such as a statement from any other individual with knowledge of the circumstances that provides the basis for the claim, or physical evidence of the act or acts of domestic violence.

750 ILCS 45/14 Judgment.

(a)(1) The judgment shall contain or explicitly reserve provisions concerning any duty and amount of child support and may contain provisions concerning the custody and guardianship of the child, visitation privileges with the child, the furnishing of bond or other security for the payment of the judgment, which the court shall determine in accordance with the relevant factors set forth in the Illinois Marriage and Dissolution of Marriage Act and any other applicable law of Illinois, to guide the court in a finding in the best interests of the child. In determining custody, joint custody, removal, or visitation, the court shall apply the relevant standards of the Illinois Marriage and Dissolution of Marriage Act, including Section 609. Specifically, in determining the amount of any child support award or child health insurance coverage, the court shall use the guidelines and standards set forth in subsection (a) of Section 505 and in Section 505.2 of the Illinois Marriage and Dissolution of Marriage Act. For purposes of Section 505 of the Illinois Marriage and Dissolution of Marriage Act, "net income" of the non-custodial parent shall include any benefits available to that person under the Illinois Public Aid Code or from other federal, State or local government-funded

programs. The court shall, in any event and regardless of the amount of the non-custodial parent's net income, in its judgment order the non-custodial parent to pay child support to the custodial parent in a minimum amount of not less than $10 per month. In an action brought within 2 years after a child's birth, the judgment or order may direct either parent to pay the reasonable expenses incurred by either parent related to the mother's pregnancy and the delivery of the child. The judgment or order shall contain the father's social security number, which the father shall disclose to the court; however, failure to include the father's social security number on the judgment or order does not invalidate the judgment or order.

(2) If a judgment of parentage contains no explicit award of custody, the establishment of a support obligation or of visitation rights in one parent shall be considered a judgment granting custody to the other parent. If the parentage judgment contains no such provisions, custody shall be presumed to be with the mother; however, the presumption shall not apply if the father has had physical custody for at least 6 months prior to the date that the mother seeks to enforce custodial rights.

(b) The court shall order all child support payments, determined in accordance with such guidelines, to commence with the date summons is served. The level of current periodic support payments shall not be reduced because of payments set for the period prior to the date of entry of the support order. The Court may order any child support payments to be made for a period prior to the commencement of the action. In determining whether and the extent to which the payments shall be made for any prior period, the court shall consider all relevant facts, including the factors for determining the amount of support specified in the Illinois Marriage and Dissolution of Marriage Act and other equitable factors including but not limited to:

(1) The father's prior knowledge of the fact and circumstances of the child's birth.

(2) The father's prior willingness or refusal to help raise or support the child.

(3) The extent to which the mother or the public agency bringing the action previously informed the father of the child's needs or attempted to seek or require his help in raising or supporting the child.

(4) The reasons the mother or the public agency did not file the action earlier.

(5) The extent to which the father would be prejudiced by the delay in bringing the action.

For purposes of determining the amount of child support to be paid for any period before the date the order for current child support is entered, there is a rebuttable presumption that the father's net income for the prior period was the same as his net income at the time the order for current child support is entered.

If (i) the non-custodial parent was properly served with a request for discovery of financial information relating to the non-custodial parent's ability to provide child support, (ii) the non-custodial parent failed to comply with the request, despite having been ordered to do so by the court, and (iii) the non-custodial parent is not present at the hearing to determine support despite having received proper notice, then any relevant financial information concerning the non-custodial parent's ability to provide child support that was obtained pursuant to subpoena and proper notice shall be admitted into evidence without the need to establish any further foundation for its admission.

(c) Any new or existing support order entered by the court under this Section shall be deemed to be a series of judgments against the person obligated to pay support thereunder, each judgment to be in the amount of each payment or installment of support and each such judgment to be deemed entered as of the date the corresponding payment or installment becomes due under the terms of the support order. Each judgment shall have the full force, effect and attributes of any other judgment of this State, including the ability to be enforced. A lien arises by operation of law against the real and personal property of the noncustodial parent for each installment of overdue support owed by the noncustodial parent.

(d) If the judgment or order of the court is at variance with the child's birth certificate, the court shall order that a new birth certificate be issued under the Vital Records Act.

(e) On request of the mother and the father, the court shall order a change in the child's name. After hearing evidence the court may stay payment of support during the period of the father's minority or period of disability.

(f) If, upon a showing of proper service, the father fails to appear in court, or otherwise appear as provided by law, the court may proceed to hear the cause upon testimony of the mother or other parties taken in open court and shall enter a judgment by default. The court may reserve any order as to the amount of child support until the father has received notice, by regular mail, of a hearing on the matter.

(g) A one-time charge of 20% is imposable upon the amount of past-due child support owed on July 1, 1988 which has accrued under a support order entered by the court. The charge shall be imposed in accordance with the provisions of Section 10-21 of the Illinois Public Aid Code and shall be enforced by the court upon petition.

(h) All orders for support, when entered or modified, shall include a provision requiring the non-custodial parent to notify the court and, in cases in which party is receiving child support enforcement services under Article X of the Illinois Public Aid Code, the Illinois Department of Public Aid, within 7 days, (i) of the name and address of any new employer of the non-custodial parent, (ii) whether the non-custodial parent has access to health insurance coverage through the employer or other group coverage and, if so, the policy name and number and the names of persons covered under the policy, and (iii) of any new residential or mailing address or telephone number of the non-custodial parent. In any subsequent action to enforce a support order, upon a sufficient showing that a diligent effort has been made to ascertain the location of the non-custodial parent, service of process or provision of notice necessary in the case may be made at the last known address of the non-custodial parent in any manner expressly provided by the Code

of Civil Procedure or this Act, which service shall be sufficient for purposes of due process.

(i) An order for support shall include a date on which the current support obligation terminates. The termination date shall be no earlier than the date on which the child covered by the order will attain the age of 18. However, if the child will not graduate from high school until after attaining the age of 18, then the termination date shall be no earlier than the earlier of the date on which the child's high school graduation will occur or the date on which the child will attain the age of 19. The order for support shall state that the termination date does not apply to any arrearage that may remain unpaid on that date. Nothing in this subsection shall be construed to prevent the court from modifying the order or terminating the order in the event the child is otherwise emancipated.

(i-5) If there is an unpaid arrearage or delinquency (as those terms are defined in the Income Withholding for Support Act) equal to at least one month's support obligation on the termination date stated in the order for support or, if there is no termination date stated in the order, on the date the child attains the age of majority or is otherwise emancipated, the periodic amount required to be paid for current support of that child immediately prior to that date shall automatically continue to be an obligation, not as current support but as periodic payment toward satisfaction of the unpaid arrearage or delinquency. That periodic payment shall be in addition to any periodic payment previously required for satisfaction of the arrearage or delinquency. The total periodic amount to be paid toward satisfaction of the arrearage or delinquency may be enforced and collected by any method provided by law for enforcement and collection of child support, including but not limited to income withholding under the Income Withholding for Support Act. Each order for support entered or modified on or after the effective date of this amendatory Act of the 93rd General Assembly must contain a statement notifying the parties of the requirements of this subsection. Failure to include the statement in the order for support does not affect the validity of the order or the operation of the provisions of this subsection with regard to the order. This subsection shall not be construed to prevent or affect the establishment or modification of an order for support of a minor child or the establishment or modification of an order for support of a non-minor child or educational expenses under Section 513 of the Illinois Marriage and Dissolution of Marriage Act.

(j) An order entered under this Section shall include a provision requiring the obligor to report to the obligee and to the clerk of court within 10 days each time the obligor obtains new employment, and each time the obligor's employment is terminated for any reason. The report shall be in writing and shall, in the case of new employment, include the name and address of the new employer. Failure to report new employment or the termination of current employment, if coupled with nonpayment of support for a period in excess of 60 days, is indirect criminal contempt. For any obligor arrested for failure to report new employment bond shall be set in the amount of the child support that should have been paid during the period of unreported employment. An order entered under this Section shall also include a provision requiring the obligor and obligee parents to advise each other of a change in residence within 5 days of the change except when the court finds that the physical, mental, or emotional health of a party or that of a minor child, or both, would be seriously endangered by disclosure of the party's address.

750 ILCS 45/14.1 Information to State Case Registry.

(a) In this Section:

"Order for support", "obligor", "obligee", and "business day" are defined as set forth in the Income Withholding for Support Act.

"State Case Registry" means the State Case Registry established under Section 10-27 of the Illinois Public Aid Code.

(b) Each order for support entered or modified by the circuit court under this Act shall require that the obligor and obligee (i) file with the clerk of the circuit court the information required by this Section (and any other information required under Title IV, Part D of the Social Security Act or by the federal Department of Health and Human Services) at the time of entry or modification of the order for support and (ii) file updated information with the clerk within 5 business days of any change. Failure of the obligor or obligee to file or update the required information shall be punishable as in cases of contempt. The failure shall not prevent the court from entering or modifying the order for support, however.

(c) The obligor shall file the following information: the obligor's name, date of birth, social security number, and mailing address.

If either the obligor or the obligee receives child support enforcement services from the Illinois Department of Public Aid under Article X of the Illinois Public Aid Code, the obligor shall also file the following information: the obligor's telephone number, driver's license number, and residential address (if different from the obligor's mailing address), and the name, address, and telephone number of the obligor's employer or employers.

(d) The obligee shall file the following information:

(1) The names of the obligee and the child or children covered by the order for support.

(2) The dates of birth of the obligee and the child or children covered by the order for support.

(3) The social security numbers of the obligee and the child or children covered by the order for support.

(4) The obligee's mailing address.

(e) In cases in which the obligee receives child support enforcement services from the Illinois Department of Public Aid under Article X of the Illinois Public Aid Code, the order for support shall (i) require that the obligee file the information required under subsection (d) with the Illinois Department of Public Aid for inclusion in the State Case Registry, rather than file the information with the clerk, and (ii) require that the obligee include the following additional information:

(1) The obligee's telephone and driver's license numbers.

(2) The obligee's residential address, if different

from the obligee's mailing address.

(3) The name, address, and telephone number of the obligee's employer or employers.

The order for support shall also require that the obligee update the information filed with the Illinois Department of Public Aid within 5 business days of any change.

(f) The clerk shall provide the information filed under this Section, together with the court docket number and county in which the order for support was entered, to the State Case Registry within 5 business days after receipt of the information.

(g) In a case in which a party is receiving child support enforcement services under Article X of the Illinois Public Aid Code, the clerk shall provide the following additional information to the State Case Registry within 5 business days after entry or modification of an order for support or request from the Illinois Department of Public Aid:

(1) The amount of monthly or other periodic support owed under the order for support and other amounts, including arrearage, interest, or late payment penalties and fees, due or overdue under the order.

(2) Any such amounts that have been received by the clerk, and the distribution of those amounts by the clerk.

(h) Information filed by the obligor and obligee under this Section that is not specifically required to be included in the body of an order for support under other laws is not a public record and shall be treated as confidential and subject to disclosure only in accordance with the provisions of this Section, Section 10-27 of the Illinois Public Aid Code, and Title IV, Part D of the Social Security Act.

750 ILCS 45/14.5 Information to locate putative fathers and noncustodial parents.

(a) Upon request by a public office, employers, labor unions, and telephone companies shall provide location information concerning putative fathers and noncustodial parents for the purpose of establishing a child's paternity or establishing, enforcing, or modifying a child support obligation. The term "public office" is defined as set forth in the Income Withholding for Support Act. In this Section, "location information" means information about (i) the physical whereabouts of a putative father or noncustodial parent, (ii) the employer of the putative father or noncustodial parent, or (iii) the salary, wages, and other compensation paid and the health insurance coverage provided to the putative father or noncustodial parent by the employer of the putative father or noncustodial parent or by a labor union of which the putative father or noncustodial parent is a member. An employer, labor union, or telephone company shall respond to the request of the public office within 15 days after receiving the request. Any employer, labor union, or telephone company that willfully fails to fully respond within the 15-day period shall be subject to a penalty of $100 for each day that the response is not provided to the public office after the 15-day period has expired. The penalty may be collected in a civil action, which may be brought against the employer, labor union, or telephone company in favor of the public office.

(b) Upon being served with a subpoena (including an

administrative subpoena as authorized by law), a utility company or cable television company must provide location information to a public office for the purpose of establishing a child's paternity or establishing, enforcing, or modifying a child support obligation.

(c) Notwithstanding the provisions of any other State or local law to the contrary, an employer, labor union, telephone company, utility company, or cable television company shall not be liable to any person for disclosure of location information under the requirements of this Section, except for willful and wanton misconduct.

750 ILCS 45/15 Enforcement of Judgment or Order.

(a) If existence of the parent and child relationship is declared, or paternity or duty of support has been established under this Act or under prior law or under the law of any other jurisdiction, the judgment rendered thereunder may be enforced in the same or other proceedings by any party or any person or agency that has furnished or may furnish financial assistance or services to the child. The Income Withholding for Support Act and Sections 14 and 16 of this Act shall also be applicable with respect to entry, modification and enforcement of any support judgment entered under provisions of the "Paternity Act", approved July 5, 1957, as amended, repealed July 1, 1985.

(b) Failure to comply with any order of the court shall be punishable as contempt as in other cases of failure to comply under the "Illinois Marriage and Dissolution of Marriage Act", as now or hereafter amended. In addition to other penalties provided by law, the court may, after finding the party guilty of contempt, order that the party be:

(1) Placed on probation with such conditions of probation as the court deems advisable;

(2) Sentenced to periodic imprisonment for a period not to exceed 6 months. However, the court may permit the party to be released for periods of time during the day or night to work or conduct business or other self-employed occupation. The court may further order any part of all the earnings of a party during a sentence of periodic imprisonment to be paid to the Clerk of the Circuit Court or to the person or parent having custody of the minor child for the support of said child until further order of the court.

(2.5) The court may also pierce the ownership veil of a person, persons, or business entity to discover assets of a non-custodial parent held in the name of that person, those persons, or that business entity if there is a unity of interest and ownership sufficient to render no financial separation between the non-custodial parent and that person, those persons, or the business entity. The following circumstances are sufficient for a court to order discovery of the assets of a person, persons, or business entity and to compel the application of any discovered assets toward payment on the judgment for support:

(A) the non-custodial parent and the person, persons, or business entity maintain records together.

(B) the non-custodial parent and the person, persons, or business entity fail to maintain an arms

length relationship between themselves with regard to any assets.

(C) the non-custodial parent transfers assets to the person, persons, or business entity with the intent to perpetrate a fraud on the custodial parent.

With respect to assets which are real property, no order entered under this subdivision (2.5) shall affect the rights of bona fide purchasers, mortgagees, judgment creditors, or other lien holders who acquire their interests in the property prior to the time a notice of lis pendens pursuant to the Code of Civil Procedure or a copy of the order is placed of record in the office of the recorder of deeds for the county in which the real property is located.

(3) The court may also order that in cases where the party is 90 days or more delinquent in payment of support or has been adjudicated in arrears in an amount equal to 90 days obligation or more, that the party's Illinois driving privileges be suspended until the court determines that the party is in compliance with the judgement or duty of support. The court may also order that the parent be issued a family financial responsibility driving permit that would allow limited driving privileges for employment and medical purposes in accordance with Section 7-702.1 of the Illinois Vehicle Code. The clerk of the circuit court shall certify the order suspending the driving privileges of the parent or granting the issuance of a family financial responsibility driving permit to the Secretary of State on forms prescribed by the Secretary. Upon receipt of the authenticated documents, the Secretary of State shall suspend the party's driving privileges until further order of the court and shall, if ordered by the court, subject to the provisions of Section 7-702.1 of the Illinois Vehicle Code, issue a family financial responsibility driving permit to the parent.

In addition to the penalties or punishment that may be imposed under this Section, any person whose conduct constitutes a violation of Section 15 of the Non-Support Punishment Act may be prosecuted under that Act, and a person convicted under that Act may be sentenced in accordance with that Act. The sentence may include but need not be limited to a requirement that the person perform community service under Section 50 of that Act or participate in a work alternative program under Section 50 of that Act. A person may not be required to participate in a work alternative program under Section 50 of that Act if the person is currently participating in a work program pursuant to Section 15.1 of this Act.

(c) In any post-judgment proceeding to enforce or modify the judgment the parties shall continue to be designated as in the original proceeding.

750 ILCS 45/15.1 (a) Whenever it is determined in a proceeding to establish or enforce a child support obligation that the person owing a duty of support is unemployed, the court may order the person to seek employment and report periodically to the court with a diary, listing or other memorandum of his or her efforts in accordance with such order. Additionally, the court may order the unemployed person to report to the Department of Employment Security for job search services or to make application with the local Job Training Partnership Act

provider for participation in job search, training or work programs and where the duty of support is owed to a child receiving child support enforcement services under Article X of the Illinois Public Aid Code, as amended, the court may order the unemployed person to report to the Illinois Department of Public Aid for participation in job search, training or work programs established under Section 9-6 and Article IXA of that Code.

(b) Whenever it is determined that a person owes past-due support for a child, and the child is receiving assistance under the Illinois Public Aid Code, the court shall order the following at the request of the Illinois Department of Public Aid:

(1) that the person pay the past-due support in accordance with a plan approved by the court; or

(2) if the person owing past-due support is unemployed, is subject to such a plan, and is not incapacitated, that the person participate in such job search, training, or work programs established under Section 9-6 and Article IXA of the Illinois Public Aid Code as the court deems appropriate.

750 ILCS 45/15.2 Order of protection; status. Whenever relief is sought under this Act, the court, before granting relief, shall determine whether any order of protection has previously been entered in the instant proceeding or any other proceeding in which any party, or a child of any party, or both, if relevant, has been designated as either a respondent or a protected person.

750 ILCS 45/16 Modification of Judgment. The court has continuing jurisdiction to modify an order for support, custody, visitation, or removal included in a judgment entered under this Act. Any custody, visitation, or removal judgment modification shall be in accordance with the relevant factors specified in the Illinois Marriage and Dissolution of Marriage Act, including Section 609. Any support judgment is subject to modification or termination only in accordance with Section 510 of the Illinois Marriage and Dissolution of Marriage Act.

750 ILCS 45/17 Costs. Except as otherwise provided in this Act, the court may order reasonable fees of counsel, experts, and other costs of the action, pre-trial proceedings, post-judgment proceedings to enforce or modify the judgment, and the appeal or the defense of an appeal of the judgment, to be paid by the parties in accordance with the relevant factors specified in Section 508 of the Illinois Marriage and Dissolution of Marriage Act, as amended.

750 ILCS 45/18 Right to Counsel; Free Transcript on Appeal.

(a) Any party may be represented by counsel at all proceedings under this Act.

(a-5) In any proceedings involving the support, custody, visitation, education, parentage, property interest, or general welfare of a minor or dependent child, the court may, on its own motion or that of any party, and subject to the terms or specifications the court determines, appoint an attorney to serve in one of the following capacities:

(1) as an attorney to represent the child;

(2) as a guardian ad litem to address issues the court delineates;

(3) as a child's representative whose duty shall be to advocate what the representative finds to be in the best interests of the child after reviewing the facts and circumstances of the case. The child's representative shall have the same power and authority to take part in the conduct of the litigation as does an attorney for a party and shall possess all the powers of investigation and recommendation as does a guardian ad litem. The child's representative shall consider, but not be bound by, the expressed wishes of the child. A child's representative shall have received training in child advocacy or shall possess such experience as determined to be equivalent to such training by the chief judge of the circuit where the child's representative has been appointed. The child's representative shall not disclose confidential communications made by the child, except as required by law or by the Rules of Professional Conduct. The child's representative shall not be called as a witness regarding the issues set forth in this subsection.

During the proceedings the court may appoint an additional attorney to serve in another of the capacities described in subdivisions (1), (2), or (3) of the preceding paragraph on its own motion or that of a party only for good cause shown and when the reasons for the additional appointment are set forth in specific findings.

The court shall enter an order as appropriate for costs, fees, and disbursements, including a retainer, when the attorney, guardian ad litem, or child's representative is appointed, and thereafter as necessary. Such orders shall require payment by either or both parents, by any other party or source, or from the marital estate or the child's separate estate. The court may not order payment by the Illinois Department of Public Aid in cases in which the Department is providing child support enforcement services under Article X of the Illinois Public Aid Code. Unless otherwise ordered by the court at the time fees and costs are approved, all fees and costs payable to an attorney, guardian ad litem, or child's representative under this Section are by implication deemed to be in the nature of support of the child and are within the exceptions to discharge in bankruptcy under 11 U.S.C.A. 523. The provisions of Sections 501 and 508 of this Act shall apply to fees and costs for attorneys appointed under this Section.

(b) Upon the request of a mother or child seeking to establish the existence of a father and child relationship, the State's Attorney shall represent the mother or child in the trial court. If the child is an applicant for or a recipient of assistance as defined in Section 2-6 of "The Illinois Public Aid Code", approved April 11, 1967, as amended, or has applied to the Illinois Department of Public Aid for services under Article X of such Code, the Department may file a complaint in the child's behalf under this Act. The Department shall refer the complaint to the Public Aid Claims Enforcement Division of the Office of the Attorney General as provided in Section 12-16 of "The Illinois Public Aid Code" for enforcement by the Attorney General. Legal representation by the State's Attorney or the Attorney General shall be limited to the establishment and enforcement of an order for support, and shall not extend to visitation, custody, property or other matters. If visitation, custody, property or other matters are raised by a party and considered by the court in any proceeding under this Act, the court shall provide a continuance sufficient to enable the mother or child to obtain representation for such matters.

(c) The Court may appoint counsel to represent any indigent defendant in the trial court, except that this representation shall be limited to the establishment of a parent and child relationship and an order for support, and shall not extend to visitation, custody, property, enforcement of an order for support, or other matters. If visitation, custody, property or other matters are raised by a party and considered by the court in any proceeding under this Act, the court shall provide a continuance sufficient to enable the defendant to obtain representation for such matters.

(d) The court shall furnish on request of any indigent party a transcript for purposes of appeal.

750 ILCS 45/19 Action to Declare Mother and Child Relationship. Any interested party may bring an action to determine the existence or non-existence of a mother and child relationship. Insofar as practicable, the provisions of this Act applicable to the father and child relationship shall apply to the mother and child relationship, including, but not limited to the obligation to support.

750 ILCS 45/20 Withholding of Income to Secure Payment of Support. Orders for support entered under this Act are subject to the Income Withholding for Support Act.

750 ILCS 45/20.5 Information concerning obligors.

(a) In this Section:

"Arrearage", "delinquency", "obligor", and "order for support" have the meanings attributed to those terms in the Income Withholding for Support Act.

"Consumer reporting agency" has the meaning attributed to that term in Section 603(f) of the Fair Credit Reporting Act, 15 U.S.C. 1681a(f).

(b) Whenever a court of competent jurisdiction finds that an obligor either owes an arrearage of more than $10,000 or is delinquent in payment of an amount equal to at least 3 months' support obligation pursuant to an order for support, the court shall direct the clerk of the court to make information concerning the obligor available to consumer reporting agencies.

(c) Whenever a court of competent jurisdiction finds that an obligor either owes an arrearage of more than $10,000 or is delinquent in payment of an amount equal to at least 3 months' support obligation pursuant to an order for support, the court shall direct the clerk of the court to cause the obligor's name and address to be published in a newspaper of general circulation in the area in which the obligor resides. The clerk shall cause the obligor's name and address to be published only after sending to the obligor at the obligor's last known address, by certified mail, return receipt requested, a notice of intent to publish the information. This subsection (c) applies only if the obligor resides in the county in which the clerk of the court holds office.

750 ILCS 45/20.7 Interest on support obligations. A support obligation, or any portion of a support obligation, which becomes due and remains unpaid as of the end of each month,

excluding the child support that was due for that month to the extent that it was not paid in that month, shall accrue simple interest as set forth in Section 12-109 of the Code of Civil Procedure. An order for support entered or modified on or after January 1, 2006 shall contain a statement that a support obligation required under the order, or any portion of a support obligation required under the order, that becomes due and remains unpaid as of the end of each month, excluding the child support that was due for that month to the extent that it was not paid in that month, shall accrue simple interest as set forth in Section 12-109 of the Code of Civil Procedure. Failure to include the statement in the order for support does not affect the validity of the order or the accrual of interest as provided in this Section.

750 ILCS 45/21 Support payments; receiving and disbursing agents.

(1) In an action filed in a county of less than 3 million population in which an order for child support is entered, and in supplementary proceedings in such a county to enforce or vary the terms of such order arising out of an action filed in such a county, the court, except in actions or supplementary proceedings in which the pregnancy and delivery expenses of the mother or the child support payments are for a recipient of aid under the Illinois Public Aid Code, shall direct that child support payments be made to the clerk of the court unless in the discretion of the court exceptional circumstances warrant otherwise. In cases where payment is to be made to persons other than the clerk of the court the judgment or order of support shall set forth the facts of the exceptional circumstances.

(2) In an action filed in a county of 3 million or more population in which an order for child support is entered, and in supplementary proceedings in such a county to enforce or vary the terms of such order arising out of an action filed in such a county, the court, except in actions or supplementary proceedings in which the pregnancy and delivery expenses of the mother or the child support payments are for a recipient of aid under the Illinois Public Aid Code, shall direct that child support payments be made either to the clerk of the court or to the Court Service Division of the County Department of Public Aid, or to the clerk of the court or to the Illinois Department of Public Aid, unless in the discretion of the court exceptional circumstances warrant otherwise. In cases where payment is to be made to persons other than the clerk of the court, the Court Service Division of the County Department of Public Aid, or the Illinois Department of Public Aid, the judgment or order of support shall set forth the facts of the exceptional circumstances.

(3) Where the action or supplementary proceeding is in behalf of a mother for pregnancy and delivery expenses or for child support, or both, and the mother, child, or both, are recipients of aid under the Illinois Public Aid Code, the court shall order that the payments be made directly to (a) the Illinois Department of Public Aid if the mother or child, or both, are recipients under Articles IV or V of the Code, or (b) the local governmental unit responsible for the support of the mother or child, or both, if they are recipients under Articles VI or VII of the Code. In accordance with federal law and

regulations, the Illinois Department of Public Aid may continue to collect current maintenance payments or child support payments, or both, after those persons cease to receive public assistance and until termination of services under Article X of the Illinois Public Aid Code. The Illinois Department of Public Aid shall pay the net amount collected to those persons after deducting any costs incurred in making the collection or any collection fee from the amount of any recovery made. The Illinois Department of Public Aid or the local governmental unit, as the case may be, may direct that payments be made directly to the mother of the child, or to some other person or agency in the child's behalf, upon the removal of the mother and child from the public aid rolls or upon termination of services under Article X of the Illinois Public Aid Code; and upon such direction, the Illinois Department or the local governmental unit, as the case requires, shall give notice of such action to the court in writing or by electronic transmission.

(4) All clerks of the court and the Court Service Division of a County Department of Public Aid and the Illinois Department of Public Aid, receiving child support payments under paragraphs (1) or (2) shall disburse the same to the person or persons entitled thereto under the terms of the order. They shall establish and maintain clear and current records of all moneys received and disbursed and of defaults and delinquencies in required payments. The court, by order or rule, shall make provision for the carrying out of these duties.

Payments under this Section to the Illinois Department of Public Aid pursuant to the Child Support Enforcement Program established by Title IV-D of the Social Security Act shall be paid into the Child Support Enforcement Trust Fund. All payments under this Section to the Illinois Department of Human Services shall be deposited in the DHS Recoveries Trust Fund. Disbursement from these funds shall be as provided in the Illinois Public Aid Code. Payments received by a local governmental unit shall be deposited in that unit's General Assistance Fund.

(5) The moneys received by persons or agencies designated by the court shall be disbursed by them in accordance with the order. However, the court, on petition of the state's attorney, may enter new orders designating the clerk of the court or the Illinois Department of Public Aid, as the person or agency authorized to receive and disburse child support payments and, in the case of recipients of public aid, the court, on petition of the Attorney General or State's Attorney, shall direct subsequent payments to be paid to the Illinois Department of Public Aid or to the appropriate local governmental unit, as provided in paragraph (3). Payments of child support by principals or sureties on bonds, or proceeds of any sale for the enforcement of a judgment shall be made to the clerk of the court, the Illinois Department of Public Aid or the appropriate local governmental unit, as the respective provisions of this Section require.

(6) For those cases in which child support is payable to the clerk of the circuit court for transmittal to the Illinois Department of Public Aid by order of court or upon notification by the Illinois Department of Public Aid, the clerk shall transmit all such payments, within 4 working days of receipt, to insure that funds are available for immediate distribution by the Department to the person or entity entitled thereto in accordance with standards of the Child Support Enforcement Program established under Title IV-D of the Social Security Act. The clerk shall notify the Department of the date of receipt and amount thereof at the time of transmittal. Where the clerk has entered into an agreement of cooperation with the Department to record the terms of child support orders and payments made thereunder directly into the Department's automated data processing system, the clerk shall account for, transmit and otherwise distribute child support payments in accordance with such agreement in lieu of the requirements contained herein.

(7) To the extent the provisions of this Section are inconsistent with the requirements pertaining to the State Disbursement Unit under Section 21.1 of this Act and Section 10-26 of the Illinois Public Aid Code, the requirements pertaining to the State Disbursement Unit shall apply.

750 ILCS 45/21.1 Payment of Support to State Disbursement Unit.

(a) As used in this Section:

"Order for support", "obligor", "obligee", and "payor" mean those terms as defined in the Income Withholding for Support Act, except that "order for support" shall not mean orders providing for spousal maintenance under which there is no child support obligation.

(b) Notwithstanding any other provision of this Act to the contrary, each order for support entered or modified on or after October 1, 1999 shall require that support payments be made to the State Disbursement Unit established under Section 10-26 of the Illinois Public Aid Code if:

(1) a party to the order is receiving child support enforcement services under Article X of the Illinois Public Aid Code; or

(2) no party to the order is receiving child support enforcement services, but the support payments are made through income withholding.

(c) Support payments shall be made to the State Disbursement Unit if:

(1) the order for support was entered before October 1, 1999, and a party to the order is receiving child support enforcement services under Article X of the Illinois Public Aid Code; or

(2) no party to the order is receiving child support enforcement services, and the support payments are being made through income withholding.

(c-5) If no party to the order is receiving child support enforcement services under Article X of the Illinois Public Aid Code, and the support payments are not made through income withholding, then support payments shall be made as directed by the order for support.

(c-10) At any time, and notwithstanding the existence of an order directing payments to be made elsewhere, the Department of Public Aid may provide notice to the obligor and, where applicable, to the obligor's payor:

(1) to make support payments to the State

Disbursement Unit if:

(A) a party to the order for support is receiving child support enforcement services under Article X of the Illinois Public Aid Code; or

(B) no party to the order for support is receiving child support enforcement services under Article X of the Illinois Public Aid Code, but the support payments are made through income withholding; or

(2) to make support payments to the State Disbursement Unit of another state upon request of another state's Title IV-D child support enforcement agency, in accordance with the requirements of Title IV, Part D of the Social Security Act and regulations promulgated under that Part D.

The Department of Public Aid shall provide a copy of the notice to the obligee and to the clerk of the circuit court.

(c-15) Within 15 days after the effective date of this amendatory Act of the 91st General Assembly, the clerk of the circuit court shall provide written notice to the obligor to directly to the clerk of the circuit court if no party to the order is receiving child support enforcement services under Article X of the Illinois Public Aid Code, the support payments are not made through income withholding, and the order for support requires support payments to be made directly to the clerk of the circuit court. The clerk shall provide a copy of the notice to the obligee.

(c-20) If the State Disbursement Unit receives a support payment that was not appropriately made to the Unit under this Section, the Unit shall immediately return the payment to the sender, including, if possible, instructions detailing where to send the support payments.

(d) The notices under subsections (c-10) and (c-15) may be sent by ordinary mail, certified mail, return receipt requested, facsimile transmission, or other electronic process, or may be served upon the obligor or payor using any method provided by law for service of a summons.

750 ILCS 45/22 In all cases instituted by the Illinois Department of Public Aid on behalf of a child or spouse, other than one receiving a grant of financial aid under Article IV of The Illinois Public Aid Code, on whose behalf an application has been made and approved for child support enforcement services as provided by Section 10-1 of that Code, the court shall impose a collection fee on the individual who owes a child or spouse support obligation in an amount equal to 10% of the amount so owed as long as such collection is required by federal law, which fee shall be in addition to the support obligation. The imposition of such fee shall be in accordance with provisions of Title IV, Part D, of the Social Security Act and regulations duly promulgated thereunder. The fee shall be payable to the clerk of the circuit court for transmittal to the Illinois Department of Public Aid and shall continue until support services are terminated by that Department.

750 ILCS 45/23 Notice to Clerk of Circuit Court of Payment Received by Illinois Department of Public Aid for Recording. For those cases in which support is payable to the clerk of the circuit court for transmittal to the Illinois Department of Public Aid by order of court, and the Illinois Department of Public Aid

collects support by assignment offset, withhold, deduction or other process permitted by law, the Illinois Department of Public Aid shall notify the clerk of the date and amount of such collection. Upon notification, the clerk shall record the collection on the payment record for the case.

750 ILCS 45/25 Except as provided in Section 8 of this Act, the repeal of the "Paternity Act", approved July 5, 1957, as amended, shall not affect rights or liabilities which have accrued thereunder and which have been determined, settled or adjudicated prior to the effective date of this Act or which are the subject of proceedings pending thereunder on such effective date. Provided further, this Act shall not be construed to bar an action which would have been barred because the action had not been filed within the then applicable time limitation, or which could not have been maintained under the "Paternity Act," approved July 5, 1957 and repealed hereunder, as long as the limitations periods set forth in Section 8 of this Act are complied with.

750 ILCS 45/26

Sec. 26. If any provision of this Act or the application thereof to any person or circumstance is held invalid, the invalidity does not affect other provisions or applications of the Act which can be given effect without the invalid provision or application, and to this end the provisions of this Act are severable.

750 ILCS 45/27 Other states' establishments of paternity. Establishments of paternity made under the laws of other states shall be given full faith and credit in this State regardless of whether paternity was established through voluntary acknowledgment, tests to determine inherited characteristics, or judicial or administrative processes.

750 ILCS 45/28 Notice of child support enforcement services. The Illinois Department of Public Aid may provide notice at any time to the parties to an action filed under this Act that child support enforcement services are being provided by the Illinois Department under Article X of the Illinois Public Aid Code. The notice shall be sent by regular mail to the party's last known address on file with the clerk of the court or the State Case Registry established under Section 10-27 of the Illinois Public Aid Code. After notice is provided pursuant to this Section, the Illinois Department shall be entitled, as if it were a party, to notice of any further proceedings brought in the case. The Illinois Department shall provide the clerk of the court with copies of the notices sent to the parties. The clerk shall file the copies in the court file.

*   *   *

750 ILCS 47/1 Short title. This Act may be cited as the Gestational Surrogacy Act.

750 ILCS 47/5 Purpose. The purpose of this Act is to establish consistent standards and procedural safeguards for the protection of all parties involved in a gestational surrogacy contract in this State and to confirm the legal status of children born as a result of these contracts. These standards and safeguards are meant to facilitate the use of this type of reproductive contract in accord with the public policy of this State.

750 ILCS 47/10 Definitions. As used in this Act:

"Compensation" means payment of any valuable consideration

for services in excess of reasonable medical and ancillary costs.

"Donor" means an individual who contributes a gamete or gametes for the purpose of in vitro fertilization or implantation in another.

"Gamete" means either a sperm or an egg.

"Gestational surrogacy" means the process by which a woman attempts to carry and give birth to a child created through in vitro fertilization using the gamete or gametes of at least one of the intended parents and to which the gestational surrogate has made no genetic contribution.

"Gestational surrogate" means a woman who agrees to engage in a gestational surrogacy.

"Gestational surrogacy contract" means a written agreement regarding gestational surrogacy.

"Health care provider" means a person who is duly licensed to provide health care, including all medical, psychological, or counseling professionals.

"Intended parent" means a person or persons who enters into a gestational surrogacy contract with a gestational surrogate pursuant to which he or she will be the legal parent of the resulting child. In the case of a married couple, any reference to an intended parent shall include both husband and wife for all purposes of this Act. This term shall include the intended mother, intended father, or both.

"In vitro fertilization" means all medical and laboratory procedures that are necessary to effectuate the extracorporeal fertilization of egg and sperm.

"Medical evaluation" means an evaluation and consultation of a physician meeting the requirements of Section 60.

"Mental health evaluation" means an evaluation and consultation of a mental health professional meeting the requirements of Section 60.

"Physician" means a person licensed to practice medicine in all its branches in Illinois.

"Pre-embryo" means a fertilized egg prior to 14 days of development.

"Pre-embryo transfer" means all medical and laboratory procedures that are necessary to effectuate the transfer of a pre-embryo into the uterine cavity.

750 ILCS 47/15 Rights of Parentage.

(a) Except as provided in this Act, the woman who gives birth to a child is presumed to be the mother of that child for purposes of State law.

(b) In the case of a gestational surrogacy satisfying the requirements set forth in subsection (d) of this Section:

(1) the intended mother shall be the mother of the child for purposes of State law immediately upon the birth of the child;

(2) the intended father shall be the father of the child for purposes of State law immediately upon the birth of the child;

(3) the child shall be considered the legitimate child of the intended parent or parents for purposes of State law immediately upon the birth of the child;

(4) parental rights shall vest in the intended parent

or parents immediately upon the birth of the child;

(5) sole custody of the child shall rest with the intended parent or parents immediately upon the birth of the child; and

(6) neither the gestational surrogate nor her husband, if any, shall be the parents of the child for purposes of State law immediately upon the birth of the child.

(c) In the case of a gestational surrogacy meeting the requirements set forth in subsection (d) of this Section, in the event of a laboratory error in which the resulting child is not genetically related to either of the intended parents, the intended parents will be the parents of the child for purposes of State law unless otherwise determined by a court of competent jurisdiction.

(d) The parties to a gestational surrogacy shall assume the rights and obligations of subsections (b) and (c) of this Section if:

(1) the gestational surrogate satisfies the eligibility requirements set forth in subsection (a) of Section 20;

(2) the intended parent or parents satisfy the eligibility requirements set forth in subsection (b) of Section 20; and

(3) the gestational surrogacy occurs pursuant to a gestational surrogacy contract meeting the requirements set forth in Section 25.

750 ILCS 47/20 Eligibility.

(a) A gestational surrogate shall be deemed to have satisfied the requirements of this Act if she has met the following requirements at the time the gestational surrogacy contract is executed:

(1) she is at least 21 years of age;

(2) she has given birth to at least one child;

(3) she has completed a medical evaluation;

(4) she has completed a mental health evaluation;

(5) she has undergone legal consultation with independent legal counsel regarding the terms of the gestational surrogacy contract and the potential legal consequences of the gestational surrogacy; and

(6) she has obtained a health insurance policy that covers major medical treatments and hospitalization and the health insurance policy has a term that extends throughout the duration of the expected pregnancy and for 8 weeks after the birth of the child; provided, however, that the policy may be procured by the intended parents on behalf of the gestational surrogate pursuant to the gestational surrogacy contract.

(b) The intended parent or parents shall be deemed to have satisfied the requirements of this Act if he, she, or they have met the following requirements at the time the gestational surrogacy contract is executed:

(1) he, she, or they contribute at least one of the gametes resulting in a pre-embryo that the gestational surrogate will attempt to carry to term;

(2) he, she, or they have a medical need for the gestational surrogacy as evidenced by a qualified physician's affidavit attached to the gestational surrogacy contract

and as required by the Illinois Parentage Act of 1984;

(3) he, she, or they have completed a mental health evaluation; and

(4) he, she, or they have undergone legal consultation with independent legal counsel regarding the terms of the gestational surrogacy contract and the potential legal consequences of the gestational surrogacy.

750 ILCS 47/25 Requirements for a gestational surrogacy contract.

(a) A gestational surrogacy contract shall be presumed enforceable for purposes of State law only if:

(1) it meets the contractual requirements set forth in subsection (b) of this Section; and

(2) it contains at a minimum each of the terms set forth in subsection (c) of this Section.

(b) A gestational surrogacy contract shall meet the following requirements:

(1) it shall be in writing;

(2) it shall be executed prior to the commencement of any medical procedures (other than medical or mental health evaluations necessary to determine eligibility of the parties pursuant to Section 20 of this Act) in furtherance of the gestational surrogacy:

(i) by a gestational surrogate meeting the eligibility requirements of subsection (a) of Section 20 of this Act and, if married, the gestational surrogate's husband; and

(ii) by the intended parent or parents meeting the eligibility requirements of subsection (b) of Section 20 of this Act. In the event an intended parent is married, both husband and wife must execute the gestational surrogacy contract;

(3) each of the gestational surrogate and the intended parent or parents shall have been represented by separate counsel in all matters concerning the gestational surrogacy and the gestational surrogacy contract;

(3.5) each of the gestational surrogate and the intended parent or parents shall have signed a written acknowledgement that he or she received information about the legal, financial, and contractual rights, expectations, penalties, and obligations of the surrogacy agreement;

(4) if the gestational surrogacy contract provides for the payment of compensation to the gestational surrogate, the compensation shall have been placed in escrow with an independent escrow agent prior to the gestational surrogate's commencement of any medical procedure (other than medical or mental health evaluations necessary to determine the gestational surrogate's eligibility pursuant to subsection (a) of Section 20 of this Act); and

(5) it shall be witnessed by 2 competent adults.

(c) A gestational surrogacy contract shall provide for:

(1) the express written agreement of the gestational surrogate to:

(i) undergo pre-embryo transfer and attempt to carry and give birth to the child; and

(ii) surrender custody of the child to the intended parent or parents immediately upon the birth of the child;

(2) if the gestational surrogate is married, the express agreement of her husband to:

(i) undertake the obligations imposed on the gestational surrogate pursuant to the terms of the gestational surrogacy contract;

(ii) surrender custody of the child to the intended parent or parents immediately upon the birth of the child;

(3) the right of the gestational surrogate to utilize the services of a physician of her choosing, after consultation with the intended parents, to provide her care during the pregnancy; and

(4) the express written agreement of the intended parent or parents to:

(i) accept custody of the child immediately upon his or her birth; and

(ii) assume sole responsibility for the support of the child immediately upon his or her birth.

(d) A gestational surrogacy contract shall be presumed enforceable for purposes of State law even though it contains one or more of the following provisions:

(1) the gestational surrogate's agreement to undergo all medical exams, treatments, and fetal monitoring procedures that the physician recommended for the success of the pregnancy;

(2) the gestational surrogate's agreement to abstain from any activities that the intended parent or parents or the physician reasonably believes to be harmful to the pregnancy and future health of the child, including, without limitation, smoking, drinking alcohol, using nonprescribed drugs, using prescription drugs not authorized by a physician aware of the gestational surrogate's pregnancy, exposure to radiation, or any other activities proscribed by a health care provider;

(3) the agreement of the intended parent or parents to pay the gestational surrogate reasonable compensation; and

(4) the agreement of the intended parent or parents to pay for or reimburse the gestational surrogate for reasonable expenses (including, without limitation, medical, legal, or other professional expenses) related to the gestational surrogacy and the gestational surrogacy contract.

(e) In the event that any of the requirements of this Section are not met, a court of competent jurisdiction shall determine parentage based on evidence of the parties' intent.

750 ILCS 47/30 Duty to support.

(a) Any person who is considered to be the parent of a child pursuant to Section 15 of this Act shall be obligated to support the child.

(b) The breach of the gestational surrogacy contract by the intended parent or parents shall not relieve such intended parent or parents of the support obligations imposed by this Act.

(c) A gamete donor may be liable for child support only if he or she fails to enter into a legal agreement with the intended parent or parents in which the intended parent or parents agree to assume all rights and responsibilities for any resulting child, and the gamete donor relinquishes his or her rights to any gametes, resulting embryos, or children.

750 ILCS 47/35 Establishment of the parent-child relationship.

(a) For purposes of the Illinois Parentage Act of 1984, a parent-child relationship shall be established prior to the birth of a child born through gestational surrogacy if, in addition to satisfying the requirements of Sections 5 and 6 of the Illinois Parentage Act of 1984, the attorneys representing both the gestational surrogate and the intended parent or parents certify that the parties entered into a gestational surrogacy contract intended to satisfy the requirements of Section 25 of this Act with respect to the child.

(b) The attorneys' certifications required by subsection (a) of this Section shall be filed on forms prescribed by the Illinois Department of Public Health and in a manner consistent with the requirement of the Illinois Parentage Act of 1984.

750 ILCS 47/40 Immunities. Except as provided in this Act, no person shall be civilly or criminally liable for non-negligent actions taken pursuant to the requirements of this Act.

750 ILCS 47/45 Noncompliance. Noncompliance by the gestational surrogate or the intended parent or parents occurs when that party breaches a provision of the gestational surrogacy contract.

750 ILCS 47/50 Effect of Noncompliance.

(a) Except as otherwise provided in this Act, in the event of noncompliance with the requirements of subsection (d) of Section 15 of this Act, a court of competent jurisdiction shall determine the respective rights and obligations of the parties.

(b) There shall be no specific performance remedy available for a breach by the gestational surrogate of a gestational surrogacy contract term that requires her to be impregnated.

(750 ILCS 47/55 Damages.

(a) Except as expressly provided in the gestational surrogacy contract, the intended parent or parents shall be entitled to all remedies available at law or equity.

(b) Except as expressly provided in the gestational surrogacy contract, the gestational surrogate shall be entitled to all remedies available at law or equity.

750 ILCS 47/60 Rulemaking. The Department of Public Health may adopt rules pertaining to the required medical and mental health evaluations for a gestational surrogacy contract. Until the Department of Public Health adopts such rules, medical and mental health evaluations and procedures shall be conducted in accordance with the recommended guidelines published by the American Society for Reproductive Medicine and the American College of Obstetricians and Gynecologists. The rules may adopt these guidelines or others by reference.

750 ILCS 47/65 Severability. If any provision of this Act or its application to any person or circumstance is held invalid, the invalidity of that provision or application does not affect other provisions or applications of this Act that can be given effect without the invalid provision or application.

750 ILCS 47/70 Irrevocability. No action to invalidate a gestational surrogacy meeting the requirements of subsection (d)

of Section 15 of this Act or to challenge the rights of parentage established pursuant to Section 15 of this Act and the Illinois Parentage Act of 1984 shall be commenced after 12 months from the date of birth of the child.

*   *   *

750 ILCS 60/101 Short Title. This Act shall be known and may be cited as the "Illinois Domestic Violence Act of 1986".

750 ILCS 60/102 Purposes; rules of construction. This Act shall be liberally construed and applied to promote its underlying purposes, which are to:

(1) Recognize domestic violence as a serious crime against the individual and society which produces family disharmony in thousands of Illinois families, promotes a pattern of escalating violence which frequently culminates in intra-family homicide, and creates an emotional atmosphere that is not conducive to healthy childhood development;

(2) Recognize domestic violence against high risk adults with disabilities, who are particularly vulnerable due to impairments in ability to seek or obtain protection, as a serious problem which takes on many forms, including physical abuse, sexual abuse, neglect, and exploitation, and facilitate accessibility of remedies under the Act in order to provide immediate and effective assistance and protection.

(3) Recognize that the legal system has ineffectively dealt with family violence in the past, allowing abusers to escape effective prosecution or financial liability, and has not adequately acknowledged the criminal nature of domestic violence; that, although many laws have changed, in practice there is still widespread failure to appropriately protect and assist victims;

(4) Support the efforts of victims of domestic violence to avoid further abuse by promptly entering and diligently enforcing court orders which prohibit abuse and, when necessary, reduce the abuser's access to the victim and address any related issues of child custody and economic support, so that victims are not trapped in abusive situations by fear of retaliation, loss of a child, financial dependence, or loss of accessible housing or services;

(5) Clarify the responsibilities and support the efforts of law enforcement officers to provide immediate, effective assistance and protection for victims of domestic violence, recognizing that law enforcement officers often become the secondary victims of domestic violence, as evidenced by the high rates of police injuries and deaths that occur in response to domestic violence calls; and

(6) Expand the civil and criminal remedies for victims of domestic violence; including, when necessary, the remedies which effect physical separation of the parties to prevent further abuse.

750 ILCS 60/103 Definitions. For the purposes of this Act, the following terms shall have the following meanings:

(1) "Abuse" means physical abuse, harassment, intimidation of a dependent, interference with personal liberty or willful deprivation but does not include reasonable direction of a minor child by a parent or person in loco parentis.

(2) "Adult with disabilities" means an elder adult with disabilities or a high-risk adult with disabilities. A person may be an

adult with disabilities for purposes of this Act even though he or she has never been adjudicated an incompetent adult. However, no court proceeding may be initiated or continued on behalf of an adult with disabilities over that adult's objection, unless such proceeding is approved by his or her legal guardian, if any.

(3) "Domestic violence" means abuse as defined in paragraph (1).

(4) "Elder adult with disabilities" means an adult prevented by advanced age from taking appropriate action to protect himself or herself from abuse by a family or household member.

(5) "Exploitation" means the illegal, including tortious, use of a high-risk adult with disabilities or of the assets or resources of a high-risk adult with disabilities. Exploitation includes, but is not limited to, the misappropriation of assets or resources of a high-risk adult with disabilities by undue influence, by breach of a fiduciary relationship, by fraud, deception, or extortion, or the use of such assets or resources in a manner contrary to law.

(6) "Family or household members" include spouses, former spouses, parents, children, stepchildren and other persons related by blood or by present or prior marriage, persons who share or formerly shared a common dwelling, persons who have or allegedly have a child in common, persons who share or allegedly share a blood relationship through a child, persons who have or have had a dating or engagement relationship, persons with disabilities and their personal assistants, and caregivers as defined in paragraph (3) of subsection (b) of Section 12-21 of the Criminal Code of 1961. For purposes of this paragraph, neither a casual acquaintanceship nor ordinary fraternization between 2 individuals in business or social contexts shall be deemed to constitute a dating relationship. In the case of a high-risk adult with disabilities, "family or household members" includes any person who has the responsibility for a high-risk adult as a result of a family relationship or who has assumed responsibility for all or a portion of the care of a high-risk adult with disabilities voluntarily, or by express or implied contract, or by court order.

(7) "Harassment" means knowing conduct which is not necessary to accomplish a purpose that is reasonable under the circumstances; would cause a reasonable person emotional distress; and does cause emotional distress to the petitioner. Unless the presumption is rebutted by a preponderance of the evidence, the following types of conduct shall be presumed to cause emotional distress:

(i) creating a disturbance at petitioner's place of employment or school;

(ii) repeatedly telephoning petitioner's place of employment, home or residence;

(iii) repeatedly following petitioner about in a public place or places;

(iv) repeatedly keeping petitioner under surveillance by remaining present outside his or her home, school, place of employment, vehicle or other place occupied by petitioner or by peering in petitioner's windows;

(v) improperly concealing a minor child from

petitioner, repeatedly threatening to improperly remove a minor child of petitioner's from the jurisdiction or from the physical care of petitioner, repeatedly threatening to conceal a minor child from petitioner, or making a single such threat following an actual or attempted improper removal or concealment, unless respondent was fleeing an incident or pattern of domestic violence; or

(vi) threatening physical force, confinement or restraint on one or more occasions.

(8) "High-risk adult with disabilities" means a person aged 18 or over whose physical or mental disability impairs his or her ability to seek or obtain protection from abuse, neglect, or exploitation.

(9) "Interference with personal liberty" means committing or threatening physical abuse, harassment, intimidation or willful deprivation so as to compel another to engage in conduct from which she or he has a right to abstain or to refrain from conduct in which she or he has a right to engage.

(10) "Intimidation of a dependent" means subjecting a person who is dependent because of age, health or disability to participation in or the witnessing of: physical force against another or physical confinement or restraint of another which constitutes physical abuse as defined in this Act, regardless of whether the abused person is a family or household member.

(11) (A) "Neglect" means the failure to exercise that degree of care toward a high-risk adult with disabilities which a reasonable person would exercise under the circumstances and includes but is not limited to:

(i) the failure to take reasonable steps to protect a high-risk adult with disabilities from acts of abuse;

(ii) the repeated, careless imposition of unreasonable confinement;

(iii) the failure to provide food, shelter, clothing, and personal hygiene to a high-risk adult with disabilities who requires such assistance;

(iv) the failure to provide medical and rehabilitative care for the physical and mental health needs of a high-risk adult with disabilities; or

(v) the failure to protect a high-risk adult with disabilities from health and safety hazards.

(B) Nothing in this subsection (10) shall be construed to impose a requirement that assistance be provided to a high-risk adult with disabilities over his or her objection in the absence of a court order, nor to create any new affirmative duty to provide support to a high-risk adult with disabilities.

(12) "Order of protection" means an emergency order, interim order or plenary order, granted pursuant to this Act, which includes any or all of the remedies authorized by Section 214 of this Act.

(13) "Petitioner" may mean not only any named petitioner for the order of protection and any named victim of abuse on whose behalf the petition is brought, but also any other person protected by this Act.

(14) "Physical abuse" includes sexual abuse and means any of the following:

(i) knowing or reckless use of physical force,

confinement or restraint;

(ii) knowing, repeated and unnecessary sleep deprivation; or

(iii) knowing or reckless conduct which creates an immediate risk of physical harm.

(14.5) "Stay away" means for the respondent to refrain from both physical presence and nonphysical contact with the petitioner whether direct, indirect (including, but not limited to, telephone calls, mail, email, faxes, and written notes), or through third parties who may or may not know about the order of protection.

(15) "Willful deprivation" means wilfully denying a person who because of age, health or disability requires medication, medical care, shelter, accessible shelter or services, food, therapeutic device, or other physical assistance, and thereby exposing that person to the risk of physical, mental or emotional harm, except with regard to medical care or treatment when the dependent person has expressed an intent to forgo such medical care or treatment. This paragraph does not create any new affirmative duty to provide support to dependent persons.

750 ILCS 60/201 Persons protected by this Act.

(a) The following persons are protected by this Act:

(i) any person abused by a family or household member;

(ii) any high-risk adult with disabilities who is abused, neglected, or exploited by a family or household member;

(iii) any minor child or dependent adult in the care of such person; and

(iv) any person residing or employed at a private home or public shelter which is housing an abused family or household member.

(b) A petition for an order of protection may be filed only: (i) by a person who has been abused by a family or household member or by any person on behalf of a minor child or an adult who has been abused by a family or household member and who, because of age, health, disability, or inaccessibility, cannot file the petition, or (ii) by any person on behalf of a high-risk adult with disabilities who has been abused, neglected, or exploited by a family or household member. However, any petition properly filed under this Act may seek protection for any additional persons protected by this Act.

750 ILCS 60/201.1 Access of high-risk adults. No person shall obstruct or impede the access of a high-risk adult with disabilities to any agency or organization authorized to file a petition for an order of protection under Section 201 of this Act for the purpose of a private visit relating to legal rights, entitlements, claims and services under this Act and Section 1 of "An Act in relation to domestic relations and domestic violence shelters and service programs", approved September 24, 1981, as now or hereafter amended. If a person does so obstruct or impede such access of a high-risk adult with disabilities, local law enforcement agencies shall take all appropriate action to assist the party seeking access in petitioning for a search warrant or an ex parte injunctive order. Such warrant or order may

issue upon a showing of probable cause to believe that the high-risk adult with disabilities is the subject of abuse, neglect, or exploitation which constitutes a criminal offense or that any other criminal offense is occurring which affects the interests or welfare of the high-risk adult with disabilities. When, from the personal observations of a law enforcement officer, it appears probable that delay of entry in order to obtain a warrant or order would cause the high-risk adult with disabilities to be in imminent danger of death or great bodily harm, entry may be made by the law enforcement officer after an announcement of the officer's authority and purpose.

750 ILCS 60/202 Commencement of action; filing fees; dismissal.

(a) How to commence action. Actions for orders of protection are commenced:

(1) Independently: By filing a petition for an order of protection in any civil court, unless specific courts are designated by local rule or order.

(2) In conjunction with another civil proceeding: By filing a petition for an order of protection under the same case number as another civil proceeding involving the parties, including but not limited to: (i) any proceeding under the Illinois Marriage and Dissolution of Marriage Act, Illinois Parentage Act of 1984, Nonsupport of Spouse and Children Act, Revised Uniform Reciprocal Enforcement of Support Act or an action for nonsupport brought under Article 10 of the Illinois Public Aid Code, provided that a petitioner and the respondent are a party to or the subject of that proceeding or (ii) a guardianship proceeding under the Probate Act of 1975, or a proceeding for involuntary commitment under the Mental Health and Developmental Disabilities Code, or any proceeding, other than a delinquency petition, under the Juvenile Court Act of 1987, provided that a petitioner or the respondent is a party to or the subject of such proceeding.

(3) In conjunction with a delinquency petition or a criminal prosecution: By filing a petition for an order of protection, under the same case number as the delinquency petition or criminal prosecution, to be granted during pre-trial release of a defendant, with any dispositional order issued under Section 5-710 of the Juvenile Court Act of 1987 or as a condition of release, supervision, conditional discharge, probation, periodic imprisonment, parole or mandatory supervised release, or in conjunction with imprisonment or a bond forfeiture warrant; provided that:

(i) the violation is alleged in an information, complaint, indictment or delinquency petition on file, and the alleged offender and victim are family or household members or persons protected by this Act; and

(ii) the petition, which is filed by the State's Attorney, names a victim of the alleged crime as a petitioner.

(b) Filing, certification, and service fees. No fee shall be charged by the clerk for filing, amending, vacating, certifying, or photocopying petitions or orders; or for issuing alias summons; or for any related filing service. No fee shall be charged by the sheriff for service by the sheriff of a petition, rule, motion, or order in an action commenced under this Section.

(c) Dismissal and consolidation. Withdrawal or dismissal of any petition for an order of protection prior to adjudication where the petitioner is represented by the State shall operate as a dismissal without prejudice. No action for an order of protection shall be dismissed because the respondent is being prosecuted for a crime against the petitioner. An independent action may be consolidated with another civil proceeding, as provided by paragraph (2) of subsection (a) of this Section. For any action commenced under paragraph (2) or (3) of subsection (a) of this Section, dismissal of the conjoined case (or a finding of not guilty) shall not require dismissal of the action for the order of protection; instead, it may be treated as an independent action and, if necessary and appropriate, transferred to a different court or division. Dismissal of any conjoined case shall not affect the validity of any previously issued order of protection, and thereafter subsections (b)(1) and (b)(2) of Section 220 shall be inapplicable to such order.

(d) Pro se petitions. The court shall provide, through the office of the clerk of the court, simplified forms and clerical assistance to help with the writing and filing of a petition under this Section by any person not represented by counsel. In addition, that assistance may be provided by the state's attorney.

750 ILCS 60/203 Pleading; non-disclosure of address; non-disclosure of schools.

(a) A petition for an order of protection shall be in writing and verified or accompanied by affidavit and shall allege that petitioner has been abused by respondent, who is a family or household member. The petition shall further set forth whether there is any other pending action between the parties. During the pendency of this proceeding, each party has a continuing duty to inform the court of any subsequent proceeding for an order of protection in this or any other state.

(b) If the petition states that disclosure of petitioner's address would risk abuse of petitioner or any member of petitioner's family or household or reveal the confidential address of a shelter for domestic violence victims, that address may be omitted from all documents filed with the court. If disclosure is necessary to determine jurisdiction or consider any venue issue, it shall be made orally and in camera. If petitioner has not disclosed an address under this subsection, petitioner shall designate an alternative address at which respondent may serve notice of any motions.

(c) If the petitioner is seeking to have a child protected by the order of protection, and if that child is enrolled in any day-care facility, pre-school, pre-kindergarten, private school, public school district, college, or university, the petitioner may provide the name and address of the day-care facility, pre-school, pre-kindergarten, private school, public school district, college, or university to the court. However, if the petition states that disclosure of this information would risk abuse to petitioner or to the child protected under the order, this information may be omitted from all documents filed with the court.

750 ILCS 60/205 Application of rules of civil procedure; Domestic abuse advocates.

(a) Any proceeding to obtain, modify, reopen or appeal an order of protection, whether commenced alone or in conjunction with a civil or criminal proceeding, shall be governed by the rules of civil procedure of this State. The standard of proof in such a proceeding is proof by a preponderance of the evidence, whether the proceeding is heard in criminal or civil court. The Code of Civil Procedure and Supreme Court and local court rules applicable to civil proceedings, as now or hereafter amended, shall apply, except as otherwise provided by this law.

(b) (1) In all circuit court proceedings under this Act, domestic abuse advocates shall be allowed to attend and sit at counsel table and confer with the victim, unless otherwise directed by the court.

(2) In criminal proceedings in circuit courts, domestic abuse advocates shall be allowed to accompany the victim and confer with the victim, unless otherwise directed by the court.

(3) Court administrators shall allow domestic abuse advocates to assist victims of domestic violence in the preparation of petitions for orders of protection.

(4) Domestic abuse advocates are not engaged in the unauthorized practice of law when providing assistance of the types specified in this subsection (b).

750 ILCS 60/206 Trial by jury. There shall be no right to trial by jury in any proceeding to obtain, modify, vacate or extend any order of protection under this Act. However, nothing in this Section shall deny any existing right to trial by jury in a criminal proceeding.

750 ILCS 60/207 Subject matter jurisdiction. Each of the circuit courts shall have the power to issue orders of protection.

750 ILCS 60/208 Jurisdiction over persons. In child custody proceedings, the court's personal jurisdiction is determined by this State's Uniform Child-Custody Jurisdiction and Enforcement Act. Otherwise, the courts of this State have jurisdiction to bind (i) State residents and (ii) non-residents having minimum contacts with this State, to the extent permitted by the long-arm statute, Section 2-209 of the Code of Civil Procedure, as now or hereafter amended.

750 ILCS 60/209 Venue.

(a) Filing. A petition for an order of protection may be filed in any county where (i) petitioner resides, (ii) respondent resides, (iii) the alleged abuse occurred or (iv) the petitioner is temporarily located if petitioner left petitioner's residence to avoid further abuse and could not obtain safe, accessible, and adequate temporary housing in the county of that residence.

(b) Exclusive Possession. With respect to requests for exclusive possession of the residence under this Act, venue is proper only in the county where the residence is located, except in the following circumstances:

(1) If a request for exclusive possession of the residence is made under this Act in conjunction with a proceeding under the Illinois Marriage and Dissolution of Marriage Act, venue is proper in the county or judicial circuit where the residence is located or in a contiguous county or judicial circuit.

(2) If a request for exclusive possession of the residence is made under this Act in any other proceeding,

provided the petitioner meets the requirements of item (iv) of subsection (a), venue is proper in the county or judicial circuit where the residence is located or in a contiguous county or judicial circuit. In such case, however, if the court is not located in the county where the residence is located, it may grant exclusive possession of the residence under subdivision (b)(2) of Section 214 only in an emergency order under Section 217, and such grant may be extended thereafter beyond the maximum initial period only by a court located in the county where the residence is located.

(c) Inconvenient forum. If an order of protection is issued by a court in a county in which neither of the parties resides, the court may balance hardships to the parties and accordingly transfer any proceeding to extend, modify, re-open, vacate or enforce any such order to a county wherein a party resides.

(d) Objection. Objection to venue is waived if not made within such time as respondent's response is due, except as otherwise provided in subsection (b). In no event shall venue be deemed jurisdictional.

750 ILCS 60/210 Process.

(a) Summons. Any action for an order of protection, whether commenced alone or in conjunction with another proceeding, is a distinct cause of action and requires that a separate summons be issued and served, except that in pending cases the following methods may be used:

(1) By delivery of the summons to respondent personally in open court in pending civil or criminal cases.

(2) By notice in accordance with Section 210.1 in civil cases in which the defendant has filed a general appearance.

The summons shall be in the form prescribed by Supreme Court Rule 101(d), except that it shall require respondent to answer or appear within 7 days. Attachments to the summons or notice shall include the petition for order of protection and supporting affidavits, if any, and any emergency order of protection that has been issued. The enforcement of an order of protection under Section 223 shall not be affected by the lack of service, delivery, or notice, provided the requirements of subsection (d) of that Section are otherwise met.

(b) Blank.

(c) Expedited service. The summons shall be served by the sheriff or other law enforcement officer at the earliest time and shall take precedence over other summonses except those of a similar emergency nature. Special process servers may be appointed at any time, and their designation shall not affect the responsibilities and authority of the sheriff or other official process servers.

(d) Remedies requiring actual notice. The counseling, payment of support, payment of shelter services, and payment of losses remedies provided by paragraphs 4, 12, 13, and 16 of subsection (b) of Section 214 may be granted only if respondent has been personally served with process, has answered or has made a general appearance.

(e) Remedies upon constructive notice. Service of process on a member of respondent's household or by publication shall be adequate for the remedies provided by paragraphs 1, 2, 3,

5, 6, 7, 8, 9, 10, 11, 14, 15, and 17 of subsection (b) of Section 214, but only if: (i) petitioner has made all reasonable efforts to accomplish actual service of process personally upon respondent, but respondent cannot be found to effect such service and (ii) petitioner files an affidavit or presents sworn testimony as to those efforts.

(f) Default. A plenary order of protection may be entered by default as follows:

(1) For any of the remedies sought in the petition, if respondent has been served or given notice in accordance with subsection (a) and if respondent then fails to appear as directed or fails to appear on any subsequent appearance or hearing date agreed to by the parties or set by the court; or

(2) For any of the remedies provided in accordance with subsection (e), if respondent fails to answer or appear in accordance with the date set in the publication notice or the return date indicated on the service of a household member.

750 ILCS 60/210.1 Service of notice in conjunction with a pending civil case.

(a) Notice. When an action for an order of protection is sought in conjunction with a pending civil case in which the court has obtained jurisdiction over respondent, and respondent has filed a general appearance, then a separate summons need not issue. Original notice of a hearing on a petition for an order of protection may be given, and the documents served, in accordance with Illinois Supreme Court Rules 11 and 12. When, however, an emergency order of protection is sought in such a case on an ex parte application, then the procedure set forth in subsection (a) of Section 210 (other than in subsection (a)(2)) shall be followed. If an order of protection is issued using the notice provisions of this Section, then the order of protection or extensions of that order may survive the disposition of the main civil case. The enforcement of any order of protection under Section 223 shall not be affected by the lack of notice under this Section, provided the requirements of subsection (d) of that Section are otherwise met.

(b) Default. The form of notice described in subsection (a) shall include the following language directed to the respondent:

A 2-year plenary order of protection may be entered by default for any of the remedies sought in the petition if you fail to appear on the specified hearing date or on any subsequent hearing date agreed to by the parties or set by the court.

(c) Party to give notice. Notice in the pending civil case shall be given (i) by either party under this Section, with respect to extensions, modifications, hearings, or other relief pertinent to an order of protection, in accordance with Illinois Supreme Court Rules 11 and 12 or (ii) by the respondent as provided in subsection (c) of Section 224.

750 ILCS 60/211 Service of notice of hearings. Except as provided in Sections 210 and 210.1, notice of hearings on petitions or motions shall be served in accordance with Supreme Court Rules 11 and 12, unless notice is excused by Section 217 of this Act, or by the Code of Civil Procedure, Supreme Court Rules, or local rules, as now or hereafter amended.

750 ILCS 60/212 Hearings.

(a) A petition for an order of protection shall be treated as an expedited proceeding, and no court shall transfer or otherwise decline to decide all or part of such petition except as otherwise provided herein. Nothing in this Section shall prevent the court from reserving issues when jurisdiction or notice requirements are not met.

(b) Any court or a division thereof which ordinarily does not decide matters of child custody and family support may decline to decide contested issues of physical care, custody, visitation, or family support unless a decision on one or more of those contested issues is necessary to avoid the risk of abuse, neglect, removal from the state or concealment within the state of the child or of separation of the child from the primary caretaker. If the court or division thereof has declined to decide any or all of these issues, then it shall transfer all undecided issues to the appropriate court or division. In the event of such a transfer, a government attorney involved in the criminal prosecution may, but need not, continue to offer counsel to petitioner on transferred matters.

(c) If the court transfers or otherwise declines to decide any issue, judgment on that issue shall be expressly reserved and ruling on other issues shall not be delayed or declined.

750 ILCS 60/213 Continuances.

(a) Petitions for emergency orders. Petitions for emergency remedies shall be granted or denied in accordance with the standards of Section 217, regardless of respondent's appearance or presence in court.

(b) Petitions for interim and plenary orders. Any action for an order of protection is an expedited proceeding. Continuances should be granted only for good cause shown and kept to the minimum reasonable duration, taking into account the reasons for the continuance. If the continuance is necessary for some, but not all, of the remedies requested, hearing on those other remedies shall not be delayed.

750 ILCS 60/213 Hearsay exception. In an action for an order of protection on behalf of a high-risk adult with disabilities, a finding of lack of capacity to testify shall not render inadmissible any statement as long as the reliability of the statement is ensured by circumstances bringing it within the scope of a hearsay exception. The following evidence shall be admitted as an exception to the hearsay rule whether or not the declarant is available as a witness:

(1) A statement relating to a startling event or condition made spontaneously while the declarant was under the contemporaneous or continuing stress of excitement caused by the event or condition.

(2) A statement made for the purpose of obtaining, receiving, or promoting medical diagnosis or treatment, including psychotherapy, and describing medical history, or past or present symptoms, pain, or sensations, or the inception or general character of the cause or external source thereof insofar as reasonably pertinent to diagnosis or treatment. For purposes of obtaining a protective order, the identity of any person inflicting abuse or neglect as defined in this Act shall be deemed reasonably pertinent to diagnosis or treatment.

(3) A statement not specifically covered by any of the foregoing exceptions but having equivalent circumstantial guarantees of trustworthiness, if the court determines that (A) the statement is offered as evidence of a material fact, and (B) the statement is more probative on the point for which it is offered than any other evidence which the proponent can procure through reasonable efforts.

Circumstantial guarantees of trustworthiness include:

(1) the credibility of the witness who testifies the statement was made;

(2) assurance of the declarant's personal knowledge of the event;

(3) the declarant's interest or bias and the presence or absence of capacity or motive to fabricate;

(4) the presence or absence of suggestiveness or prompting at the time the statement was made;

(5) whether the declarant has ever reaffirmed or recanted the statement; and

(6) corroboration by physical evidence or behavioral changes in the declarant.

The record shall reflect the court's findings of fact and conclusions of law as to the trustworthiness requirement.

A statement shall not be admitted under the exception set forth in this Section unless its proponent gives written notice stating his or her intention to offer the statement and the particulars of it to the adverse party sufficiently in advance of offering the statement to provide the adverse party with a fair opportunity to prepare to meet the statement.

(750 ILCS 60/213.2 Waiver of privilege. When the subject of any proceeding under this Act is a high-risk adult with disabilities for whom no guardian has been appointed, no party other than the high-risk adult or the attorney for the high-risk adult shall be entitled to invoke or waive a common law or statutory privilege on behalf of the high-risk adult which results in the exclusion of evidence.

750 ILCS 60/213.3 Independent counsel; temporary substitute guardian. If the petitioner is a high-risk adult with disabilities for whom a guardian has been appointed, the court shall appoint independent counsel other than a guardian ad litem and, may appoint a temporary substitute guardian under the provisions of Article XIa of the Probate Act of 1975. The court shall appoint a temporary substitute guardian if the guardian is named as a respondent in a petition under this Act.

750 ILCS 60/214 Order of protection; remedies.

(a) Issuance of order. If the court finds that petitioner has been abused by a family or household member or that petitioner is a high-risk adult who has been abused, neglected, or exploited, as defined in this Act, an order of protection prohibiting the abuse, neglect, or exploitation shall issue; provided that petitioner must also satisfy the requirements of one of the following Sections, as appropriate: Section 217 on emergency orders, Section 218 on interim orders, or Section 219 on plenary orders. Petitioner shall not be denied an order of protection because petitioner or respondent is a minor. The court, when determining whether or not to issue an order of protection, shall not require physical manifestations of abuse on the person of the victim. Modification and extension of prior orders of protection shall be in accordance with this Act.

(b) Remedies and standards. The remedies to be included in an order of protection shall be determined in accordance with this Section and one of the following Sections, as appropriate: Section 217 on emergency orders, Section 218 on interim orders, and Section 219 on plenary orders. The remedies listed in this subsection shall be in addition to other civil or criminal remedies available to petitioner.

(1) Prohibition of abuse, neglect, or exploitation.

Prohibit respondent's harassment, interference with personal liberty, intimidation of a dependent, physical abuse, or willful deprivation, neglect or exploitation, as defined in this Act, or stalking of the petitioner, as defined in Section 12-7.3 of the Criminal Code of 1961, if such abuse, neglect, exploitation, or stalking has occurred or otherwise appears likely to occur if not prohibited.

(2) Grant of exclusive possession of residence.

Prohibit respondent from entering or remaining in any residence or household of the petitioner, including one owned or leased by respondent, if petitioner has a right to occupancy thereof. The grant of exclusive possession of the residence shall not affect title to real property, nor shall the court be limited by the standard set forth in Section 701 of the Illinois Marriage and Dissolution of Marriage Act.

(A) Right to occupancy. A party has a right to occupancy of a residence or household if it is solely or jointly owned or leased by that party, that party's spouse, a person with a legal duty to support that party or a minor child in that party's care, or by any person or entity other than the opposing party that authorizes that party's occupancy (e.g., a domestic violence shelter). Standards set forth in subparagraph (B) shall not preclude equitable relief.

(B) Presumption of hardships. If petitioner and respondent each has the right to occupancy of a residence or household, the court shall balance (i) the hardships to respondent and any minor child or dependent adult in respondent's care resulting from entry of this remedy with (ii) the hardships to petitioner and any minor child or dependent adult in petitioner's care resulting from continued exposure to the risk of abuse (should petitioner remain at the residence or household) or from loss of possession of the residence or household (should petitioner leave to avoid the risk of abuse). When determining the balance of hardships, the court shall also take into account the accessibility of the residence or household. Hardships need not be balanced if respondent does not have a right to occupancy.

The balance of hardships is presumed to favor possession by petitioner unless the presumption is rebutted by a preponderance of the evidence, showing that the hardships to respondent substantially outweigh the hardships to petitioner and any minor child or dependent adult in petitioner's care. The court, on the request of petitioner or on its own motion, may order respondent to provide suitable, accessible, alternate housing for petitioner instead of excluding respondent from a mutual residence or household.

(3) Stay away order and additional prohibitions.

Order respondent to stay away from petitioner or any other person protected by the order of protection, or prohibit respondent from entering or remaining present at petitioner's school, place of employment, or other specified places at times when petitioner is present, or both, if reasonable, given the balance of hardships. Hardships need not be balanced for the court to enter a stay away order or prohibit entry if respondent has no right to enter the premises.

If an order of protection grants petitioner exclusive possession of the residence, or prohibits respondent from entering the residence, or orders respondent to stay away from petitioner or other protected persons, then the court may allow respondent access to the residence to remove items of clothing and personal adornment used exclusively by respondent, medications, and other items as the court directs. The right to access shall be exercised on only one occasion as the court directs and in the presence of an agreed-upon adult third party or law enforcement officer.

(4) Counseling. Require or recommend the respondent to undergo counseling for a specified duration with a social worker, psychologist, clinical psychologist, psychiatrist, family service agency, alcohol or substance abuse program, mental health center guidance counselor, agency providing services to elders, program designed for domestic violence abusers or any other guidance service the court deems appropriate.

(5) Physical care and possession of the minor child.

In order to protect the minor child from abuse, neglect, or unwarranted separation from the person who has been the minor child's primary caretaker, or to otherwise protect the well-being of the minor child, the court may do either or both of the following: (i) grant petitioner physical care or possession of the minor child, or both, or (ii) order respondent to return a minor child to, or not remove a minor child from, the physical care of a parent or person in loco parentis.

If a court finds, after a hearing, that respondent has committed abuse (as defined in Section 103) of a minor child, there shall be a rebuttable presumption that awarding physical care to respondent would not be in the minor child's best interest.

(6) Temporary legal custody. Award temporary legal custody to petitioner in accordance with this Section, the Illinois Marriage and Dissolution of Marriage Act, the Illinois Parentage Act of 1984, and this State's Uniform Child-Custody Jurisdiction and Enforcement Act.

If a court finds, after a hearing, that respondent has committed abuse (as defined in Section 103) of a minor child, there shall be a rebuttable presumption that awarding temporary legal custody to respondent would not be in the child's best interest.

(7) Visitation. Determine the visitation rights, if any, of respondent in any case in which the court awards physical care or temporary legal custody of a minor child to petitioner. The court shall restrict or deny respondent's visitation with a minor child if the court finds that respondent has done or is likely to do any of the following: (i) abuse or

endanger the minor child during visitation; (ii) use the visitation as an opportunity to abuse or harass petitioner or petitioner's family or household members; (iii) improperly conceal or detain the minor child; or (iv) otherwise act in a manner that is not in the best interests of the minor child. The court shall not be limited by the standards set forth in Section 607.1 of the Illinois Marriage and Dissolution of Marriage Act. If the court grants visitation, the order shall specify dates and times for the visitation to take place or other specific parameters or conditions that are appropriate. No order for visitation shall refer merely to the term "reasonable visitation".

Petitioner may deny respondent access to the minor child if, when respondent arrives for visitation, respondent is under the influence of drugs or alcohol and constitutes a threat to the safety and well-being of petitioner or petitioner's minor children or is behaving in a violent or abusive manner.

If necessary to protect any member of petitioner's family or household from future abuse, respondent shall be prohibited from coming to petitioner's residence to meet the minor child for visitation, and the parties shall submit to the court their recommendations for reasonable alternative arrangements for visitation. A person may be approved to supervise visitation only after filing an affidavit accepting that responsibility and acknowledging accountability to the court.

(8) Removal or concealment of minor child. Prohibit respondent from removing a minor child from the State or concealing the child within the State.

(9) Order to appear. Order the respondent to appear in court, alone or with a minor child, to prevent abuse, neglect, removal or concealment of the child, to return the child to the custody or care of the petitioner or to permit any court-ordered interview or examination of the child or the respondent.

(10) Possession of personal property. Grant petitioner exclusive possession of personal property and, if respondent has possession or control, direct respondent to promptly make it available to petitioner, if:

(i) petitioner, but not respondent, owns the property; or

(ii) the parties own the property jointly; sharing it would risk abuse of petitioner by respondent or is impracticable; and the balance of hardships favors temporary possession by petitioner.

If petitioner's sole claim to ownership of the property is that it is marital property, the court may award petitioner temporary possession thereof under the standards of subparagraph (ii) of this paragraph only if a proper proceeding has been filed under the Illinois Marriage and Dissolution of Marriage Act, as now or hereafter amended.

No order under this provision shall affect title to property.

(11) Protection of property. Forbid the respondent from taking, transferring, encumbering, concealing, damaging or otherwise disposing of any real or personal property, except as explicitly authorized by the court, if:

(i) petitioner, but not respondent, owns the property; or

(ii) the parties own the property jointly, and the balance of hardships favors granting this remedy.

If petitioner's sole claim to ownership of the property is that it is marital property, the court may grant petitioner relief under subparagraph (ii) of this paragraph only if a proper proceeding has been filed under the Illinois Marriage and Dissolution of Marriage Act, as now or hereafter amended.

The court may further prohibit respondent from improperly using the financial or other resources of an aged member of the family or household for the profit or advantage of respondent or of any other person.

(12) Order for payment of support. Order respondent to pay temporary support for the petitioner or any child in the petitioner's care or custody, when the respondent has a legal obligation to support that person, in accordance with the Illinois Marriage and Dissolution of Marriage Act, which shall govern, among other matters, the amount of support, payment through the clerk and withholding of income to secure payment. An order for child support may be granted to a petitioner with lawful physical care or custody of a child, or an order or agreement for physical care or custody, prior to entry of an order for legal custody. Such a support order shall expire upon entry of a valid order granting legal custody to another, unless otherwise provided in the custody order.

(13) Order for payment of losses. Order respondent to pay petitioner for losses suffered as a direct result of the abuse, neglect, or exploitation. Such losses shall include, but not be limited to, medical expenses, lost earnings or other support, repair or replacement of property damaged or taken, reasonable attorney's fees, court costs and moving or other travel expenses, including additional reasonable expenses for temporary shelter and restaurant meals.

(i) Losses affecting family needs. If a party is entitled to seek maintenance, child support or property distribution from the other party under the Illinois Marriage and Dissolution of Marriage Act, as now or hereafter amended, the court may order respondent to reimburse petitioner's actual losses, to the extent that such reimbursement would be "appropriate temporary relief", as authorized by subsection (a)(3) of Section 501 of that Act.

(ii) Recovery of expenses. In the case of an improper concealment or removal of a minor child, the court may order respondent to pay the reasonable expenses incurred or to be incurred in the search for and recovery of the minor child, including but not limited to legal fees, court costs, private investigator fees, and travel costs.

(14) Prohibition of entry. Prohibit the respondent from entering or remaining in the residence or household while the respondent is under the influence of alcohol or drugs and constitutes a threat to the safety and well-being of the petitioner or the petitioner's children.

(14.5) Prohibition of firearm possession.

(a) When a complaint is made under a request for an order of protection, that the respondent has threatened or is likely to use firearms illegally against the petitioner, and the respondent is present in court, or has failed to appear after receiving actual notice, the court shall examine on oath the petitioner, and any witnesses who may be produced. If the court is satisfied that there is any danger of the illegal use of firearms, it shall issue an order that any firearms in the possession of the respondent, except as provided in subsection (b), be turned over to the local law enforcement agency for safekeeping. If the respondent has failed to appear, the court shall issue a warrant for seizure of any firearm in the possession of the respondent. The period of safekeeping shall be for a stated period of time not to exceed 2 years. The firearm or firearms shall be returned to the respondent at the end of the stated period or at expiration of the order of protection, whichever is sooner.

(b) If the respondent is a peace officer as defined in Section 2-13 of the Criminal Code of 1961, the court shall order that any firearms used by the respondent in the performance of his or her duties as a peace officer be surrendered to the chief law enforcement executive of the agency in which the respondent is employed, who shall retain the firearms for safekeeping for the stated period not to exceed 2 years as set forth in the court order.

(15) Prohibition of access to records. If an order of protection prohibits respondent from having contact with the minor child, or if petitioner's address is omitted under subsection (b) of Section 203, or if necessary to prevent abuse or wrongful removal or concealment of a minor child, the order shall deny respondent access to, and prohibit respondent from inspecting, obtaining, or attempting to inspect or obtain, school or any other records of the minor child who is in the care of petitioner.

(16) Order for payment of shelter services. Order respondent to reimburse a shelter providing temporary housing and counseling services to the petitioner for the cost of the services, as certified by the shelter and deemed reasonable by the court.

(17) Order for injunctive relief. Enter injunctive relief necessary or appropriate to prevent further abuse of a family or household member or further abuse, neglect, or exploitation of a high-risk adult with disabilities or to effectuate one of the granted remedies, if supported by the balance of hardships. If the harm to be prevented by the injunction is abuse or any other harm that one of the remedies listed in paragraphs (1) through (16) of this subsection is designed to prevent, no further evidence is necessary that the harm is an irreparable injury.

(c) Relevant factors; findings.

(1) In determining whether to grant a specific remedy, other than payment of support, the court shall consider relevant factors, including but not limited to the following:

(i) the nature, frequency, severity, pattern and consequences of the respondent's past abuse, neglect or exploitation of the petitioner or any family or household member, including the concealment of his or her location in order to evade service of process or notice, and the likelihood of danger of future abuse, neglect, or exploitation to petitioner or any member of petitioner's or respondent's family or household; and

(ii) the danger that any minor child will be abused or neglected or improperly removed from the jurisdiction, improperly concealed within the State or improperly separated from the child's primary caretaker.

(2) In comparing relative hardships resulting to the parties from loss of possession of the family home, the court shall consider relevant factors, including but not limited to the following:

(i) availability, accessibility, cost, safety, adequacy, location and other characteristics of alternate housing for each party and any minor child or dependent adult in the party's care;

(ii) the effect on the party's employment; and

(iii) the effect on the relationship of the party, and any minor child or dependent adult in the party's care, to family, school, church and community.

(3) Subject to the exceptions set forth in paragraph (4) of this subsection, the court shall make its findings in an official record or in writing, and shall at a minimum set forth the following:

(i) That the court has considered the applicable relevant factors described in paragraphs (1) and (2) of this subsection.

(ii) Whether the conduct or actions of respondent, unless prohibited, will likely cause irreparable harm or continued abuse.

(iii) Whether it is necessary to grant the requested relief in order to protect petitioner or other alleged abused persons.

(4) For purposes of issuing an ex parte emergency order of protection, the court, as an alternative to or as a supplement to making the findings described in paragraphs (c)(3)(i) through (c)(3)(iii) of this subsection, may use the following procedure:

When a verified petition for an emergency order of protection in accordance with the requirements of Sections 203 and 217 is presented to the court, the court shall examine petitioner on oath or affirmation. An emergency order of protection shall be issued by the court if it appears from the contents of the petition and the examination of petitioner that the averments are sufficient to indicate abuse by respondent and to support the granting of relief under the issuance of the emergency order of protection.

(5) Never married parties. No rights or responsibilities for a minor child born outside of marriage attach to a putative father until a father and child relationship has been established under the Illinois Parentage Act of 1984, the Illinois Public Aid Code, Section 12 of the Vital Records Act, the Juvenile Court Act of 1987, the Probate Act of 1985, the Revised Uniform Reciprocal Enforcement of Support Act, the Uniform Interstate Family Support Act, the Expedited Child Support Act of 1990, any judicial, administrative, or other act of another state or territory, any other Illinois statute, or by any

foreign nation establishing the father and child relationship, any other proceeding substantially in conformity with the Personal Responsibility and Work Opportunity Reconciliation Act of 1996 (Pub. L. 104-193), or where both parties appeared in open court or at an administrative hearing acknowledging under oath or admitting by affirmation the existence of a father and child relationship. Absent such an adjudication, finding, or acknowledgement, no putative father shall be granted temporary custody of the minor child, visitation with the minor child, or physical care and possession of the minor child, nor shall an order of payment for support of the minor child be entered.

(d) Balance of hardships; findings. If the court finds that the balance of hardships does not support the granting of a remedy governed by paragraph (2), (3), (10), (11), or (16) of subsection (b) of this Section, which may require such balancing, the court's findings shall so indicate and shall include a finding as to whether granting the remedy will result in hardship to respondent that would substantially outweigh the hardship to petitioner from denial of the remedy. The findings shall be an official record or in writing.

(e) Denial of remedies. Denial of any remedy shall not be based, in whole or in part, on evidence that:

(1) Respondent has cause for any use of force, unless that cause satisfies the standards for justifiable use of force provided by Article VII of the Criminal Code of 1961;

(2) Respondent was voluntarily intoxicated;

(3) Petitioner acted in self-defense or defense of another, provided that, if petitioner utilized force, such force was justifiable under Article VII of the Criminal Code of 1961;

(4) Petitioner did not act in self-defense or defense of another;

(5) Petitioner left the residence or household to avoid further abuse, neglect, or exploitation by respondent;

(6) Petitioner did not leave the residence or household to avoid further abuse, neglect, or exploitation by respondent;

(7) Conduct by any family or household member excused the abuse, neglect, or exploitation by respondent, unless that same conduct would have excused such abuse, neglect, or exploitation if the parties had not been family or household members.

750 ILCS 60/215 Mutual orders of protection; correlative separate orders. Mutual orders of protection are prohibited. Correlative separate orders of protection undermine the purposes of this Act and are prohibited unless both parties have properly filed written pleadings, proved past abuse by the other party, given prior written notice to the other party unless excused under Section 217, satisfied all prerequisites for the type of order and each remedy granted, and otherwise complied with this Act. In these cases, the court shall hear relevant evidence, make findings, and issue separate orders in accordance with Sections 214 and 221. The fact that correlative separate orders are issued shall not be a sufficient basis to deny any remedy to petitioner or to prove that the parties are equally at fault or equally endangered.

750 ILCS 60/216 Accountability for Actions of Others. For the purposes of issuing an order of protection, deciding what remedies should be included and enforcing the order, Article 5 of the Criminal Code of 1961 shall govern whether respondent is legally accountable for the conduct of another person.

750 ILCS 60/217 Emergency order of protection.

(a) Prerequisites. An emergency order of protection shall issue if petitioner satisfies the requirements of this subsection for one or more of the requested remedies. For each remedy requested, petitioner shall establish that:

(1) The court has jurisdiction under Section 208;

(2) The requirements of Section 214 are satisfied; and

(3) There is good cause to grant the remedy, regardless of prior service of process or of notice upon the respondent, because:

(i) For the remedies of "prohibition of abuse" described in Section 214(b)(1), "stay away order and additional prohibitions" described in Section 214(b)(3), "removal or concealment of minor child" described in Section 214(b)(8), "order to appear" described in Section 214(b)(9), "physical care and possession of the minor child" described in Section 214(b)(5), "protection of property" described in Section 214(b)(11), "prohibition of entry" described in Section 214(b)(14), "prohibition of access to records" described in Section 214(b)(15), and "injunctive relief" described in Section 214(b)(16), the harm which that remedy is intended to prevent would be likely to occur if the respondent were given any prior notice, or greater notice than was actually given, of the petitioner's efforts to obtain judicial relief;

(ii) For the remedy of "grant of exclusive possession of residence" described in Section 214(b)(2), the immediate danger of further abuse of petitioner by respondent, if petitioner chooses or had chosen to remain in the residence or household while respondent was given any prior notice or greater notice than was actually given of petitioner's efforts to obtain judicial relief, outweighs the hardships to respondent of an emergency order granting petitioner exclusive possession of the residence or household. This remedy shall not be denied because petitioner has or could obtain temporary shelter elsewhere while prior notice is given to respondent, unless the hardships to respondent from exclusion from the home substantially outweigh those to petitioner;

(iii) For the remedy of "possession of personal property" described in Section 214(b)(10), improper disposition of the personal property would be likely to occur if respondent were given any prior notice, or greater notice than was actually given, of petitioner's efforts to obtain judicial relief, or petitioner has an immediate and pressing need for possession of that property.

An emergency order may not include the counseling, legal custody, payment of support or monetary compensation remedies.

(b) Appearance by respondent. If respondent appears in court for this hearing for an emergency order, he or she may elect to file a general appearance and testify. Any resulting order may be an emergency order, governed by this Section.

Notwithstanding the requirements of this Section, if all requirements of Section 218 have been met, the court may issue a 30-day interim order.

(c) Emergency orders: court holidays and evenings.

(1) Prerequisites. When the court is unavailable at the close of business, the petitioner may file a petition for a 21-day emergency order before any available circuit judge or associate judge who may grant relief under this Act. If the judge finds that there is an immediate and present danger of abuse to petitioner and that petitioner has satisfied the prerequisites set forth in subsection (a) of Section 217, that judge may issue an emergency order of protection.

(1.5) Issuance of order. The chief judge of the circuit court may designate for each county in the circuit at least one judge to be reasonably available to issue orally, by telephone, by facsimile, or otherwise, an emergency order of protection at all times, whether or not the court is in session.

(2) Certification and transfer. Any order issued under this Section and any documentation in support thereof shall be certified on the next court day to the appropriate court. The clerk of that court shall immediately assign a case number, file the petition, order and other documents with the court, and enter the order of record and file it with the sheriff for service, in accordance with Section 222. Filing the petition shall commence proceedings for further relief under Section 202. Failure to comply with the requirements of this subsection shall not affect the validity of the order.

750 ILCS 60/218 30-Day interim order of protection.

(a) Prerequisites. An interim order of protection shall issue if petitioner has served notice of the hearing for that order on respondent, in accordance with Section 211, and satisfies the requirements of this subsection for one or more of the requested remedies. For each remedy requested, petitioner shall establish that:

(1) The court has jurisdiction under Section 208;

(2) The requirements of Section 214 are satisfied; and

(3) A general appearance was made or filed by or for respondent; or process was served on respondent in the manner required by Section 210; or the petitioner is diligently attempting to complete the required service of process.

An interim order may not include the counseling, payment of support or monetary compensation remedies, unless the respondent has filed a general appearance or has been personally served.

(b) Appearance by respondent. If respondent appears in court for this hearing for an interim order, he or she may elect to file a general appearance and testify. Any resulting order may be an interim order, governed by this Section. Notwithstanding the requirements of this Section, if all requirements of Section 219 have been met, the Court may issue a plenary order of protection.

750 ILCS 60/219 Plenary Order of Protection. A plenary order of protection shall issue if petitioner has served notice of the hearing for that order on respondent, in accordance with Section 211, and satisfies the requirements of this Section for

one or more of the requested remedies. For each remedy requested, petitioner must establish that:

(1) The court has jurisdiction under Section 208;

(2) The requirements of Section 214 are satisfied; and

(3) A general appearance was made or filed by or for respondent or process was served on respondent in the manner required by Section 210; and

(4) Respondent has answered or is in default.

750 ILCS 60/220 Duration and extension of orders.

(a) Duration of emergency and interim orders. Unless re-opened or extended or voided by entry of an order of greater duration:

(1) Emergency orders issued under Section 217 shall be effective for not less than 14 nor more than 21 days;

(2) Interim orders shall be effective for up to 30 days.

(b) Duration of plenary orders. Except as otherwise provided in this Section, a plenary order of protection shall be valid for a fixed period of time, not to exceed two years.

(1) A plenary order of protection entered in conjunction with another civil proceeding shall remain in effect as follows:

(i) if entered as preliminary relief in that other proceeding, until entry of final judgment in that other proceeding;

(ii) if incorporated into the final judgment in that other proceeding, until the order of protection is vacated or modified; or

(iii) if incorporated in an order for involuntary commitment, until termination of both the involuntary commitment and any voluntary commitment, or for a fixed period of time not exceeding 2 years.

(2) A plenary order of protection entered in conjunction with a criminal prosecution shall remain in effect as follows:

(i) if entered during pre-trial release, until disposition, withdrawal, or dismissal of the underlying charge; if, however, the case is continued as an independent cause of action, the order's duration may be for a fixed period of time not to exceed 2 years;

(ii) if in effect in conjunction with a bond forfeiture warrant, until final disposition or an additional period of time not exceeding 2 years; no order of protection, however, shall be terminated by a dismissal that is accompanied by the issuance of a bond forfeiture warrant;

(iii) until expiration of any supervision, conditional discharge, probation, periodic imprisonment, parole or mandatory supervised release and for an additional period of time thereafter not exceeding 2 years; or

(iv) until the date set by the court for expiration of any sentence of imprisonment and subsequent parole or mandatory supervised release and for an additional period of time thereafter not exceeding 2 years.

(c) Computation of time. The duration of an order of protection shall not be reduced by the duration of any prior order of protection.

(d) Law enforcement records. When a plenary order of protection expires upon the occurrence of a specified event, rather than upon a specified date as provided in subsection (b), no expiration date shall be entered in Department of State Police records. To remove the plenary order from those records, either party shall request the clerk of the court to file a certified copy of an order stating that the specified event has occurred or that the plenary order has been vacated or modified with the Sheriff, and the Sheriff shall direct that law enforcement records shall be promptly corrected in accordance with the filed order.

(e) Extension of orders. Any emergency, interim or plenary order may be extended one or more times, as required, provided that the requirements of Section 217, 218 or 219, as appropriate, are satisfied. If the motion for extension is uncontested and petitioner seeks no modification of the order, the order may be extended on the basis of petitioner's motion or affidavit stating that there has been no material change in relevant circumstances since entry of the order and stating the reason for the requested extension. Extensions may be granted only in open court and not under the provisions of subsection (c) of Section 217, which applies only when the court is unavailable at the close of business or on a court holiday.

(f) Termination date. Any order of protection which would expire on a court holiday shall instead expire at the close of the next court business day.

(g) Statement of purpose. The practice of dismissing or suspending a criminal prosecution in exchange for the issuance of an order of protection undermines the purposes of this Act. This Section shall not be construed as encouraging that practice.

750 ILCS 60/221 Contents of orders.

(a) Any order of protection shall describe the following:

(1) Each remedy granted by the court, in reasonable detail and not by reference to any other document, so that respondent may clearly understand what he or she must do or refrain from doing. Pre-printed form orders of protection shall include the definitions of the types of abuse, neglect, and exploitation, as provided in Section 103. Remedies set forth in pre-printed form orders shall be numbered consistently with and corresponding to the numerical sequence of remedies listed in Section 214 (at least as of the date the form orders are printed).

(2) The reason for denial of petitioner's request for any remedy listed in Section 214.

(b) An order of protection shall further state the following:

(1) The name of each petitioner that the court finds was abused, neglected, or exploited by respondent, and that respondent is a member of the family or household of each such petitioner, and the name of each other person protected by the order and that such person is protected by this Act.

(2) For any remedy requested by petitioner on which the court has declined to rule, that that remedy is reserved.

(3) The date and time the order of protection was issued, whether it is an emergency, interim or plenary order and the duration of the order.

(4) The date, time and place for any scheduled hearing for extension of that order of protection or for another order of greater duration or scope.

(5) For each remedy in an emergency order of protection, the reason for entering that remedy without prior notice to respondent or greater notice than was actually given.

(6) For emergency and interim orders of protection, that respondent may petition the court, in accordance with Section 224, to re-open that order if he or she did not receive actual prior notice of the hearing, in accordance with Section 211, and alleges that he or she had a meritorious defense to the order or that the order or any of its remedies was not authorized by this Act.

(c) Any order of protection shall include the following notice, printed in conspicuous type: "Any knowing violation of an order of protection forbidding physical abuse, neglect, exploitation, harassment, intimidation, interference with personal liberty, willful deprivation, or entering or remaining present at specified places when the protected person is present, or granting exclusive possession of the residence or household, or granting a stay away order is a Class A misdemeanor. Grant of exclusive possession of the residence or household shall constitute notice forbidding trespass to land. Any knowing violation of an order awarding legal custody or physical care of a child or prohibiting removal or concealment of a child may be a Class 4 felony. Any willful violation of any order is contempt of court. Any violation may result in fine or imprisonment."

(d) An emergency order of protection shall state, "This Order of Protection is enforceable, even without registration, in all 50 states, the District of Columbia, tribal lands, and the U.S. territories pursuant to the Violence Against Women Act (18 U.S.C. 2265). Violating this Order of Protection may subject the respondent to federal charges and punishment (18 U.S.C. 2261-2262)."

(e) An interim or plenary order of protection shall state, "This Order of Protection is enforceable, even without registration, in all 50 states, the District of Columbia, tribal lands, and the U.S. territories pursuant to the Violence Against Women Act (18 U.S.C. 2265). Violating this Order of Protection may subject the respondent to federal charges and punishment (18 U.S.C. 2261-2262). The respondent may be subject to federal criminal penalties for possessing, transporting, shipping, or receiving any firearm or ammunition under the Gun Control Act (18 U.S.C. 922(g)(8) and (9))."

750 ILCS 60/222 Notice of orders.

(a) Entry and issuance. Upon issuance of any order of protection, the clerk shall immediately, or on the next court day if an emergency order is issued in accordance with subsection (c) of Section 217, (i) enter the order on the record and file it in accordance with the circuit court procedures and (ii) provide a file stamped copy of the order to respondent, if present, and to petitioner.

(b) Filing with sheriff. The clerk of the issuing judge shall, or the petitioner may, on the same day that an order of protection is issued, file a certified copy of that order with the sheriff or other law enforcement officials charged with maintaining Department of State Police records or charged with serving the order upon respondent. If the order was issued in accordance with subsection (c) of Section 217, the clerk shall on the next court day, file a certified copy of the order with the Sheriff or other law enforcement officials charged with maintaining Department of State Police records.

(c) Service by sheriff. Unless respondent was present in court when the order was issued, the sheriff, other law enforcement official or special process server shall promptly serve that order upon respondent and file proof of such service, in the manner provided for service of process in civil proceedings. Instead of serving the order upon the respondent, however, the sheriff, other law enforcement official, or special process server may serve the respondent with a short form notification as provided in Section 222.10. If process has not yet been served upon the respondent, it shall be served with the order or short form notification. A single fee may be charged for service of an order obtained in civil court, or for service of such an order together with process, unless waived or deferred under Section 210.

(c-5) If the person against whom the order of protection is issued is arrested and the written order is issued in accordance with subsection (c) of Section 217 and received by the custodial law enforcement agency before the respondent or arrestee is released from custody, the custodial law enforcement agent shall promptly serve the order upon the respondent or arrestee before the respondent or arrestee is released from custody. In no event shall detention of the respondent or arrestee be extended for hearing on the petition for order of protection or receipt of the order issued under Section 217 of this Act.

(d) Extensions, modifications and revocations. Any order extending, modifying or revoking any order of protection shall be promptly recorded, issued and served as provided in this Section.

(e) Notice to schools. Upon the request of the petitioner, within 24 hours of the issuance of an order of protection, the clerk of the issuing judge shall send written notice of the order of protection along with a certified copy of the order of protection to the day-care facility, pre-school or pre-kindergarten, or private school or the principal office of the public school district or any college or university in which any child who is a protected person under the order of protection or any child of the petitioner is enrolled. If the child transfers enrollment to another day-care facility, pre-school, pre-kindergarten, private school, public school, college, or university, the petitioner may, within 24 hours of the transfer, send to the clerk written notice of the transfer, including the name and address of the institution to which the child is transferring. Within 24 hours of receipt of notice from the petitioner that a child is transferring to another day-care facility, pre-school, pre-kindergarten, private school, public school, college, or university, the clerk shall send written notice of the order of protection, along with a certified copy of the order, to the institution to which the child is transferring.

(f) Disclosure by schools. After receiving a certified copy of an order of protection that prohibits a respondent's access to records, neither a day-care facility, pre-school, pre-kindergarten, public or private school, college, or university nor its employees shall allow a respondent access to a protected child's records or release information in those records to the respondent. The school shall file the copy of the order of protection in the records of a child who is a protected person under the order of protection. When a child who is a protected person under the order of protection transfers to another day-care facility, pre-school, pre-kindergarten, public or private school, college, or university, the institution from which the child is transferring may, at the request of the petitioner, provide, within 24 hours of the transfer, written notice of the order of protection, along with a certified copy of the order, to the institution to which the child is transferring.

750 ILCS 60/222.5 Filing of an order of protection issued in another state.

(a) A person entitled to protection under an order of protection issued by the court of another state, tribe, or United States territory may file a certified copy of the order of protection with the clerk of the court in a judicial circuit in which the person believes that enforcement may be necessary.

(b) The clerk shall:

(1) treat the foreign order of protection in the same manner as a judgment of the circuit court for any county of this State in accordance with the provisions of the Uniform Enforcement of Foreign Judgments Act, except that the clerk shall not mail notice of the filing of the foreign order to the respondent named in the order; and

(2) on the same day that a foreign order of protection is filed, file a certified copy of that order with the sheriff or other law enforcement officials charged with maintaining Department of State Police records as set forth in Section 222 of this Act.

(c) Neither residence in this State nor filing of a foreign order of protection shall be required for enforcement of the order by this State. Failure to file the foreign order shall not be an impediment to its treatment in all respects as an Illinois order of protection.

(d) The clerk shall not charge a fee to file a foreign order of protection under this Section.

(e) The sheriff shall inform the Department of State Police as set forth in Section 302 of this Act.

750 ILCS 60/222.10 Short form notification.

(a) Instead of personal service of an order of protection under Section 222, a sheriff, other law enforcement official, or special process server may serve a respondent with a short form notification. The short form notification must include the following items:

(1) The respondent's name.
(2) The respondent's date of birth, if known.
(3) The petitioner's name.
(4) The names of other protected parties.
(5) The date and county in which the order of protection was filed.
(6) The court file number.

(7) The hearing date and time, if known.

(8) The conditions that apply to the respondent, either in checklist form or handwritten.

(9) The name of the judge who signed the order.

(b) The short form notification must contain the following notice in bold print:

"The order of protection is now enforceable. You must report to the office of the sheriff or the office of the circuit court in (name of county) County to obtain a copy of the order of protection. You are subject to arrest and may be charged with a misdemeanor or felony if you violate any of the terms of the order of protection."

(c) Upon verification of the identity of the respondent and the existence of an unserved order of protection against the respondent, a sheriff or other law enforcement official may detain the respondent for a reasonable time necessary to complete and serve the short form notification.

(d) When service is made by short form notification under this Section, it may be proved by the affidavit of the sheriff, other law enforcement official, or special process server making the service.

(e) The Attorney General shall provide adequate copies of the short form notification form to law enforcement agencies in this State.

750 ILCS 60/223 Enforcement of orders of protection.

(a) When violation is crime. A violation of any order of protection, whether issued in a civil or criminal proceeding, shall be enforced by a criminal court when:

(1) The respondent commits the crime of violation of an order of protection pursuant to Section 12-30 of the Criminal Code of 1961, by having knowingly violated:

(i) remedies described in paragraphs (1), (2), (3), (14), or (14.5) of subsection (b) of Section 214 of this Act; or

(ii) a remedy, which is substantially similar to the remedies authorized under paragraphs (1), (2), (3), (14), and (14.5) of subsection (b) of Section 214 of this Act, in a valid order of protection which is authorized under the laws of another state, tribe, or United States territory; or

(iii) any other remedy when the act constitutes a crime against the protected parties as defined by the Criminal Code of 1961.

Prosecution for a violation of an order of protection shall not bar concurrent prosecution for any other crime, including any crime that may have been committed at the time of the violation of the order of protection; or

(2) The respondent commits the crime of child abduction pursuant to Section 10-5 of the Criminal Code of 1961, by having knowingly violated:

(i) remedies described in paragraphs (5), (6) or (8) of subsection (b) of Section 214 of this Act; or

(ii) a remedy, which is substantially similar to the remedies authorized under paragraphs (5), (6), or (8) of subsection (b) of Section 214 of this Act, in a valid order of protection which is authorized under the laws of another state, tribe, or United States territory.

(b) When violation is contempt of court. A violation of any valid Illinois order of protection, whether issued in a civil or criminal proceeding, may be enforced through civil or criminal contempt procedures, as appropriate, by any court with jurisdiction, regardless where the act or acts which violated the order of protection were committed, to the extent consistent with the venue provisions of this Act. Nothing in this Act shall preclude any Illinois court from enforcing any valid order of protection issued in another state. Illinois courts may enforce orders of protection through both criminal prosecution and contempt proceedings, unless the action which is second in time is barred by collateral estoppel or the constitutional prohibition against double jeopardy.

(1) In a contempt proceeding where the petition for a rule to show cause sets forth facts evidencing an immediate danger that the respondent will flee the jurisdiction, conceal a child, or inflict physical abuse on the petitioner or minor children or on dependent adults in petitioner's care, the court may order the attachment of the respondent without prior service of the rule to show cause or the petition for a rule to show cause. Bond shall be set unless specifically denied in writing.

(2) A petition for a rule to show cause for violation of an order of protection shall be treated as an expedited proceeding.

(c) Violation of custody or support orders. A violation of remedies described in paragraphs (5), (6), (8), or (9) of subsection (b) of Section 214 of this Act may be enforced by any remedy provided by Section 611 of the Illinois Marriage and Dissolution of Marriage Act. The court may enforce any order for support issued under paragraph (12) of subsection (b) of Section 214 in the manner provided for under Articles V and VII of the Illinois Marriage and Dissolution of Marriage Act.

(d) Actual knowledge. An order of protection may be enforced pursuant to this Section if the respondent violates the order after the respondent has actual knowledge of its contents as shown through one of the following means:

(1) By service, delivery, or notice under Section 210.

(2) By notice under Section 210.1 or 211.

(3) By service of an order of protection under Section 222.

(4) By other means demonstrating actual knowledge of the contents of the order.

(e) The enforcement of an order of protection in civil or criminal court shall not be affected by either of the following:

(1) The existence of a separate, correlative order, entered under Section 215.

(2) Any finding or order entered in a conjoined criminal proceeding.

(f) Circumstances. The court, when determining whether or not a violation of an order of protection has occurred, shall not require physical manifestations of abuse on the person of the victim.

(g) Penalties.

(1) Except as provided in paragraph (3) of this subsection, where the court finds the commission of a

crime or contempt of court under subsections (a) or (b) of this Section, the penalty shall be the penalty that generally applies in such criminal or contempt proceedings, and may include one or more of the following: incarceration, payment of restitution, a fine, payment of attorneys' fees and costs, or community service.

(2) The court shall hear and take into account evidence of any factors in aggravation or mitigation before deciding an appropriate penalty under paragraph (1) of this subsection.

(3) To the extent permitted by law, the court is encouraged to:

(i) increase the penalty for the knowing violation of any order of protection over any penalty previously imposed by any court for respondent's violation of any order of protection or penal statute involving petitioner as victim and respondent as defendant;

(ii) impose a minimum penalty of 24 hours imprisonment for respondent's first violation of any order of protection; and

(iii) impose a minimum penalty of 48 hours imprisonment for respondent's second or subsequent violation of an order of protection

unless the court explicitly finds that an increased penalty or that period of imprisonment would be manifestly unjust.

(4) In addition to any other penalties imposed for a violation of an order of protection, a criminal court may consider evidence of any violations of an order of protection:

(i) to increase, revoke or modify the bail bond on an underlying criminal charge pursuant to Section 110-6 of the Code of Criminal Procedure of 1963;

(ii) to revoke or modify an order of probation, conditional discharge or supervision, pursuant to Section 5-6-4 of the Unified Code of Corrections;

(iii) to revoke or modify a sentence of periodic imprisonment, pursuant to Section 5-7-2 of the Unified Code of Corrections.

(5) In addition to any other penalties, the court shall impose an additional fine of $20 as authorized by Section 5-9-1.11 of the Unified Code of Corrections upon any person convicted of or placed on supervision for a violation of an order of protection. The additional fine shall be imposed for each violation of this Section.

750 ILCS 60/223.1 Order of protection; status. Whenever relief is sought under this Act, the court, before granting relief, shall determine whether any order of protection has previously been entered in the instant proceeding or any other proceeding in which any party, or a child of any party, or both, if relevant, has been designated as either a respondent or a protected person.

750 ILCS 60/224 Modification and re-opening of orders.

(a) Except as otherwise provided in this Section, upon motion by petitioner, the court may modify an emergency, interim, or plenary order of protection:

(1) If respondent has abused petitioner since the hearing for that order, by adding or altering one or more

remedies, as authorized by Section 214; and

(2) Otherwise, by adding any remedy authorized by Section 214 which was:

(i) reserved in that order of protection;

(ii) not requested for inclusion in that order of protection; or

(iii) denied on procedural grounds, but not on the merits.

(b) Upon motion by petitioner or respondent, the court may modify any prior order of protection's remedy for custody, visitation or payment of support in accordance with the relevant provisions of the Illinois Marriage and Dissolution of Marriage Act. Each order of protection shall be entered in the Law Enforcement Automated Data System on the same day it is issued by the court.

(c) After 30 days following entry of a plenary order of protection, a court may modify that order only when changes in the applicable law or facts since that plenary order was entered warrant a modification of its terms.

(d) Upon 2 days' notice to petitioner, in accordance with Section 211 of this Act, or such shorter notice as the court may prescribe, a respondent subject to an emergency or interim order of protection issued under this Act may appear and petition the court to re-hear the original or amended petition. Any petition to re-hear shall be verified and shall allege the following:

(1) that respondent did not receive prior notice of the initial hearing in which the emergency, interim, or plenary order was entered under Sections 211 and 217; and

(2) that respondent had a meritorious defense to the order or any of its remedies or that the order or any of its remedies was not authorized by this Act.

(e) In the event that the emergency or interim order granted petitioner exclusive possession and the petition of respondent seeks to re-open or vacate that grant, the court shall set a date for hearing within 14 days on all issues relating to exclusive possession. Under no circumstances shall a court continue a hearing concerning exclusive possession beyond the 14th day, except by agreement of the parties. Other issues raised by the pleadings may be consolidated for the hearing if neither party nor the court objects.

(f) This Section does not limit the means, otherwise available by law, for vacating or modifying orders of protection.

750 ILCS 60/225 Immunity from prosecution. Any individual or organization acting in good faith to report the abuse of any person 60 years of age or older or to do any of the following in complying with the provisions of this Act shall not be subject to criminal prosecution or civil liability as a result of such action: providing any information to the appropriate law enforcement agency, providing that the giving of any information does not violate any privilege of confidentiality under law; assisting in any investigation; assisting in the preparation of any materials for distribution under this Act; or by providing services ordered under an order of protection.

Any individual, agency, or organization acting in good faith to report or investigate alleged abuse, neglect, or exploitation of a high-risk adult with disabilities, to testify in any proceeding on behalf of a high-risk adult with disabilities, to take photographs or perform an examination, or to perform any other act in compliance with the provisions of this Act shall not be the subject of criminal prosecution, civil liability, or other penalty, sanction, restriction, or retaliation as a result of such action.

750 ILCS 60/226 Untrue statements. Allegations and denials, made without reasonable cause and found to be untrue, shall subject the party pleading them to the payment of reasonable expenses actually incurred by the other party by reason of the untrue pleading, together with a reasonable attorney's fee, to be summarily taxed by the court upon motion made within 30 days of the judgment or dismissal, as provided in Supreme Court Rule 137. The court may direct that a copy of an order entered under this Section be provided to the State's Attorney so that he or she may determine whether to prosecute for perjury. This Section shall not apply to proceedings heard in Criminal Court or to criminal contempt of court proceedings, whether heard in Civil or Criminal Court.

750 ILCS 60/227 Privileged communications between domestic violence counselors and victims.

(a) As used in this Section:

(1) "Domestic violence program" means any unit of local government, organization, or association whose major purpose is to provide one or more of the following: information, crisis intervention, emergency shelter, referral, counseling, advocacy, or emotional support to victims of domestic violence.

(2) "Domestic violence advocate or counselor" means any person (A) who has undergone a minimum of forty hours of training in domestic violence advocacy, crisis intervention, and related areas, and (B) who provides services to victims through a domestic violence program either on an employed or volunteer basis.

(3) "Confidential communication" means any communication between an alleged victim of domestic violence and a domestic violence advocate or counselor in the course of providing information, counseling, or advocacy. The term includes all records kept by the advocate or counselor or by the domestic violence program in the course of providing services to an alleged victim concerning the alleged victim and the services provided. The confidential nature of the communication is not waived by the presence at the time of the communication of any additional persons, including but not limited to an interpreter, to further express the interests of the domestic violence victim or by the advocate's or counselor's disclosure to such an additional person with the consent of the victim when reasonably necessary to accomplish the purpose for which the advocate or counselor is consulted.

(4) "Domestic violence victim" means any person who consults a domestic violence counselor for the purpose of securing advice, counseling or assistance related to one or more alleged incidents of domestic violence.

(5) "Domestic violence" means abuse as defined in the Illinois Domestic Violence Act.

(b) No domestic violence advocate or counselor shall disclose any confidential communication or be examined as a witness in any civil or criminal case or proceeding or in any legislative or administrative proceeding without the written consent of the domestic violence victim except (1) in accordance with the provisions of the Abused and Neglected Child Reporting Act or (2) in cases where failure to disclose is likely to result in an imminent risk of serious bodily harm or death of the victim or another person.

(c) A domestic violence advocate or counselor who knowingly discloses any confidential communication in violation of this Act commits a Class A misdemeanor.

(d) When a domestic violence victim is deceased or has been adjudged incompetent by a court of competent jurisdiction, the guardian of the domestic violence victim or the executor or administrator of the estate of the domestic violence victim may waive the privilege established by this Section, except where the guardian, executor or administrator of the estate has been charged with a violent crime against the domestic violence victim or has had an Order of Protection entered against him or her at the request of or on behalf of the domestic violence victim or otherwise has an interest adverse to that of the domestic violence victim with respect to the waiver of the privilege. In that case, the court shall appoint an attorney for the estate of the domestic violence victim.

(e) A minor may knowingly waive the privilege established by this Section. Where a minor is, in the opinion of the court, incapable of knowingly waiving the privilege, the parent or guardian of the minor may waive the privilege on behalf of the minor, except where such parent or guardian has been charged with a violent crime against the minor or has had an Order of Protection entered against him or her on request of or on behalf of the minor or otherwise has any interest adverse to that of the minor with respect to the waiver of the privilege. In that case, the court shall appoint an attorney for the minor child who shall be compensated in accordance with Section 506 of the Illinois Marriage and Dissolution of Marriage Act.

(f) Nothing in this Section shall be construed to limit in any way any privilege that might otherwise exist under statute or common law.

(g) The assertion of any privilege under this Section shall not result in an inference unfavorable to the State's cause or to the cause of the domestic violence victim.

750 ILCS 60/227.1 Other privileged information. Except as otherwise provided in this Section, no court or administrative or legislative body shall compel any person or domestic violence program to disclose the location of any domestic violence program or the identity of any domestic violence advocate or counselor in any civil or criminal case or proceeding or in any administrative or legislative proceeding. A court may compel disclosure of the location of a domestic violence program or the identity of a domestic violence advocate or counselor if the court finds, following a hearing, that there is clear and convincing evidence that failure to disclose would be likely to result in an imminent risk of serious bodily harm or death to

a domestic violence victim or another person. If the court makes such a finding, then disclosure shall take place in camera, under a restrictive protective order that does not frustrate the purposes of compelling the disclosure, and the information disclosed shall not be made a part of the written record of the case.

750 ILCS 60/301 Arrest without warrant.

(a) Any law enforcement officer may make an arrest without warrant if the officer has probable cause to believe that the person has committed or is committing any crime, including but not limited to violation of an order of protection, under Section 12-30 of the Criminal Code of 1961, even if the crime was not committed in the presence of the officer.

(b) The law enforcement officer may verify the existence of an order of protection by telephone or radio communication with his or her law enforcement agency or by referring to the copy of the order provided by the petitioner or respondent.

(c) Any law enforcement officer may make an arrest without warrant if the officer has reasonable grounds to believe a defendant at liberty under the provisions of subdivision (d)(1) or (d)(2) of Section 110-10 of the Code of Criminal Procedure of 1963 has violated a condition of his or her bail bond or recognizance.

750 ILCS 60/301.1 Law enforcement policies. Every law enforcement agency shall develop, adopt, and implement written policies regarding arrest procedures for domestic violence incidents consistent with the provisions of this Act. In developing these policies, each law enforcement agency is encouraged to consult with community organizations and other law enforcement agencies with expertise in recognizing and handling domestic violence incidents.

750 ILCS 60/302 Data maintenance by law enforcement agencies.

(a) All sheriffs shall furnish to the Department of State Police, on the same day as received, in the form and detail the Department requires, copies of any recorded emergency, interim, or plenary orders of protection issued by the court, and any foreign orders of protection filed by the clerk of the court, and transmitted to the sheriff by the clerk of the court pursuant to subsection (b) of Section 222 of this Act. Each order of protection shall be entered in the Law Enforcement Automated Data System on the same day it is issued by the court. If an emergency order of protection was issued in accordance with subsection (c) of Section 217, the order shall be entered in the Law Enforcement Automated Data System as soon as possible after receipt from the clerk.

(b) The Department of State Police shall maintain a complete and systematic record and index of all valid and recorded orders of protection issued pursuant to this Act. The data shall be used to inform all dispatchers and law enforcement officers at the scene of an alleged incident of abuse, neglect, or exploitation or violation of an order of protection of any recorded prior incident of abuse, neglect, or exploitation involving the abused, neglected, or exploited party and the effective dates and terms of any recorded order of protection.

(c) The data, records and transmittals required under this Section shall pertain to any valid emergency, interim or plenary order of protection, whether issued in a civil or criminal proceeding or authorized under the laws of another state, tribe, or United States territory.

750 ILCS 60/303 Reports by law enforcement officers.

(a) Every law enforcement officer investigating an alleged incident of abuse, neglect, or exploitation between family or household members shall make a written police report of any bona fide allegation and the disposition of such investigation. The police report shall include the victim's statements as to the frequency and severity of prior incidents of abuse, neglect, or exploitation by the same family or household member and the number of prior calls for police assistance to prevent such further abuse, neglect, or exploitation.

(b) Every police report completed pursuant to this Section shall be recorded and compiled as a domestic crime within the meaning of Section 5.1 of the Criminal Identification Act.

750 ILCS 60/304 Assistance by law enforcement officers.

(a) Whenever a law enforcement officer has reason to believe that a person has been abused, neglected, or exploited by a family or household member, the officer shall immediately use all reasonable means to prevent further abuse, neglect, or exploitation, including:

(1) Arresting the abusing, neglecting and exploiting party, where appropriate;

(2) If there is probable cause to believe that particular weapons were used to commit the incident of abuse, subject to constitutional limitations, seizing and taking inventory of the weapons;

(3) Accompanying the victim of abuse, neglect, or exploitation to his or her place of residence for a reasonable period of time to remove necessary personal belongings and possessions;

(4) Offering the victim of abuse, neglect, or exploitation immediate and adequate information (written in a language appropriate for the victim or in Braille or communicated in appropriate sign language), which shall include a summary of the procedures and relief available to victims of abuse under subsection (c) of Section 217 and the officer's name and badge number;

(5) Providing the victim with one referral to an accessible service agency;

(6) Advising the victim of abuse about seeking medical attention and preserving evidence (specifically including photographs of injury or damage and damaged clothing or other property); and

(7) Providing or arranging accessible transportation for the victim of abuse (and, at the victim's request, any minors or dependents in the victim's care) to a medical facility for treatment of injuries or to a nearby place of shelter or safety; or, after the close of court business hours, providing or arranging for transportation for the victim (and, at the victim's request, any minors or dependents in the victim's care) to the nearest available circuit judge or associate judge so the victim may file a petition for an emergency order of protection under subsection (c) of Section 217. When a victim of abuse chooses

to leave the scene of the offense, it shall be presumed that it is in the best interests of any minors or dependents in the victim's care to remain with the victim or a person designated by the victim, rather than to remain with the abusing party.

(b) Whenever a law enforcement officer does not exercise arrest powers or otherwise initiate criminal proceedings, the officer shall:

(1) Make a police report of the investigation of any bona fide allegation of an incident of abuse, neglect, or exploitation and the disposition of the investigation, in accordance with subsection (a) of Section 303;

(2) Inform the victim of abuse neglect, or exploitation of the victim's right to request that a criminal proceeding be initiated where appropriate, including specific times and places for meeting with the State's Attorney's office, a warrant officer, or other official in accordance with local procedure; and

(3) Advise the victim of the importance of seeking medical attention and preserving evidence (specifically including photographs of injury or damage and damaged clothing or other property).

(c) Except as provided by Section 24-6 of the Criminal Code of 1961 or under a court order, any weapon seized under subsection (a)(2) shall be returned forthwith to the person from whom it was seized when it is no longer needed for evidentiary purposes.

750 ILCS 60/305 Limited law enforcement liability. Any act of omission or commission by any law enforcement officer acting in good faith in rendering emergency assistance or otherwise enforcing this Act shall not impose civil liability upon the law enforcement officer or his or her supervisor or employer, unless the act is a result of willful or wanton misconduct.

Appendix B: Sample Visitation Schedule

The Mother shall be the primary residential parent. The Father shall be entitled to reasonable visitation, which at a minimum shall include the following days.

The Father shall have the children from 6:00 p.m. every other Friday until 6:00 p.m. the following Sunday, except as provided below, as special provisions for holidays shall supersede the Father's regular visitation:

On the following holidays, the Father shall have the children from 6:00 p.m. the day before the holiday until 6:00 p.m. on the actual holiday:

During even-numbered years:

New Year's Day

Easter

Independence Day

Columbus Day

Thanksgiving

During odd-numbered years, the Mother shall have the children on these holidays, even if such holidays occur on a day that is regularly the Father's day for visitation.

During odd-numbered years:

Martin Luther King Jr.'s birthday

President's Day

Memorial Day

Labor Day

Halloween

During even-numbered years, the Mother shall have the children on these holidays, even if such holidays occur on a day that is regularly the Father's day for visitation.

The Father shall have the children every year from 6:00 p.m. on the day before, until 6:00 p.m. on the actual day of, the following:

Father's Day

Father's birthday

If either of these days shall fall upon a day that the Mother is scheduled to have the children, the Father's right to visitation shall supersede the Mother's.

The Mother shall have the children every year from 6:00 p.m. on the day before, until 6:00 p.m. on the actual day of, the following:

Mother's Day

Mother's birthday

These days shall supersede the Father's regular visitation.

The Father shall have the children during extended breaks from school according to the following schedule:

Spring Break—The Father shall have the children during even-numbered years from 6:00 p.m. on the Friday when Spring Break begins until 6:00 p.m. on the Sunday when Spring Break ends. The Mother shall have the children for Spring Break during odd-numbered years and her visitation shall supersede the Father's regular weekend visitation during the time of Spring Break only.

Winter Break—During odd-numbered years, the Father shall have the children from 6:00 p.m. on the Friday on which Winter Break begins until 6:00 p.m. on the second Sunday following, including Christmas Eve and Christmas Day. The Mother shall have the children from 6:00 p.m. on the second Sunday of Winter Break until 6:00 p.m. on New Year's Eve. During even-numbered years, the Mother shall have the children from 6:00 p.m. on the Friday on which Winter Break begins until 6:00 p.m. on the second Sunday following, including Christmas Eve and Christmas Day. The Father shall have the children from the second Sunday of Winter Break until 6:00 p.m. on New Year's Eve and then from 6:00 p.m. on New Year's Day until 6:00 p.m. on the last day of Winter Break.

Summer Break—The Father shall have the children for five (5) consecutive weeks of each summer. During even-numbered years, this period shall commence on the first Monday following the last day of the school year. During odd-numbered years, this period shall commence on the first Monday following the 4th of July. During this period, the Mother shall be entitled to visitation with the children every other weekend according to the same schedule as the Father's regular visitation. The Father's regular weekend visitation shall remain in effect for the remainder of the Summer Break.

Appendix C:
Illinois Organizations Providing Pro Bono or Reduced-Rate Services

NOTE: *Although the author has attempted to provide a list of resources for the use of the reader, the information contained herein was obtained from secondary sources. Thus, the author makes no guarantee as to the accuracy or comprehensiveness of the information or the availability of pro bono or reduced-rate services.*

Land of Lincoln Legal Assistance Foundation
413 East Broadway
Alton, IL 62002
800-642-5570
www.lollaf.org

Southern Illinois University School of Law Legal Clinic
Lesar Law Building
Mail Code 6821
Southern Illinois University
1150 Douglas Drive
Carbondale, IL 62901
618-453-3217
www.law.siu.edu

American Bar Association for Pro Bono
321 North Clark Street
Chicago, IL 60610
312-988-5759

Chicago Volunteer Legal Services Foundation
100 North LaSalle Street
Suite 900
Chicago, IL 60602
312-332-1624
www.cvls.org

Legal Assistance Foundation of Metropolitan Chicago
111 West Jackson Boulevard
3rd Floor
Chicago, IL 60604
312-341-1070
www.lafchicago.org

Loyola University
Civitas Child Law Clinic
childlaw-center@luc.edu
312-915-6481

Metropolitan Family Services
Legal Aid Bureau
One North Dearborn
Chicago, IL 60602
312-986-4200
www.metrofamily.org

Northwestern University
Bluhm Legal Clinic
357 East Chicago Avenue
Chicago, IL 60611
312-503-3100
www.law.northwestern.edu/
legalclinic

University of Chicago Law School
Mandel Legal Aid Clinic
6020 South University Avenue
Chicago, IL 60637
773-702-9611
www.law.uchicago.edu

Land of Lincoln Legal Assisstance
Foundation, Inc.
8787 State Street
Suite 201
East St. Louis, IL 62203
618-398-0958

Will County Legal Assistance
5 East Van Buren Street
Suite 310
Joliet, IL 60432
815-727-5123
www.willcolegalaid.org

Chicago Legal Clinic
Pro Bono Program
2938 East 91st Street
Chicago, IL 60617
773-731-1762

Volunteer Lawyer Project of Rock
Island County
208 18th Street
Suite 202
Rock Island, IL 61201
309-794-1328

McLean County Pro Bono Program
Prairie State Legal Services, Inc.
316 West Washington Street
Bloomington, IL 61701
309-827-5021
www.pslegal.org

Kane County Pro Bono Program
Prairie State Legal Services, Inc.
201 Houston
Suite 102
Batavia, IL 60510
630-232-9415
www.pslegal.com

Public Interest Law Initiative
321 North Clark Street
28th Floor
Chicago, IL 60610
312-832-5127
http://pili-law.org

Peoria County Pro Bono Plan
Prairie State Legal Services, Inc.
331 Fulton Street
Suite 600
Peoria, IL 61602
309-674-9831
www.pslegal.org

Prairie State Legal Services
975 North Main Street
Rockford, IL 61103
815-965-2134
www.pslegal.org

Northern Illinois University
College of Law
Zeke Giorgi Legal Clinic
319 West State Street
Rockford, IL 61101
815-962-9980
http://law.niu.edu

**Lake County Bar Association
Volunteer Lawyers Program**
7 North County Street
Waukegan, IL 60085
847-244-3143

**DuPage County Bar Association
Legal Aid Service**
126 South County Farm Road
Wheaton, IL 60187
630-653-6212
www.dcba.org
www.metrofamily.org

**McHenry County Bar Association
Legal Aid**
1212 North Seminary Avenue
Woodstock, IL 60098
815-338-9559

**Coordinated Advice and Referral
Program for Legal Services
(CARPLS)**
17 North State
Street Suite 1850
Chicago, IL 60602
312-738-9494
www.carpls.org

**Champaign County Bar Association
Pro Bono Program**
1817 South Neil Street
Suite 203
Champaign, IL 61820
217-356-1351

**Civil Court Clinic for Orders of
Protection Pro Bono Advocates**
28 North Clark Street
Suite 630
Chicago, IL 60602
312-827-2420
http://probonoadvocates.com

Appendix D: Sample Forms

The following compilation of forms is based on general child custody, visitation, and support principles. These forms will give the reader an idea of what his or her own pleadings should look like. Of course, the forms are only a guide, and must be drafted to reflect the actual circumstances of the reader's case.

PETITION FOR CHILD CUSTODY AND SUPPORT

STATE OF ILLINOIS
IN THE CIRCUIT COURT OF THE __26th__ JUDICIAL CIRCUIT
__Sphinx__ COUNTY

JOAN DOE,	)	
Petitioner,	)	
	)	
v.	)	Case No. __12345__
	)	
	)	
JOHN SMITH,	)	
Respondent.	)	

PETITION FOR CHILD CUSTODY AND SUPPORT

NOW COMES the Petitioner, __JOAN DOE__ (hereinafter "Petitioner"), by and through her attorney, __Lawrence Lawyer__, and for her Petition for Child Custody and Support against the Respondent, __JOHN SMITH__ (hereinafter "Respondent") states as follows:

1. Petitioner resides in __Sphinx County, Illinois__.

2. Respondent resides in __Sphinx County, Illinois__.

3. Petitioner and Respondent __are not and have never been married__.

4. Petitioner and Respondent are the __biological parents of the following two children__:

John Smith, Jr., born 5/3/96

Jill Smith, born 8/5/98

5.	The above-named children reside in DuPage County with their mother, the Petitioner herein.

6.	Petitioner was not married on the birthdates of the above-named children, and was not married within three hundred days before the birthdates of the above-named children.

7.	Respondent is employed and has the ability to financially support the above-named children, but has refused to do so.

8.	No previous court order exists, in this or any other jurisdiction, concerning custody or support of the above-named children.

WHEREFORE, the Petitioner respectfully requests this Honorable Court to order the following:

that full legal and physical custody of the above-named children be granted to Petitioner, with reasonable visitation awarded to Respondent;

that Respondent be ordered to pay Petitioner the percentage of Respondent's monthly income that the Court deems necessary for the support of the above-named children; and

that Respondent be ordered to provide health care insurance for the benefit of the above-named children.

Any further relief that the Court deems proper.

_____*Joan Doe*_____
Petitioner

RESPONSE TO PETITION FOR CHILD CUSTODY AND SUPPORT

STATE OF ILLINOIS

IN THE CIRCUIT COURT OF THE <u>TWENTY-SIXTH</u> JUDICIAL CIRCUIT

<u>Sphinx</u>   COUNTY

JOAN DOE,)	
Petitioner,)	
V.)	CASE No. <u>12345</u>
)	
)	
JOHN SMITH,)	
Respondent.)	
)	

RESPONSE TO PETITION FOR CHILD CUSTODY AND SUPPORT

NOW COMES the Respondent, <u>JOHN SMITH</u> (hereinafter "Respondent"), by and through his attorney, <u>Brenda Barrister</u>, and in response to Petitioner's Petition for Child Custody and Support states as follows:

1. Respondent <u>admits</u> the allegations of Petitioner's paragraph 1.

2. Respondent <u>admits</u> the allegations of Petitioner's paragraph 2.

3. Respondent <u>admits</u> the allegations of Petitioner's paragraph 3.

4. Respondent <u>admits</u> the allegations of Petitioner's paragraph 4.

5. Respondent <u>admits</u> the allegations of Petitioner's paragraph 5.

6. Respondent <u>admits</u> the allegations of Petitioner's paragraph 6.

7. Respondent admits that he is employed and has the ability to contribute to the financial support for the above-named children, but denies that he has refused to do so. Respondent further states that Petitioner has a greater income than Respondent, and is capable of providing the majority of the financial support for the children.

8. Respondent admits the allegations of Petitioner's paragraph 8.

Further, Respondent states that Petitioner has unreasonably refused to allow Respondent to have telephone or in-person contact with the children, even though Respondent has repeatedly requested that he be allowed to see and speak with the children.

WHEREFORE, the Respondent respectfully requests this Honorable Court to order the following:

that full legal and physical custody of the above-named children be granted to Respondent, with reasonable visitation awarded to Petitioner;

that Petitioner be ordered to pay Respondent the percentage of Petitioner's monthly income that the Court deems necessary for the support of the above-named children; and

that Petitioner be ordered to provide health care insurance for the benefit of the above-named children.

Any further relief that the Court deems proper.

John Smith

Respondent

SUMMONS

STATE OF ILLINOIS

IN THE CIRCUIT COURT OF THE _____26th____ JUDICIAL CIRCUIT

____Sphinx_____ COUNTY

JOAN DOE,	)	
Petitioner,	)	
v.	)	Case No. _____12345_____
	)	
JOHN SMITH,	)	
Respondent.	)	

SUMMONS

ILLINOIS MARRIAGE AND DISSOLUTION OF MARRIAGE ACT

To each Defendant:

You are summoned and required to file an answer to the complaint in this case, a copy of which is hereto attached, or otherwise file your appearance in the office of the Clerk of this court, _364 Sycamore St., Wheeler_ (address), Illinois, within 30 days after service of this summons, not counting the day of service. IF YOU FAIL TO DO SO, A JUDGMENT BY DEFAULT MAY BE TAKEN AGAINST YOU FOR THE RELIEF ASKED IN THE COMPLAINT.

YOU ARE FURTHER NOTIFIED THAT A DISSOLUTION ACTION STAY IS IN FULL FORCE AND EFFECT UPON SERVICE OF THIS SUMMONS.

THE CONDITIONS OF THE STAY ARE SET FORTH ON THE REVERSE SIDE OF THIS SUMMONS, WHICH WAS SERVED UPON YOU, AND ARE APPLICABLE TO THE PARTIES AS SET FORTH IN THE STATUTE.

To the Officer:

This summons must be returned by the Officer or other person to whom it was given for service, with the endorsement of service and fees, if any, immediately after service. If service cannot be made, this summons shall be returned so endorsed. THIS SUMMONS MAY NOT BE SERVED LATER THAN 30 DAYS AFTER ITS DATE.

(Seal of Court)
Circuit

WITNESS: <u>Jo Crow</u>, Clerk of the <u>26th</u> Judicial

and the seal thereof, at <u>Wheeler</u>, Illinois

DATED: <u>March 20, 2007</u>

Petitioner's Attorney (or Petitioner,

if not represented by attorney)

Clerk of the <u>26th</u> Judicial Circuit

<u>364 Sycamore Street</u>

<u>Wheeler, IL 12345</u>

Address

Date of Service <u>March 20</u>, 20 <u>07</u>

<u>630-555-6677</u>

(To be inserted by officer on copy left with defendant

Telephone

or other person)

CONDITIONS OF DISSOLUTION ACTION STAY

Upon service of a summons and petition or praecipe filed under the Illinois Marriage and Dissolution of Marriage Act or upon the filing of the respondent's appearance in the proceeding, whichever first occurs, a dissolution action stay shall be in effect against both parties and their agents and employees, without bond or further notice, until a final judgment is entered, the proceeding is dismissed, or until further order of the court restraining both parties from physically abusing, harassing, intimidating, striking, or interfering with the personal liberty of the other party or the minor children of either party (750 ILCS 5/501.1 (a)(2)) and restraining both parties from removing any minor child or either party from the State of Illinois or from concealing any such child from the other party, without the consent of the party or an order of the court (750 ILCS 5/501.1(a)(3)).

APPEARANCE

STATE OF ILLINOIS

IN THE CIRCUIT COURT OF THE ___26th___ JUDICIAL CIRCUIT

<u>Sphinx</u> COUNTY

JOAN DOE,   )

    Petitioner,   )

v.   )   Case No. ___12345___

)

JOHN SMITH,   )

    Respondent.   )

APPEARANCE

I HEREBY ENTER THE APPEARANCE OF ___Jill Smith___

(Insert the name of the party for whom you are entering an appearance)

AND MY OWN AS

___ REGULAR COUNSEL	___ TRIAL COUNSEL
___ SPECIAL APPEARANCE	___ SUBSTITUTE COUNSEL
___ PRO SE	___ COUNSEL IN FORCIBLE ENTRY
___ ADDITIONAL COUNSEL	___ APPELLATE COUNSEL
_X_ GUARDIAN AD LITEM	___ COURT APPOINTED COUNSEL

AND AS (HIS) (HER) (THEIR) COUNSEL IN THE ABOVE ENTITLED CASE.

SIGNED ___*Abbey Attorney*___

(Signature of Attorney filing Appearance)

Name ___Abbey Attorney___

Attorney for ___Jill Smith___

Address ___567 Business Drive___

City, State, Zip ___Anytown, IL___

Phone ___987-123-4567___

UCCJEA AFFIDAVIT

STATE OF ILLINOIS

IN THE CIRCUIT COURT OF THE ___26th___ JUDICIAL CIRCUIT

___Sphinx___ COUNTY

JOAN DOE,	)
Petitioner,	)
v.	) Case No. _____12345_____
	)
JOHN SMITH,	)
Respondent.	)

AFFIDAVIT PURSUANT TO UNIFORM CHILD CUSTODY JURISDICTION AND ENFORCEMENT ACT

<u>JOAN DOE</u>, Petitioner herein, being duly sworn, deposes and states as follows:

1. Petitioner resides at <u>1234 Poplar Street, Anytown, Illinois</u>.

2. Upon information and belief, the children who are subject to this proceeding currently reside at:

Name	Date of Birth	Address
Jill Smith	8/5/98	1234 Poplar Street, Anytown, IL
John Smith, Jr.	5/3/96	1234 Poplar Street, Anytown, IL

3.   Upon information and belief, the children who are subject to this proceeding have, during the previous five years, resided at the following:

Name	Address	Dates of Residence
Jill Smith	1234 Poplar St.	5-3-98 to present
John Smith, Jr.	1234 Poplar St.	8-5-96 to present

4.   Upon information and belief, the children who are subject to this proceeding have, during the previous five years, resided with the following persons:

Name	Address	Dates of Residence
Joan Doe	1234 Poplar St.	6/95 to present

5.   Petitioner _____ Joan Doe _____ ~~has~~/has not participated as a party/witness/other_____(indicate capacity) in other litigation concerning the custody of the same children in this or any other state.

6.   Petitioner __ Joan Doe __ ~~has~~/does not have information of any custody proceeding concerning the child pending in a court of this or any other state.

7.   Petitioner __ Joan Doe __ ~~knows~~/does not know of any person not a party to the proceedings who has physical custody of the child or claims to have custody or visitation rights with respect to the children.

If the declarations in either paragraph 5, 6, or 7 is in the affirmative, Petitioner shall provide additional information to the Court under oath. Petitioner understands that she has a continuing duty to inform the court of any custody proceeding concerning the child in this or any other state of which she obtained information during this proceeding.

STATE OF ILLINOIS   )

)SS.

COUNTY OF __ Sphinx __)

_____ Joan Doe _____, being first duly sworn on oath, deposes and states that she has read the foregoing document, and the answers made herein are true, correct, and complete to the best of her knowledge and belief.

___ *Joan Doe* ___

SIGNATURE

SUBSCRIBED and SWORN to before me this ___10___ day of __April__ , 20 _07_ .

_____C.U. Sine_____

NOTARY PUBLIC

NOTICE OF MOTION

STATE OF ILLINOIS

IN THE CIRCUIT COURT OF THE ___26th___ JUDICIAL CIRCUIT

___Sphinx___ COUNTY

JOHN SMITH,	)	
Petitioner,	)	
v.	)	Case No. ___12345___
	)	
JOAN DOE,	)	
Respondent.	)	

NOTICE OF MOTION

To: Lawrence Lawyer
        Attorney at Law
        123 Main Street
        Chicago, Illinois 60600

On ___May 3___, 20_07_, at ___9___ a. m., or as soon thereafter as Counsel may be heard, I shall appear before the Honorable ___Renee Barrales___, or any Judge sitting in his/her stead, in the courtroom usually occupied by him/her in the ___Sphinx___ County Government Center, ___2642 Emmett Road, Legaltown___, Illinois, and then and there present the following Motion:

(continued on next page)

PROOF OF SERVICE

Lawrence Lawyer

123 Main Street

Chicago, Illinois 60600

The undersigned being first duly sworn on oath deposes and says that a copy of the foregoing Notice was served upon the above named by enclosing the same in an envelope, plainly addressed as is shown above, postage fully prepaid, and by depositing the same in a U.S. Post Office Box, at Chicago, Illinois, on the ___15___ th day of ___November___, A.D. 20_07_, before the hour of 4:00 p.m.

Brenda Barrister

Brenda Barrister

SUBSCRIBED and SWORN to before me this

___15th___ day of ___November___, 20 _07_.

C. U. Sine

NOTARY PUBLIC

PETITION FOR VISITATION

STATE OF ILLINOIS

IN THE CIRCUIT COURT OF THE ___26th___ JUDICIAL CIRCUIT

<u>Sphinx</u>   COUNTY

JOHN SMITH,	)	
Petitioner,	)	
v.	)	Case No. ____12345____
	)	
JOAN DOE,	)	
Respondent.	)	

PETITION FOR VISITATION

NOW COMES the Petitioner, <u>John Smith</u>, through his attorney, <u>Brenda Barrister</u>, and in support of his Petition for Visitation states as follows:

1. Petitioner resides in <u>Sphinx</u> County, Illinois.

2. Respondent resides in <u>Sphinx</u> County, Illinois.

3. Petitioner and Respondent are <u>not and have never been married</u>.

4. Petitioner and Respondent are <u>the biological parents of the following two children</u>:

<u>John Smith, Jr., born 5/3/96</u>

<u>Jill Smith, born 8/5/98</u>

5. The above-named children reside in Sphinx County with their mother, the Respondent herein.

6. No previous court order exists, in this or any other jurisdiction, concerning custody or support of the 2 above-named children

7. Respondent has not allowed Petitioner, the father of the above-named children, reasonable access to and contact with the above-named children, and does not even allow Petitioner to speak with the children over the telephone.

WHEREFORE, Petitioner prays that this Court will grant Petitioner a liberal visitation schedule with the above-named children, including in-person visitation and communication by telephone on a regular basis.

John Smith

Petitioner

RESPONSE TO PETITION FOR VISITATION

STATE OF ILLINOIS

IN THE CIRCUIT COURT OF THE ___26th___ JUDICIAL CIRCUIT

___Sphinx___ COUNTY

JOHN SMITH,	)	
Petitioner,	)	
v.	)	Case No. _____12345_____
	)	
JOAN DOE,	)	
Respondent.	)	

RESPONSE TO PETITION FOR VISITATION

NOW COMES the Respondent, <u>Joan Doe</u>, through her attorney, <u>Lawrence Lawyer</u>, and in response to Petitioner's Petition for Visitation states as follows:

1. Respondent <u>admits</u> the allegations of paragraph 1 of Petitioner's Petition.

2. Respondent <u>admits</u> the allegations of paragraph 2 of Petitioner's Petition.

3. Respondent <u>admits</u> the allegations of paragraph 3 of Petitioner's Petition.

4. Respondent <u>admits</u> the allegations of paragraph 4 of Petitioner's Petition.

5. Respondent <u>admits</u> the allegations of paragraph 5 of Petitioner's Petition.

6. Respondent <u>admits</u> the allegations of paragraph 6 of Petitioner's Petition.

7. Respondent <u>denies</u> the allegations of paragraph 7 of Petitioner's Petition, <u>and further states affirmatively that Petitioner has failed to appear for a</u>

large number of scheduled visits with the children, that Petitioner often attempts to make telephone calls after 9:00 p.m., when the children are asleep, and that Respondent believes that these late telephone calls are merely a means to find out if Respondent is at home in the evening.

WHEREFORE, Respondent prays that this Court will grant Petitioner minimal visitation, and will restrict telephone contact by Petitioner to one day a week, with telephone calls to be completed before 6:00 p.m. on the scheduled day.

Joan Doe
_____

Respondent

PETITION TO MODIFY CUSTODY

STATE OF ILLINOIS

IN THE CIRCUIT COURT OF THE __26th__ JUDICIAL CIRCUIT

Sphinx__ COUNTY

JOHN SMITH,	)
Petitioner,	)
v.	) Case No. ____12345____
	)
JOAN DOE,	)
Respondent.	)

PETITION TO MODIFY CUSTODY

NOW COMES the Petitioner, John__Smith, by and through his attorney, Brenda Barrister, and in support of his Petition to Modify Custody, states as follows:

1. Petitioner resides in __Sphinx__ County, Illinois.

2. Respondent, JOAN DOE, resides in Sphinx__ County, Illinois.

3. Petitioner and Respondent are the parents of two minor children, John Smith, Jr., d/o/b: 5/3/96, and Jill Smith, d/o/b: 8/5/98.

4. On July 1, 2007, this Court entered its order granting legal and physical custody of the above-named children to Respondent.

5. The above-named children currently reside with Respondent in Sphinx County, Illinois.

6. Since the date of the previous order regarding custody, there has been a substantial change in circumstances in this matter, in that the Respondent has moved several times in the past several years.

7. It is in the best interest of the above-named children that the Court's previous order be modified to grant legal and physical custody of the children to Petitioner.

8. More than two years have passed since the entry of the previous order regarding custody.

WHEREFORE, Petitioner requests that this Honorable Court modify its earlier custody order, such that Petitioner be granted immediate legal and physical custody of the above-named minor children.

John Smith
_____
Petitioner

VERIFICATION

STATE OF ILLINOIS   )

        SS   )

COUNTY OF SPHINX)

The undersigned, being duly sworn, hereby deposes and says that he is the Petitioner in the captioned matter, that he has read the Petition to Modify Custody herein, and that the contents thereof are true and correct.

John Smith
_____
Petitioner

Subscribed and sworn to before me

This ____10th____ day of __April__ 20 _07_

C. U. Sine
_____
Notary Public

RESPONSE TO PETITION TO MODIFY CUSTODY

STATE OF ILLINOIS

IN THE CIRCUIT COURT OF THE ___26th___ JUDICIAL CIRCUIT

__Sphinx__ COUNTY

JOHN SMITH,	)	
Petitioner,	)	
v.	)	Case No. ____12345____
	)	
JOAN DOE,	)	
Respondent.	)	

RESPONSE TO PETITION TO MODIFY CUSTODY

NOW COMES the Respondent, <u>Joan Doe</u>, by and through her attorney, <u>Lawrence Lawyer</u>, and in Response to Petitioner's Petition to Modify Custody, states as follows:

1. Respondent <u>admits</u> the allegations of paragraph 1 of Petitioner's petition.

2. Respondent <u>admits</u> the allegations of paragraph 2 of Petitioner's petition.

3. Respondent <u>admits</u> the allegations of paragraph 3 of Petitioner's petition.

4. Respondent <u>admits</u> the allegations of paragraph 4 of Petitioner's petition.

5. Respondent <u>admits</u> the allegations of paragraph 5 of Petitioner's petition.

6. Respondent <u>admits that she has moved three times in the last two years; however, she denies that this amounts to a substantial change in circumstances.</u>

7. Respondent <u>denies that it is in the best interest of the above-named children that the Court's previous order be modified.</u>

8. Respondent <u>admits the allegations of paragraph 8 of Petitioner's petition.</u>

WHEREFORE, Respondent requests that this Honorable Court deny Petitioner's Petition, and order that custody of the minor children remain with Respondent.

_____***Joan Doe***_____

Respondent

VERIFICATION

STATE OF ILLINOIS   )

            SS   )

COUNTY OF SPHINX)

The undersigned, being duly sworn, hereby deposes and says that she is the Respondent in the captioned matter, that she has read the Response herein, and that the contents thereof are true and correct.

_____***Joan Doe***_____

Respondent

Subscribed and sworn to before me

This __3rd__ day of __May__ 20 __07.__

___***C.U. Sine***___

Notary Public

PETITION FOR RULE TO SHOW CAUSE
(NON-PAYMENT OF SUPPORT)

STATE OF ILLINOIS

IN THE CIRCUIT COURT OF THE __26th__ JUDICIAL CIRCUIT
__Sphinx__ COUNTY

JOAN DOE,	)	
Petititoner,	)	
v.	)	Case No. _____12345_____
	)	
JOHN SMITH,	)	
Respondent.	)	

PETITION FOR RULE TO SHOW CAUSE

NOW COMES the Petitioner, __JOAN DOE__, by and through her attorney, __Lawrence Lawyer__, and in support of her Petition for Rule to Show Cause against the Respondent, JOHN SMITH, states as follows:

1. That on July 1, 2007, Respondent was ordered by this Court to pay monthly child support to Petitioner in the amount of $200.00, commencing on August 1, 2007.

2. That Respondent has willfully failed to pay Petitioner as ordered by this Court.

3. That, as a result of Respondent's willful failure to pay, Respondent now owes past-due support in the amount of $1,400.00.

WHEREFORE, Petitioner prays that a rule be entered against Respondent, requiring Respondent to show cause, if any he has, for failure to abide by the orders of this court as contained in the order of July 1, 2007, why he should not be held in contempt of this Court. Petitioner further respectfully requests that judgment be entered against Respondent in the amount of $1,400.00, plus costs and attorney's fees incurred in bringing this petition, as set forth in the Affidavit for Attorney's Fees, which is attached hereto and incorporated herein by reference as Exhibit "A".

_____*Joan Doe*_____
            Petitioner

PETITION FOR RULE TO SHOW CAUSE
(VISITATION INTERFERENCE)

STATE OF ILLINOIS

IN THE CIRCUIT COURT OF THE ___26th___ JUDICIAL CIRCUIT

___Sphinx___ COUNTY

JOHN SMITH,	)	
Petitioner,	)	
v.	)	Case No. ____12345____
	)	
JOAN DOE,	)	
Respondent.	)	

PETITION FOR RULE TO SHOW CAUSE

NOW COMES the Petitioner, JOHN SMITH, and in support of his Petition for Rule to Show Cause against Respondent, JOAN DOE, states as follows:

1. Petitioner and Respondent are the parents of the following minor children: John Smith, Jr., d/o/b 5/3/96, and Jill Smith, d/o/b 8/5/98.

2. Petitioner resides in Sphinx County, Illinois.

3. On July 1, 2007, this Court entered its order granting custody of the above-named children to Respondent, and granting Petitioner weekly visitation from 7:00 a.m. on Saturday until 7:00 p.m. on Sunday.

4. Respondent and the two above-named children reside together in DuPage County, Illinois.

5. Respondent has refused to allow Petitioner's visitation with the above-named children on the following dates, without cause:

[list dates]

6. Respondent has refused to allow Petitioner make-up time for the missed periods of visitation.

WHEREFORE, Petitioner respectfully asks the Court to enter a rule against Respondent, requiring Respondent to show cause, if any she has, for failure to abide by the orders of this Court as contained in the order of July 1, 2007, why she should not be held in contempt of this Court. Petitioner further respectfully requests that Respondent be ordered to provide make-up visitation at a time that suits the convenience of the Petitioner. Petitioner also asks for an award of attorney's fees incurred in bringing this petition, as set forth in the Affidavit for Attorney's Fees, which is attached hereto and incorporated herein by reference as Exhibit "A".

_____*John Smith*_____
Petitioner

NOTE: *Interrogatories will typically ask the following questions. What follows is a standard interrogatory, filled in by the hypothetical John Smith.*

SUPREME COURT RULE 213(j) STANDARD INTERROGATORIES

1. State your full name, current address, date of birth, and social security number.

```
John Smith                      March 20, 1966
123 Normal Dr., Apt. 3          333-33-3333
Normalville, IL 60123
```

2. List all employment held by you during the preceding three years and with regard to each employment state:

a. The name and address of each employer;

```
Bossman, Saylor, and Associates
999 Job Ave.
Jobvile, IL 60333
```

b. Your position, job title, or description;

```
Marketing Director
```

c. If you had an employment contract;

```
no
```

d. The date on which you commenced your employment and, if applicable, the date and reason for the termination of your employment;

```
November 15, 1986
```

e. Your current gross and net income per pay period;

```
$6,000/mo. gross, $4,000/mo net
```

f. Your gross income as shown on the last W-2 tax and wage statement received by you, your social security wages as shown on the last W-2 tax and wage statement received by you, and the amounts of all deductions shown thereon; and

```
$72,000 gross annual income
```

g. All additional benefits or perquisites received from your employment stating the type and value thereof.

3. During the preceding three years, have you had any source of income other than from your employment listed above? If so, with regard to each source of income, state the following:

      no

a. the source of income, including the type of income and name and address of the source;

b. the frequency in which you receive income from the source;

c. the amount of income received by you from the source during the immediately preceding three years; and

d. the amount of income received by you from the source for each month during the immediately preceding three years.

4. Do you own any interest in real estate? If so, with regard to each such interest state the following:

      no

a. the size and description of the parcel of real estate, including improvements thereon;

b. the name, address and interest of each person who has or claims to have an ownership interest in the parcel of real estate;

c. the date your interest in the parcel of real estate was acquired;

d. the consideration you transferred or paid for your interest in the parcel of real estate;

e. your estimate of the current fair market value of the parcel of real estate and your interest therein; and

f. the amount of any indebtedness owed on the parcel of real estate and to whom.

5. For the preceding three years, list the names and addresses of all associations, partnerships, corporations, enterprises or entities in which you have an interest or claim any interest, the nature of your interest or claim of interest therein, the amount of percentage of your interest or claim of interest therein, and an estimate of the value of your interest therein.

      n/a

6. During the preceding three years, have you had any account or investment in any type of financial institution, individually or with another or in the name of another, including checking accounts, savings accounts, certificates of deposit, and money market accounts? If so, with regard to each such account or investment, state the following:

a. the type of account or investment;

      checking account

b. the name and address of the financial institution;

```
Bank of the Universe
Moneydog Dr.
Cashtown, IL   60633
```

c. the name and address of each person in whose name the account is held; and

```
John Smith
123 Normal Dr., Apt. 3
Normalville, IL 60123
```

d. both the high and the low balance of the account or investment, stating the date of the high balance and the date of the low balance.

```
$2000.00 on 5/3/94
```

```
$5000.00 on 6/9/86
```

7. During the preceding three years, have you been the holder of or had access to any safety deposit boxes? If so, state the following:

```
no
```

a. the name of the bank or institution where such box is located;

b. the number of each box;

c. a description of the contents of each box during the immediately preceding three years and as of the date of the answer; and

d. the name and address of any joint or co-owners of such safety deposit box or any trustees holding the box for your benefit.

8. During the immediately preceding three years, has any person or entity held cash or property on your behalf? If so, state:

```
no
```

a. the name and address of the person or entity holding the cash or property; and

b. the type of cash or property held and the value thereof.

9. During the preceding three years, have you owned any stocks, bonds, securities, or other investments, including savings bonds? If so, with regard to each such stock, bond, security, or investment state:

no

a. a description of the stock, bond, security, or investment;

b. the name and address of the entity issuing the stock, bond, security, or investment;

c. the present value of such stock, bond, security, or investment;

d. the date of acquisition of the stock, bond, security, or investment;

e. the cost of the stock, bond, security, or investment;

f. the name and address of any other owner or owners in such stock, bond, security, or investment; and

g. if applicable, the date sold and the amount realized therefrom.

10. Do you own or have any incidents of ownership in any life, annuity, or endowment insurance policies? If so, with regard to each such policy state:

no

a. the name of the company;

b. the number of the policy;

c. the face value of the policy;

d. the present value of the policy;

e. the amount of any loan or encumbrance on the policy;

f. the date of acquisition of the policy; and

g. with regard to each policy, the beneficiary or beneficiaries.

11. Do you have any right, title, claim, or interest in or to a pension plan, retirement plan, or profit sharing plan, including, but not limited to, individual retirement accounts, 401(k) plans, and deferred compensation plans? If so, with regard to each such plan state:

yes

a. the name and address of the entity providing the plan;

```
E-Z Retirement, Inc.
Safeplanning St.
Safetytown, IL 60609
```

b. the date of your initial participation in the plan; and

```
December 15, 1986
```

c. the amount of funds currently held on your behalf under the plan.

```
$35,015.02
```

12. Do you have any outstanding indebtedness or financial obligations, including mortgages, promissory notes, or other oral or written contracts? If so, with regard to each obligation state the following:

```
no
```

a. the name and address of the creditor;

b. the form of the obligation;

c. the date the obligation was initially incurred;

d. the amount of the original obligation;

e. the purpose or consideration for which the obligation was incurred;

f. a description of any security connected with the obligation;

g. the rate of interest on the obligation;

h. the present unpaid balance of the obligation;

i. the dates and amounts of installment payments; and

j. the date of maturity of the obligation.

13. Are you owed any money or property? If so, state:

a. the name and address of the debtor;

b. the form of the obligation;

c. the date the obligation was initially incurred;

d. the amount of the original obligation;

e. the purpose or consideration for which the obligation was incurred;

f. the description of any security connected with the obligation;

g. the rate of interest on the obligation;

h. the present unpaid balance of the obligation;

i. the dates and amounts of installment payments; and

j. the date of maturity of the obligation.

14. State the year, make, and model of each motor or motorized vehicle, motor or mobile home, and farm machinery or equipment in which you have an ownership, estate, interest, or claim of interest, whether individually or with another, and with regard to each item state:

    2000 DW Cobracar

a. the date the item was acquired;

    3/11/00

b. the consideration paid for the item;

    $40,000

c. the name and address of each other person who has a right, title, claim, or interest in or to the item;

    Joan Doe, 1234 Poplar St., Anytown, IL

d. the approximate fair market value of the item; and

    $30,000.00

e. the amount of any indebtedness on the item and the name and address of the creditor.

    (none)

15. Have you purchased or contributed toward the payment for or provided other consideration or improvement with regard to any real estate, motorized vehicle, financial account or securities, or other property, real or personal, on behalf of another person or entity other than your spouse during the preceding three years? If so, with regard to each such transaction state:

    no

a. the name and address of the person or entity to whom you contributed;

b. the type of contribution made by you;

c. the type of property to which the contribution was made;

d. the location of the property to which the contribution was made;

e. whether or not there is written evidence of the existence of a loan; and

f. a description of the written evidence.

16. During the preceding three years, have you made any gift of cash or property, real or personal, to any person or entity not your spouse? If so, with regard to each such transaction state:

     no

a. a description of the gift;

b. the value of the gift;

c. the date of the gift;

d. the name and address of the person or entity receiving the gift;

e. whether or not there is written evidence of the existence of a gift; and

f. a description of the written evidence.

17. During the preceding three years, have you made any loans to any person or entity not your spouse and, if so, with regard to each such loan state:

     no

a. a description of the loan;

b. the value of the loan;

c. the date of the loan;

d. the name and address of the person or entity receiving the loan;

e. whether or not there is written evidence of the existence of a loan; and

f. a description of the written evidence.

18. During the preceding three years, have you sold, transferred, conveyed, encumbered, concealed, damaged, or otherwise disposed of any property owned by you and/or your spouse individually or collectively? If so, with regard to each item of property state:

     no

a. a description of the property;

b. the current location of the property;

c. the purpose or reason for the action taken by you with regard to the property;

d. the approximate fair market value of the property;

e. whether or not there is written evidence of any such transaction; and

f. a description of the written evidence.

19. During the preceding three years, have any appraisals been made with regard to any of the property listed by you under your answers to these interrogatories? If so, state:

      no

a. the name and address of the person conducting each such appraisal;

b. a description of the property appraised;

c. the date of the appraisal; and

d. the location of any copies of each such appraisal.

20. During the preceding three years, have you prepared or has anyone prepared for you any financial statements, net worth statements, or lists of assets and liabilities pertaining to your property or financial affairs? If so, with regard to each such document state:

      no

a. the name and address of the person preparing each such document;

b. the type of document prepared;

c. the date the document was prepared; and

d. the location of all copies of each such document.

21. State the name and address of any accountant, tax preparer, bookkeeper, and other person, firm, or entity who has kept or prepared books, documents, and records with regard to your income, property, business, or financial affairs during the course of this marriage.

      n/a

22. List all nonmarital property claimed by you, identifying each item of property as to the type of property, the date received, the basis on which you claim it is nonmarital property, its location, and the present value of the property.

```
Diamond cufflinks, $4,000, nonmarital property because inher-
ited during marriage.
```

23. List all marital property of this marriage, identifying each item of property as to the type of property, the basis on which you claim it to be marital property, its location, and the present value of the property.

```
house, car, savings account worth $127.00, because aquired
during marriage and titled in both names
```

24. What contribution or dissipation has your spouse made to the marital estate?

25. Pursuant to Illinois Supreme Court Rule 213(f), provide the name and address of each witness who will testify at trial and state the subject of each witness' testimony.

```
(no witnesses)
```

26. Pursuant to Illinois Supreme Court Rule 213(g), provide the name and address of each opinion witness who will offer any testimony, and state:

```
(no witnesses)
```

a. the subject matter on which the opinion witness is expected to testify;

```
n/a
```

b. the conclusions and/or opinions of the opinion witness and the basis therefor, including reports of the witness, if any;

```
n/a
```

c. the qualifications of each opinion witness, including a curriculum vitae and/or resume, if any; and

```
n/a
```

d. the identity of any written reports of the opinion witness regarding this occurrence.

```
n/a
```

27. Are you in any manner incapacitated or limited in your ability to earn income at the present time?

```
no
```

If so, define and describe such incapacity, or limitation, and state when such incapacity or limitation commenced and when it is expected to end.

28. Identify any statements, information, and/or documents known to you and requested by any of the foregoing interrogatories that you claim to be work product or subject to any common law or statutory privilege, and with respect to each interrogatory, specify the legal basis for the claim as required by Illinois Supreme Court Rule 201(n).

    n/a

ATTESTATION

STATE OF ILLINOIS   )

COUNTY OF   <u>Sphinx</u>   )^{ss.}

<u>   John Smith   </u>, being first duly sworn on oath, deposes and states that he/she is a defendant in the above-captioned matter, that he/she has read the foregoing document, and the answers made herein are true, correct, and complete to the best of his/her knowledge and belief.

<u>   *John Smith*   </u>

SIGNATURE

SUBSCRIBED and SWORN to before me this

<u> 10 </u> day of <u> April </u> 20<u> 07 </u> .

<u>   **C. U. Sine**   </u>

NOTARY PUBLIC

FINANCIAL AFFIDAVIT

STATE OF ILLINOIS
IN THE CIRCUIT COURT OF THE ___26th___ JUDICIAL CIRCUIT
___Sphinx___ COUNTY

JOHN SMITH,	)	
Petitioner,	)	
v.	)	Case No. ____12345____
	)	
JOAN DOE,	)	
Respondent.	)	

FINANCIAL AFFIDAVIT

Affiant, <u>John Smith</u>, the Petitioner in the above captioned case, having been duly sworn, hereby states the following for his Financial Affidavit:

PERSONAL DATA

A. FULL NAME   <u>John Joe Smith</u>

B. DATE OF BIRTH   <u>3-20-66</u>

C. RESIDENTIAL ADDRESS   <u>123 Normal Dr. Apt. 3</u>

                                  <u>Normal IL 60123</u>

D. EMPLOYER   <u>Bossman, Saylor, and Associates</u>

E. EMPLOYER'S ADDRESS   <u>999 Job Ave</u>

                                  <u>Jobville, IL 60333</u>

F. NUMBER OF DEPENDENTS   <u>2</u>
    CLAIMED

G. PAY PERIOD (WEEKLY, BI-WEEKLY,
    SEMI-MONTHLY, MONTHLY)   <u>Monthly</u>

H. RENT OR OWN RESIDENCE?   <u>Rent</u>

INCOME

GROSS MONTHLY INCOME FROM

EMPLOYMENT (SALARY, WAGES) $ <u>6,000</u>

CHILD SUPPORT CURRENTLY
BEING RECEIVED $ <u>0</u>

INTEREST, DIVIDEND, OR
OTHER INVESTMENT INCOME $ <u>0</u>

UNEMPLOYMENT, WORKERS'
COMP, DISABILITY INCOME $ <u>0</u>

E. OTHER INCOME $ <u>0</u>

    (SPECIFY SOURCES AND AMOUNTS)

    _____ $ ___—___

    _____ $ ___—___

TOTAL GROSS MONTHLY INCOME $ <u>6,000</u>

LIQUID ASSETS/ASSET VALUE

A.   SAVINGS/CHECKING ACCOUNTS $ <u>4,500</u>

B.   CERTIFICATES OF DEPOSIT $ ___—___

C.   MONEY MARKET ACCOUNTS $ ___—___

D.   STOCK OR BOND INSTRUMENTS $ ___—___

OTHER CASH ON HAND OR
CASH EQUIVALENT $ ____—____

TOTAL LIQUID ASSETS $ _4,500_

MANDATORY MONTHLY DEDUCTIONS FROM INCOME

FEDERAL TAX $ _1,500_

STATE TAX $ __350__

FICA $ __50__

UNION DUES $ __0__

HEALTH INSURANCE PREMIUMS
REQUIRED BY EMPLOYER $ __100__

DEDUCTIONS REQUIRED BY
COURT ORDER $ ____—____

MISCELLANEOUS REQUIRED
DEDUCTIONS $ ____—____

TOTAL MONTHLY DEDUCTIONS $ _2,000_

MONTHLY EXPENSES

A. RENT OR MORTGAGE $ _1,000_

B. PROPERTY TAXES $ _N/A_

INSURANCE (MORTGAGE,
RENTERS', HOMEOWNERS', ETC.) $ _N/A_

UTILITIES (INCLUDE WATER/SEWER,
GAS, ELECTRIC, CABLE OR SATELLITE,
TELEPHONE, REFUSE REMOVAL, ETC.) $ _300_

FOOD AND SUNDRIES (INCLUDE
RESTAURANT MEALS, PERSONAL
HYGIENE ITEMS, OFFICE/SCHOOL
SUPPLIES, PET CARE ITEMS, ETC.) $ ___200___

CLOTHING (INCLUDE PURCHASE
AND CLEANING FOR ALL MEMBERS
OF HOUSEHOLD) $ ___500___

HEALTH CARE (INCLUDE MEDICAL
AND DENTAL EXPENSES, HEALTH
CARE INSURANCE FOR ALL MEMBERS
OF HOUSEHOLD) $ ___100___

TRANSPORTATION (INCLUDE CAR
LOAN PAYMENTS, AUTO INSURANCE
OF ANY TYPE, GASOLINE, AUTO
MAINTENANCE/REPAIR, MASS TRANSIT
EXPENSES, PARKING, OTHER
TRANSPORTATION EXPENSES) $ ___300___

CHILDREN (INCLUDE TUITION, EXTRA-
CURRICULAR ACTIVITIES, DAY CARE,
BABYSITTING, ANY OTHER CHILD-
RELATED EXPENSES NOT PREVIOUSLY
ENUMERATED) $ ___300___

RECREATION (INCLUDE HOBBIES,
BOOKS/MAGAZINES, VACATIONS,
OTHER ENTERTAINMENT) $ ___500___

DEBT PAYMENTS (INCLUDE PRIOR
COURT-ORDERED SUPPORT, CREDIT
CARD BALANCES, AND OTHER DEBT
NOT PREVIOUSLY ENUMERATED) $ ___—___

MISCELLANEOUS EXPENSES
(SPECIFY TYPE AND AMOUNT) $ _____0_____

_____ $ ____—____

_____ $ ____—____

TOTAL MONTHLY EXPENSES $ __3,200__

The undersigned states under oath, under penalties as provided by law pursuant to 735 ILCS 5/1-109, that this financial affidavit includes all of his income and expenses, he has knowledge of the matters stated and he certifies that the statements set forth herein are true and correct, except as to matters stated to be on information and belief, and as to such matters the undersigned certifies as aforesaid that he believes the same to be true.

_____*John Smith*_____
AFFIANT

Appendix E: Blank Forms

The following compilation of forms is based on general child custody, visitation, and support principles. These forms will give the reader an idea of what his or her own pleadings should look like. Of course, the forms are only a guide.

STATE OF ILLINOIS

IN THE CIRCUIT COURT OF THE _____ JUDICIAL CIRCUIT

_____ COUNTY

	)	
_____	)	
Petitioner,	)	
	)	
v.	)	Case No. _____
	)	
	)	
_____	)	
Respondent.	)	

PETITION FOR CHILD CUSTODY AND SUPPORT

NOW COMES the Petitioner, _____ (hereinafter "Petitioner"), by and through her attorney, _____, and for her Petition for Child Custody and Support against the Respondent, _____ (hereinafter "Respondent") states as follows:

1. Petitioner resides in _____.

2. Respondent resides in _____.

3. Petitioner and Respondent _____

4. Petitioner and Respondent are the _____

5.   The above-named children reside in _____ County with _____, the Petitioner herein.

6.   Petitioner was not married on the birthdates of the above-named children, and was not married within three hundred days before the birthdates of the above-named children.

7.   Respondent is employed and has the ability to financially support the above-named children, but has refused to do so.

8.   No previous court order exists, in this or any other jurisdiction, concerning custody or support of the above-named children.

WHEREFORE, the Petitioner respectfully requests this Honorable Court to order the following:

_____
Petitioner

STATE OF ILLINOIS

IN THE CIRCUIT COURT OF THE _____ JUDICIAL CIRCUIT

_____ COUNTY

_____)
)
    Petitioner,   )
)
v.   )   CASE NO. _____
)
)
_____)
)
    Respondent.   )
)

RESPONSE TO PETITION FOR CHILD CUSTODY AND SUPPORT

NOW COMES the Respondent, _____ (hereinafter "Respondent"), by and through his attorney, _____, and in response to Petitioner's Petition for Child Custody and Support states as follows:

1. Respondent _____ the allegations of Petitioner's paragraph 1.

2. Respondent _____ the allegations of Petitioner's paragraph 2.

3. Respondent _____ the allegations of Petitioner's paragraph 3.

4. Respondent _____ the allegations of Petitioner's paragraph 4.

5. Respondent _____ allegations of Petitioner's paragraph 5.

6. Respondent _____ the allegations of Petitioner's paragraph 6.

Further, Respondent states _____

_____.

WHEREFORE, the Respondent respectfully requests this Honorable Court to order the following:

_____

Respondent

STATE OF ILLINOIS

IN THE CIRCUIT COURT OF THE _____ JUDICIAL CIRCUIT

_____ COUNTY

_____   )

      Petitioner,   )

v.   )   Case No. _____

)

_____   )

      Respondent.   )

SUMMONS

ILLINOIS MARRIAGE AND DISSOLUTION OF MARRIAGE ACT

To each Defendant:

      You are summoned and required to file an answer to the complaint in this case, a copy of which is hereto attached, or otherwise file your appearance in the office of the Clerk of this court, _____(address), Illinois, within 30 days after service of this summons, not counting the day of service. IF YOU FAIL TO DO SO, A JUDGMENT BY DEFAULT MAY BE TAKEN AGAINST YOU FOR THE RELIEF ASKED IN THE COMPLAINT.

YOU ARE FURTHER NOTIFIED THAT A DISSOLUTION ACTION STAY IS IN FULL FORCE AND EFFECT UPON SERVICE OF THIS SUMMONS.

THE CONDITIONS OF THE STAY ARE SET FORTH ON THE REVERSE SIDE OF THIS SUMMONS, WHICH WAS SERVED UPON YOU, AND ARE APPLICABLE TO THE PARTIES AS SET FORTH IN THE STATUTE.

To the Officer:

This summons must be returned by the Officer or other person to whom it was given for service, with the endorsement of service and fees, if any, immediately after service. If service cannot be made, this summons shall be returned so endorsed. THIS SUMMONS MAY NOT BE SERVED LATER THAN 30 DAYS AFTER ITS DATE.

(Seal of Court)　　　　　　　WITNESS: _____, Clerk of the

_____ Judicial Circuit

　　　　　　　　　　　　　　and the seal thereof, at _____, Illinois

　　　　　　　　　　　　　　DATED: _____

Petitioner's Attorney (or Petitioner,　　　_____

if not represented by attorney)

Clerk of the _____ Judicial Circuit

_____

_____

Address

　　　　　　　　　　　　Date of Service _____, 20 ____

_____　　(To be inserted by officer on copy left with defendant

Telephone　　　　　　　　or other person)

CONDITIONS OF DISSOLUTION ACTION STAY

Upon service of a summons and petition or praecipe filed under the Illinois Marriage and Dissolution of Marriage Act or upon the filing of the respondent's appearance in the proceeding, whichever first occurs, a dissolution action stay shall be in effect against both parties and their agents and employees, without bond or further notice, until a final judgment is entered, the proceeding is dismissed, or until further order of the court restraining both parties from physically abusing, harassing, intimidating, striking, or interfering with the personal liberty of the other party or the minor children of either party (750 ILCS 5/501.1 (a)(2)) and restraining both parties from removing any minor child or either party from the State of Illinois or from concealing any such child from the other party, without the consent of the party or an order of the court (750 ILCS 5/501.1(a)(3)).

This page is intentionally blank.

STATE OF ILLINOIS

IN THE CIRCUIT COURT OF THE _____ JUDICIAL CIRCUIT

_____ COUNTY

_____   )

      Petitioner,   )

v.   )   Case No. _____

)

_____   )

      Respondent.   )

APPEARANCE

I HEREBY ENTER THE APPEARANCE OF _____

            (Insert the name of the party for whom you are entering an appearance)

AND MY OWN AS

___ REGULAR COUNSEL	___ TRIAL COUNSEL
___ SPECIAL APPEARANCE	___ SUBSTITUTE COUNSEL
___ PRO SE	___ COUNSEL IN FORCIBLE ENTRY
___ ADDITIONAL COUNSEL	___ APPELLATE COUNSEL
_X_ GUARDIAN AD LITEM	___ COURT APPOINTED COUNSEL

AND AS (HIS) (HER) (THEIR) COUNSEL IN THE ABOVE ENTITLED CASE.

SIGNED _____

            (Signature of Attorney filing Appearance)

Name _____

Attorney for _____

Address _____

City, State, Zip _____

Phone _____

This page is intentionally blank.

STATE OF ILLINOIS

IN THE CIRCUIT COURT OF THE _____ JUDICIAL CIRCUIT

_____ COUNTY

_____   )

      Petitioner,   )

v.   )   Case No. _____

)

_____   )

      Respondent.   )

AFFIDAVIT PURSUANT TO UNIFORM CHILD CUSTODY JURISDICTION AND ENFORCEMENT ACT

_____, Petitioner herein, being duly sworn, deposes and states as follows:

1. Petitioner resides at _____.

2. Upon information and belief, the children who are subject to this proceeding currently reside at:

Name   Date of Birth   Address

_____   _____   _____

_____   _____   _____

3.   Upon information and belief, the children who are subject to this proceeding have, during the previous five years, resided at the following:

Name	Address	Dates of Residence
_____	_____	_____
_____	_____	_____

4.   Upon information and belief, the children who are subject to this proceeding have, during the previous five years, resided with the following persons:

Name	Address	Dates of Residence
_____	_____	_____

5.   Petitioner _____ [has/has not participated] as a party/witness/other_____(indicate capacity) in other litigation concerning the custody of the same children in this or any other state.

6.   Petitioner _____[has/does not have] information of any custody proceeding concerning the child pending in a court of this or any other state.

7.   Petitioner _____ [knows/does not know] of any person not a party to the proceedings who has physical custody of the child or claims to have custody or visitation rights with respect to the children.

If the declarations in either paragraph 5, 6, or 7 is in the affirmative, Petitioner shall provide additional information to the Court under oath. Petitioner understands that she has a continuing duty to inform the court of any custody proceeding concerning the child in this or any other state of which she obtained information during this proceeding.

STATE OF ILLINOIS   )

)SS.

COUNTY OF _____)

_____, being first duly sworn on oath, deposes and states that she has read the foregoing document, and the answers made herein are true, correct, and complete to the best of her knowledge and belief.

_____

SIGNATURE

SUBSCRIBED and SWORN to before me this _____ day of _____, 20 _____.

_____

NOTARY PUBLIC

This page is intentionally blank.

STATE OF ILLINOIS
IN THE CIRCUIT COURT OF THE _____ JUDICIAL CIRCUIT
_____ COUNTY

_____   )
     Petitioner,   )
v.   )   Case No. _____
)
_____   )
     Respondent.   )

NOTICE OF MOTION

To: _____

              _____

              _____

              _____

On _____, 20_____, at _____[a.m./p.m.], or as soon thereafter as Counsel may be heard, I shall appear before the Honorable _____, or any Judge sitting in his/her stead, in the courtroom usually occupied by him/her in the _____ County Government Center, _____, Illinois, and then and there present the following Motion:

(continued on next page)

This page is intentionally blank.

PROOF OF SERVICE

_____

_____

_____

The undersigned being first duly sworn on oath deposes and says that a copy of the foregoing Notice was served upon the above named by enclosing the same in an envelope, plainly addressed as is shown above, postage fully prepaid, and by depositing the same in a U.S. Post Office Box, at Chicago, Illinois, on the _____th day of _____, A.D. 20____, before the hour of 4:00 p.m.

_____

_____

SUBSCRIBED and SWORN to before me this

_____ day of _____, 20 ____.

_____

NOTARY PUBLIC

This page is intentionally blank.

STATE OF ILLINOIS
IN THE CIRCUIT COURT OF THE _____ JUDICIAL CIRCUIT
_____ COUNTY

_____   )

      Petitioner,   )

v.   )   Case No. _____

)

_____   )

      Respondent.   )

PETITION FOR VISITATION

NOW COMES the Petitioner, _____, through his attorney, _____, and in support of his Petition for Visitation states as follows:

1. Petitioner resides in _____ County, Illinois.

2. Respondent resides in _____ County, Illinois.

3. Petitioner and Respondent are _____.

4. Petitioner and Respondent are _____:

5. The above-named children reside in _____ County with _____, the Respondent herein.

6. No previous court order exists, in this or any other jurisdiction, concerning custody or support of the ___ above-named children

7. Respondent has not allowed Petitioner, _____

_____

_____

WHEREFORE, Petitioner prays that this Court will grant Petitioner _____

_____

_____

                                             _____

                                                        Petitioner

STATE OF ILLINOIS
IN THE CIRCUIT COURT OF THE _____ JUDICIAL CIRCUIT
_____ COUNTY

_____   )
     Petitioner,   )

v.   )   Case No. _____

)

_____   )
     Respondent.   )

RESPONSE TO PETITION FOR VISITATION

NOW COMES the Respondent, _____, through her attorney, _____, and in response to Petitioner's Petition for Visitation states as follows:

1. Respondent _____ the allegations of paragraph 1 of Petitioner's Petition.

2. Respondent _____ the allegations of paragraph 2 of Petitioner's Petition.

3. Respondent _____ the allegations of paragraph 3 of Petitioner's Petition.

4. Respondent _____ the allegations of paragraph 4 of Petitioner's Petition.

5. Respondent _____ the allegations of paragraph 5 of Petitioner's Petition.

6. Respondent _____ the allegations of paragraph 6 of Petitioner's Petition.

WHEREFORE, Respondent prays that this Court will grant Petitioner _____

_____

_____

                                                     _____

                                                           Respondent

STATE OF ILLINOIS

IN THE CIRCUIT COURT OF THE _____ JUDICIAL CIRCUIT

_____ COUNTY

_____)	
Petitioner,)	
v.)	Case No. _____
)	
_____)	
Respondent.)	

PETITION TO MODIFY CUSTODY

NOW COMES the Petitioner, _____, by and through his attorney, _____, and in support of his Petition to Modify Custody, states as follows:

1. Petitioner resides in _____ County, Illinois.

2. Respondent, _____, resides in _____ County, Illinois.

3. Petitioner and Respondent are the parents of _____ _____

4. On _____, this Court entered its order granting legal and physical custody of the above-named children to Respondent.

5. The above-named children currently reside with Respondent in _____ County, Illinois.

6. Since the date of the previous order regarding custody, there has been a substantial change in circumstances in this matter, in that the Respondent has moved several times in the past several years.

7. It is in the best interest of the above-named children that the Court's previous order be modified to grant legal and physical custody of the children to Petitioner.

8. More than _____ have passed since the entry of the previous order regarding custody.

WHEREFORE, Petitioner requests that this Honorable Court modify its earlier custody order, such that Petitioner be granted immediate legal and physical custody of the above-named minor children.

_____

                                                                  Petitioner

VERIFICATION

STATE OF ILLINOIS   )

                SS   )

COUNTY OF _____)

The undersigned, being duly sworn, hereby deposes and says that he is the Petitioner in the captioned matter, that he has read the Petition to Modify Custody herein, and that the contents thereof are true and correct.

_____

                                                                  Petitioner

Subscribed and sworn to before me

This _____ day of _____ 20 ____

_____

Notary Public

STATE OF ILLINOIS
IN THE CIRCUIT COURT OF THE _____ JUDICIAL CIRCUIT
_____ COUNTY

_____)	
Petitioner,)	
v.)	Case No. _____
)	
_____)	
Respondent.)	

RESPONSE TO PETITION TO MODIFY CUSTODY

NOW COMES the Respondent, _____, by and through her attorney, _____, and in Response to Petitioner's Petition to Modify Custody, states as follows:

1. Respondent _____ the allegations of paragraph 1 of Petitioner's petition.

2. Respondent _____ the allegations of paragraph 2 of Petitioner's petition.

3. Respondent _____ the allegations of paragraph 3 of Petitioner's petition.

4. Respondent _____ the allegations of paragraph 4 of Petitioner's petition.

5. Respondent _____ the allegations of paragraph 5 of Petitioner's petition.

WHEREFORE, Respondent requests that this Honorable Court _____

_____

_____

Respondent

VERIFICATION

STATE OF ILLINOIS   )

          SS   )

COUNTY OF _____)

The undersigned, being duly sworn, hereby deposes and says that she is the Respondent in the captioned matter, that she has read the Response herein, and that the contents thereof are true and correct.

_____

                      Respondent

Subscribed and sworn to before me

This _____ day of _____ 20 ____.

_____

Notary Public

STATE OF ILLINOIS
IN THE CIRCUIT COURT OF THE _____ JUDICIAL CIRCUIT
_____ COUNTY

_____   )
    Petititoner,   )
v.   )   Case No. _____
)
_____   )
    Respondent.   )

PETITION FOR RULE TO SHOW CAUSE
(NON-PAYMENT OF SUPPORT)

NOW COMES the Petitioner, _____, by and through her attorney, _____, and in support of her Petition for Rule to Show Cause against the Respondent, _____, states as follows:

WHEREFORE, Petitioner prays that

_____
                    Petitioner

This page is intentionally blank.

STATE OF ILLINOIS

IN THE CIRCUIT COURT OF THE _____ JUDICIAL CIRCUIT

_____ COUNTY

_____)	
Petitioner,)	
v.)	Case No. _____
)	
_____)	
Respondent.)	

PETITION FOR RULE TO SHOW CAUSE
(VISITATION INTERFERENCE)

NOW COMES the Petitioner, _____, and in support of his Petition for Rule to Show Cause against Respondent, _____, states as follows:

1. Petitioner and Respondent are the parents of the following minor children: _____ _____.

2. Petitioner resides in _____.

3. On_____, this Court entered its order granting custody of the above-named children to Respondent, and granting Petitioner the following visitation _____.

4. Respondent and the two above-named children reside together in _____ County, Illinois.

5. Respondent has refused to allow Petitioner's visitation with the above-named children on the following dates, without cause:

[list dates]

6. Respondent has refused to allow Petitioner make-up time for the missed periods of visitation.

WHEREFORE, Petitioner respectfully asks the Court to enter a rule against Respondent, requiring Respondent to show cause, if any she has, for failure to abide by the orders of this Court as contained in the order of _____, why she should not be held in contempt of this Court. Petitioner further respectfully requests that Respondent be ordered to provide make-up visitation at a time that suits the convenience of the Petitioner. Petitioner also asks for an award of attorney's fees incurred in bringing this petition, as set forth in the Affidavit for Attorney's Fees, which is attached hereto and incorporated herein by reference as Exhibit "A".

_____
Petitioner

NOTE: *Interrogatories will typically ask the following questions. What follows is a standard interrogatory, filled in by the hypothetical John Smith.*

SUPREME COURT RULE 213(j) STANDARD INTERROGATORIES

1. State your full name, current address, date of birth, and social security number.

_____   _____

_____   _____ - __ - _____

_____

2. List all employment held by you during the preceding three years and with regard to each employment state:

a. The name and address of each employer;

_____

_____

_____

b. Your position, job title, or description;

c. If you had an employment contract;

d. The date on which you commenced your employment and, if applicable, the date and reason for the termination of your employment;

e. Your current gross and net income per pay period;

f. Your gross income as shown on the last W-2 tax and wage statement received by you, your social security wages as shown on the last W-2 tax and wage statement received by you, and the amounts of all deductions shown thereon; and

g. All additional benefits or perquisites received from your employment stating the type and value thereof.

3. During the preceding three years, have you had any source of income other than from your employment listed above? If so, with regard to each source of income, state the following:

a. the source of income, including the type of income and name and address of the source;

b. the frequency in which you receive income from the source;

c. the amount of income received by you from the source during the immediately preceding three years; and

d. the amount of income received by you from the source for each month during the immediately preceding three years.

4. Do you own any interest in real estate? If so, with regard to each such interest state the following:

a. the size and description of the parcel of real estate, including improvements thereon;

b. the name, address and interest of each person who has or claims to have an ownership interest in the parcel of real estate;

c. the date your interest in the parcel of real estate was acquired;

d. the consideration you transferred or paid for your interest in the parcel of real estate;

e. your estimate of the current fair market value of the parcel of real estate and your interest therein; and

f. the amount of any indebtedness owed on the parcel of real estate and to whom.

5. For the preceding three years, list the names and addresses of all associations, partnerships, corporations, enterprises or entities in which you have an interest or claim any interest, the nature of your interest or claim of interest therein, the amount of percentage of your interest or claim of interest therein, and an estimate of the value of your interest therein.

6. During the preceding three years, have you had any account or investment in any type of financial institution, individually or with another or in the name of another, including checking accounts, savings accounts, certificates of deposit, and money market accounts? If so, with regard to each such account or investment, state the following:

a. the type of account or investment;

b. the name and address of the financial institution;

_____
_____
_____

c. the name and address of each person in whose name the account is held; and

_____
_____
_____

d. both the high and the low balance of the account or investment, stating the date of the high balance and the date of the low balance.

7. During the preceding three years, have you been the holder of or had access to any safety deposit boxes? If so, state the following:

a. the name of the bank or institution where such box is located;

b. the number of each box;

c. a description of the contents of each box during the immediately preceding three years and as of the date of the answer; and

d. the name and address of any joint or co-owners of such safety deposit box or any trustees holding the box for your benefit.

8. During the immediately preceding three years, has any person or entity held cash or property on your behalf? If so, state:

a. the name and address of the person or entity holding the cash or property; and

b. the type of cash or property held and the value thereof.

9. During the preceding three years, have you owned any stocks, bonds, securities, or other investments, including savings bonds? If so, with regard to each such stock, bond, security, or investment state:

a. a description of the stock, bond, security, or investment;

b. the name and address of the entity issuing the stock, bond, security, or investment;

c. the present value of such stock, bond, security, or investment;

d. the date of acquisition of the stock, bond, security, or investment;

e. the cost of the stock, bond, security, or investment;

f. the name and address of any other owner or owners in such stock, bond, security, or investment; and

g. if applicable, the date sold and the amount realized therefrom.

10. Do you own or have any incidents of ownership in any life, annuity, or endowment insurance policies? If so, with regard to each such policy state:

a. the name of the company;

b. the number of the policy;

c. the face value of the policy;

d. the present value of the policy;

e. the amount of any loan or encumbrance on the policy;

f. the date of acquisition of the policy; and

g. with regard to each policy, the beneficiary or beneficiaries.

11. Do you have any right, title, claim, or interest in or to a pension plan, retirement plan, or profit sharing plan, including, but not limited to, individual retirement accounts, 401(k) plans, and deferred compensation plans? If so, with regard to each such plan state:

a. the name and address of the entity providing the plan;

_____

_____

_____

b. the date of your initial participation in the plan; and

c. the amount of funds currently held on your behalf under the plan.

12. Do you have any outstanding indebtedness or financial obligations, including mortgages, promissory notes, or other oral or written contracts? If so, with regard to each obligation state the following:

a. the name and address of the creditor;

b. the form of the obligation;

c. the date the obligation was initially incurred;

d. the amount of the original obligation;

e. the purpose or consideration for which the obligation was incurred;

f. a description of any security connected with the obligation;

g. the rate of interest on the obligation;

h. the present unpaid balance of the obligation;

i. the dates and amounts of installment payments; and

j. the date of maturity of the obligation.

13. Are you owed any money or property? If so, state:

a. the name and address of the debtor;

b. the form of the obligation;

c. the date the obligation was initially incurred;

d. the amount of the original obligation;

e. the purpose or consideration for which the obligation was incurred;

f. the description of any security connected with the obligation;

g. the rate of interest on the obligation;

h. the present unpaid balance of the obligation;

i. the dates and amounts of installment payments; and

j. the date of maturity of the obligation.

14. State the year, make, and model of each motor or motorized vehicle, motor or mobile home, and farm machinery or equipment in which you have an ownership, estate, interest, or claim of interest, whether individually or with another, and with regard to each item state:

a. the date the item was acquired;

b. the consideration paid for the item;

c. the name and address of each other person who has a right, title, claim, or interest in or to the item;

d. the approximate fair market value of the item; and

e. the amount of any indebtedness on the item and the name and address of the creditor.

15. Have you purchased or contributed toward the payment for or provided other consideration or improvement with regard to any real estate, motorized vehicle, financial account or securities, or other property, real or personal, on behalf of another person or entity other than your spouse during the preceding three years? If so, with regard to each such transaction state:

a. the name and address of the person or entity to whom you contributed;

b. the type of contribution made by you;

c. the type of property to which the contribution was made;

d. the location of the property to which the contribution was made;

e. whether or not there is written evidence of the existence of a loan; and

f. a description of the written evidence.

16. During the preceding three years, have you made any gift of cash or property, real or personal, to any person or entity not your spouse? If so, with regard to each such transaction state:

a. a description of the gift;

b. the value of the gift;

c. the date of the gift;

d. the name and address of the person or entity receiving the gift;

e. whether or not there is written evidence of the existence of a gift; and

f. a description of the written evidence.

17. During the preceding three years, have you made any loans to any person or entity not your spouse and, if so, with regard to each such loan state:

a. a description of the loan;

b. the value of the loan;

c. the date of the loan;

d. the name and address of the person or entity receiving the loan;

e. whether or not there is written evidence of the existence of a loan; and

f. a description of the written evidence.

18. During the preceding three years, have you sold, transferred, conveyed, encumbered, concealed, damaged, or otherwise disposed of any property owned by you and/or your spouse individually or collectively? If so, with regard to each item of property state:

a. a description of the property;

b. the current location of the property;

c. the purpose or reason for the action taken by you with regard to the property;

d. the approximate fair market value of the property;

e. whether or not there is written evidence of any such transaction; and

f. a description of the written evidence.

19. During the preceding three years, have any appraisals been made with regard to any of the property listed by you under your answers to these interrogatories? If so, state:

a. the name and address of the person conducting each such appraisal;

b. a description of the property appraised;

c. the date of the appraisal; and

d. the location of any copies of each such appraisal.

20. During the preceding three years, have you prepared or has anyone prepared for you any financial statements, net worth statements, or lists of assets and liabilities pertaining to your property or financial affairs? If so, with regard to each such document state:

a. the name and address of the person preparing each such document;

b. the type of document prepared;

c. the date the document was prepared; and

d. the location of all copies of each such document.

21. State the name and address of any accountant, tax preparer, bookkeeper, and other person, firm, or entity who has kept or prepared books, documents, and records with regard to your income, property, business, or financial affairs during the course of this marriage.

22. List all nonmarital property claimed by you, identifying each item of property as to the type of property, the date received, the basis on which you claim it is nonmarital property, its location, and the present value of the property.

23. List all marital property of this marriage, identifying each item of property as to the type of property, the basis on which you claim it to be marital property, its location, and the present value of the property.

24. What contribution or dissipation has your spouse made to the marital estate?

25. Pursuant to Illinois Supreme Court Rule 213(f), provide the name and address of each witness who will testify at trial and state the subject of each witness' testimony.

26. Pursuant to Illinois Supreme Court Rule 213(g), provide the name and address of each opinion witness who will offer any testimony, and state:

a. the subject matter on which the opinion witness is expected to testify;

b. the conclusions and/or opinions of the opinion witness and the basis therefor, including reports of the witness, if any;

c. the qualifications of each opinion witness, including a curriculum vitae and/or resume, if any; and

d. the identity of any written reports of the opinion witness regarding this occurrence.

27. Are you in any manner incapacitated or limited in your ability to earn income at the present time?

If so, define and describe such incapacity, or limitation, and state when such incapacity or limitation commenced and when it is expected to end.

28. Identify any statements, information, and/or documents known to you and requested by any of the foregoing interrogatories that you claim to be work product or subject to any common law or statutory privilege, and with respect to each interrogatory, specify the legal basis for the claim as required by Illinois Supreme Court Rule 201(n).

ATTESTATION

STATE OF ILLINOIS   )
) ss.
COUNTY OF _____)

_____, being first duly sworn on oath, deposes and states that he/she is a defendant in the above-captioned matter, that he/she has read the foregoing document, and the answers made herein are true, correct, and complete to the best of his/her knowledge and belief.

_____

SIGNATURE

SUBSCRIBED and SWORN to before me this

_____ day of _____ 20 ____.

_____

NOTARY PUBLIC

STATE OF ILLINOIS

IN THE CIRCUIT COURT OF THE _____ JUDICIAL CIRCUIT

_____ COUNTY

_____)

    Petitioner,)

v.)   Case No. _____

)

_____)

    Respondent.)

FINANCIAL AFFIDAVIT

Affiant, _____, the Petitioner in the above captioned case, having been duly sworn, hereby states the following for his Financial Affidavit:

PERSONAL DATA

A. FULL NAME   _____

B. DATE OF BIRTH   _____

C. RESIDENTIAL ADDRESS   _____

                                     _____

D. EMPLOYER   _____

E. EMPLOYER'S ADDRESS   _____

                                     _____

F. NUMBER OF DEPENDENTS _____
    CLAIMED

G. PAY PERIOD (WEEKLY, BI-WEEKLY,
    SEMI-MONTHLY, MONTHLY) _____

H. RENT OR OWN RESIDENCE? _____

INCOME

GROSS MONTHLY INCOME FROM

EMPLOYMENT (SALARY, WAGES) $ _____

CHILD SUPPORT CURRENTLY
BEING RECEIVED $ _____

INTEREST, DIVIDEND, OR
OTHER INVESTMENT INCOME $ _____

UNEMPLOYMENT, WORKERS'
COMP, DISABILITY INCOME $ _____

E. OTHER INCOME $ _____

    (SPECIFY SOURCES AND AMOUNTS)

    _____ $ _____

    _____ $ _____

TOTAL GROSS MONTHLY INCOME $ _____

LIQUID ASSETS/ASSET VALUE

A.   SAVINGS/CHECKING ACCOUNTS $ _____

B.   CERTIFICATES OF DEPOSIT $ _____

C.   MONEY MARKET ACCOUNTS $ _____

D.   STOCK OR BOND INSTRUMENTS $ _____

OTHER CASH ON HAND OR
CASH EQUIVALENT $ _____

TOTAL LIQUID ASSETS $ _____

MANDATORY MONTHLY DEDUCTIONS FROM INCOME

FEDERAL TAX $ _____

STATE TAX $ _____

FICA $ _____

UNION DUES $ _____

HEALTH INSURANCE PREMIUMS
REQUIRED BY EMPLOYER $ _____

DEDUCTIONS REQUIRED BY
COURT ORDER $ _____

MISCELLANEOUS REQUIRED
DEDUCTIONS $ _____

TOTAL MONTHLY DEDUCTIONS $ _____

MONTHLY EXPENSES

A. RENT OR MORTGAGE $ _____

B. PROPERTY TAXES $ _____

INSURANCE (MORTGAGE,
RENTERS', HOMEOWNERS', ETC.) $ _____

UTILITIES (INCLUDE WATER/SEWER,
GAS, ELECTRIC, CABLE OR SATELLITE,
TELEPHONE, REFUSE REMOVAL, ETC.) $ _____

FOOD AND SUNDRIES (INCLUDE
RESTAURANT MEALS, PERSONAL
HYGIENE ITEMS, OFFICE/SCHOOL
SUPPLIES, PET CARE ITEMS, ETC.) $ _____

CLOTHING (INCLUDE PURCHASE
AND CLEANING FOR ALL MEMBERS
OF HOUSEHOLD) $ _____

HEALTH CARE (INCLUDE MEDICAL
AND DENTAL EXPENSES, HEALTH
CARE INSURANCE FOR ALL MEMBERS
OF HOUSEHOLD) $ _____

TRANSPORTATION (INCLUDE CAR
LOAN PAYMENTS, AUTO INSURANCE
OF ANY TYPE, GASOLINE, AUTO
MAINTENANCE/REPAIR, MASS TRANSIT
EXPENSES, PARKING, OTHER
TRANSPORTATION EXPENSES) $ _____

CHILDREN (INCLUDE TUITION, EXTRA-
CURRICULAR ACTIVITIES, DAY CARE,
BABYSITTING, ANY OTHER CHILD-
RELATED EXPENSES NOT PREVIOUSLY
ENUMERATED) $ _____

RECREATION (INCLUDE HOBBIES,
BOOKS/MAGAZINES, VACATIONS,
OTHER ENTERTAINMENT) $ _____

DEBT PAYMENTS (INCLUDE PRIOR
COURT-ORDERED SUPPORT, CREDIT
CARD BALANCES, AND OTHER DEBT
NOT PREVIOUSLY ENUMERATED) $ _____

MISCELLANEOUS EXPENSES
(SPECIFY TYPE AND AMOUNT) $ _____

_____ $ _____

_____ $ _____

TOTAL MONTHLY EXPENSES $ _____

The undersigned states under oath, under penalties as provided by law pursuant to 735 ILCS 5/1-109, that this financial affidavit includes all of his income and expenses, he has knowledge of the matters stated and he certifies that the statements set forth herein are true and correct, except as to matters stated to be on information and belief, and as to such matters the undersigned certifies as aforesaid that he believes the same to be true.

_____

AFFIANT

Index

A

B

C

V

W